D1190142

Schizophrenia: Treatment Process and Outcome

Schizophrenia: Treatment Process and Outcome

Thomas H. McGlashan, M.D.
Christopher J. Keats, M.D.

American Psychiatric Press, Inc.

1400 K Street, N.W.
Washington, DC 20005

Copyright © 1989 by Thomas H. McGlashan and Christopher J. Keats
ALL RIGHTS RESERVED
Manufactured in the United States of America
88 89 90 91 5 4 3 2 1

First Edition

The paper used in this publication meets the minimum requirements of American National Standard for Information Sciences—Permanence of Paper for Printed Library Materials, ANSI Z39.48-1984.   ∞

Library of Congress Cataloging-in-Publication Data

McGlashan, Thomas H., 1941-
   Schizophrenia: treatment process and outcome/Thomas H.
McGlashan, Christopher J. Keats.–1st ed.
   p. cm.
   Bibliography: p.
   Includes index.
   ISBN 0-88048-281-8
   1. Schizophrenia—Treatment—Case studies. I. Keats,
Christopher J., 1943–   . II. Title.
   [DNLM: 1. Schizophrenia—therapy—case studies. WM 40 M478s]
   RC514.M39 1988
   616.89'82—dc19
   DNLM/DLC
   for Library of Congress   88-24228
                                                              CIP

To
Lara and Jennifer
and to
Leo and Anthony

Contents

		Page
List of Figures		ix
Foreword		xi
Allen J. Frances, M.D.		
Preface		xv
About the Authors		xix

Part One: The Cases

1	Case Study Rationale and Method	3
	Schizophrenia and	
	Psychotherapy Research	6
	Method	10
2	Ben	13
3	Betty	27
4	Joanne	41
5	Mark	71

Part Two: The Synthesis

6	Introduction to Case Critiques	91
7	Schizophrenia: One Illness or Many?	93
	The Illness: Common Features	94
	The Illness: Disparate Features	96
	Host Factors: The Person with the	
	Illness of Personhood	110

8   Introduction to Treatment Process 119
9   Psychotherapy Process Descriptors 121
10   Case Illustrations of Psychotherapeutic
      Process Parameters 143
11   Case Illustrations of Psychotherapeutic
      Process Levels 161
         Betty 161
         Mark 162
         Ben 163
         Joanne 166
12   Research and Treatment
      Implications 175
         Research Implications 175
         Articulation Studies 175
         Psychometric Studies 178
         Treatment Efficacy Studies 179
         Treatment Implications 181
         Outcome and Natural History
            Effect 184
         Outcome and Treatment Effect 187
         A Proposed Integrated Psychotherapy
            for Schizophrenia 190

References 193
Index 197

List of Figures

		Page
1	Process levels and hypothesized correlations	128
2	Articulation studies of process dimensions	175
3	Treatment efficacy studies using process dimensions	180
4	The natural history of schizophrenia: prognostic factors and outcome	185
5	Treatment effect and natural history	188
6	Asylum and treatment effect	189

Foreword

Allen J. Frances, M.D.

Harry Stack Sullivan once made the seemingly obvious, yet poignant, observation that the people we label schizophrenic remain much more simply human than otherwise. For all sorts of reasons, we tend to forget this. Whatever schizophrenia is, people who receive the diagnosis very often have great difficulty in relating to others, including us. Many clinicians see their schizophrenic patients infrequently and come to lose touch with the pain and poetry of their experience. Researchers focus on group findings that are difficult to translate to the individual situation. As a society, we have devoted comparatively paltry resources to the research and treatment of schizophrenia. Certainly, we have never developed an adequate, integrated, and rational method of providing care.

What are the results? My guess is that there has never been a worse place or a worse time than here and now in which to be schizophrenic and this despite the remarkable recent progress in our basic understanding of the disorder and in developing powerful methods for treating it. The discovery of neuroleptic medication has certainly been a medical breakthrough benefiting millions of individuals and inspiring a revolution in neuroscience and clinical research. But neuroleptics are usually only partially effective and are often poorly tolerated by patients. Moreover, the use of neuroleptics has inadvertently justified our society's shameless abdication of responsibility for providing asylum to our severely mentally ill. We have in effect used neuroleptics to clear the hospitals and fill the streets.

Schizophrenic patients must cope with a complicated and fragmented society, usually without the support of the extended family, without the refuge of the hospital, and must live within a culture that is frightened by, and stigmatizes, diversity. We no longer burn schizophrenics at the stake, but we also do not honor them as shamans, saints, or creative misfits. We have medicalized schizophrenia but don't treat it very well. We often forget to listen and to like our patients.

Which brings us to this lovely and illuminating book by Thomas H. McGlashan and Christopher J. Keats. In great and moving detail, they have captured the lives and treatments of four patients who were hospitalized years ago at Chestnut Lodge. We learn the circumstances and psychopathology that caused these patients to enter the hospital and the nature of the psychotherapeutic and human contacts that were experienced there. These are then correlated with the patient's subsequent long-term course in an attempt to understand the factors that lead to growth and healing, or to stagnation, in their lives. Speculations are drawn linking this outcome with the level achieved by each patient in his or her psychotherapy at Chestnut Lodge. This is research, but research which generates questions from the crucible of personal encounter.

The authors are keen and compassionate observers and write with wit and style. The patients and their therapists come alive as people engaged in a sometimes desperate attempt to understand themselves and the illness. This intense and microscopic case study method has many advantages. It allows us to see each person in depth and does justice to the individual particularities that often become blurred in larger, more systematic but lower resolution studies. We are never allowed to lose touch with these four people as individuals.

The limitations of the method are also clear and stated explicitly. The four patients were relatively well-to-do and were treated a generation ago in a very special way. The authors also make clear that their purpose does not include a detailed exposition of other useful models, particularly those related to the psychoeducational, behavioral, rehabilitative, and somatic approaches. As such the case studies may not generalize very well to the larger cohort of schizophrenic patients receiving today's treatment. They do, however, help us to rediscover that which is human about schizophrenia.

A careful consideration of even a few patients meeting descriptive criteria for schizophrenia reveals them to be heterogeneous in all sorts of important ways. The diagnosis of schizophrenia captures a patient group that is highly variable in developmental and family backgrounds, premorbid functioning, interpersonal relationships, vulnerability to stressors, onset of illness, types of psychopathology, illness severity, treatment response, and course. The label schizophrenia certainly predicts something of value about the patient's behavior, problems in life, and treatment needs, but it necessarily cannot include all that is crucial.

Drs. McGlashan and Keats have also provided us with a highly sophisticated and very useful description of the stages and levels in the process of therapy with schizophrenic patients. More clearly than I have ever seen before, they have outlined the ways in which the development of the therapeutic relationship can be integrated with the technical interventions that inform psychotherapy. Their model for understanding treatment process and its relation to outcome is illustrated with case vignettes that are always pertinent and often moving. This is great stuff for a beginning therapist, a valuable aid to the supervisor, and I found myself listening much better to my next patient.

I must take special note of the most vivid and haunting of the vignettes, their description of the remarkable encounter between a great therapist, Frieda Fromm-Reichmann, and a great patient, Joanne Greenberg. Ms. Greenberg has, of course, written a beautiful book based on this experience, but it is fascinating now to hear about the treatment both from the point of view of the hospital record (with many of Dr. Fromm-Reichmann's comments) and from Ms. Greenberg's recollections many years later. Dr. Fromm-Reichmann was extraordinary in her sensitivity, simplicity, and great common sense. Ms. Greenberg was extraordinary for her creative, but uncontrolled, immersion in fantasy, and also for her insight, honesty, and personal charm. Together they make a grand treatment team and provide a wonderful example of the special magic that can occur in interpersonal relationships, including therapeutic ones. Dr. Fromm-Reichmann never forgot, nor let Ms. Greenberg forget, that both parties to the encounter were human beings. It is not surprising that what Ms. Greenberg appreciated most in Dr. Fromm-Reichmann and in the others who had helped her was "a kind of matter-of-factness, an ordinariness; they looked across at me, not up or down at me, but across at me." Ms. Greenberg grew up to become a wise, funny, and wonderfully productive woman. Perhaps this would have happened in the natural course of maturation, but I think not.

The moral of the story—and, I think, of the book—is that we must not give up on our patients, and we must not lose touch with them as people.

Preface

Most people, seeing a newborn, wish the baby well. Given this auspicious start, how do any of us, including our patients, become estranged? Distancing may begin when we no longer understand, when the place of another's intentions in a mental sequence (to paraphrase Freud) cannot be discerned. Contrariwise, alienation recedes the more we as clinicians know just why, from the patient's perspective, their behavior makes sense.

This lends new meaning to the phrase "to know him is to love him." What happens to the infant, regarded so fondly through the glass of the hospital nursery, is that we stop "knowing" him as he develops a mind of his own. In extreme instances he seems "unknowable," and though there are many contributing factors, this is an aspect of mental illness. A big part of our work as clinicians is to "know" the patient again. In our experience at Chestnut Lodge, this is not so easy to do, especially when the patient suffers from schizophrenia.

This is a book about schizophrenia, about living with it over time as a patient, and about dealing with it over time as a therapist. This is also a book about individuals with schizophrenia. Our method is the old fashioned clinical case study. Each patient described here was part of a larger research project tracking the outcomes of several hundred patients from Chestnut Lodge. This book, however, is not about that research or about patients with schizophrenia as a group. The results of such studies are readily available in existing scientific journals. We wanted to present here individual schizophrenic patients just as we encounter them daily in our role as treating clinicians.

The research project referred to above, and the process of psychotherapy project described in this book, in fact, arose out of our frustrations as clinicians. Our failure at being effective psychotherapists with many of our schizophrenic patients led us on a journey back into the voluminous Chestnut Lodge archives for descriptions of how psychotherapy was done by our esteemed predecessors. We discovered to our dismay (but also to our relief) that no therapist proved consistently effective. It became clear that we had to look beyond the therapist to the dyad and that we had to let outcome, not a therapist's professional reputation, determine the value of any treatment encounter. In the selection of cases, therefore, we placed no special emphasis on who the therapist was.

Our choice of Joanne Greenberg and Frieda Fromm-Reichmann as one of the dyads seems to belie this assertion. Certainly Dr. Fromm-Reichmann is a special therapist with a place in the hall of fame of American psychiatry. Yet when we unearthed her from the archives, we found someone very familiar and everyday, quite straightforward and emulatable. She was indeed special, but her specialness was of a kind many could achieve with the proper mix of empathy, common sense, and good training.

We chose Joanne as one of our cases for several reasons, besides her therapist. She provided an excellent example of a good outcome and she was the best case in our project for illustrating the psychotherapeutic process at the upper end of the spectrum. We also felt that presenting her case from the hospital's perspective might add a certain factual validation and richness to her own fictionalized account (*I Never Promised You a Rose Garden*). For this and other reasons, we are grateful to her for permission to use her name. Despite the lack of anonymity, her case study has not been treated any differently from the others (we did not, for example, expunge more sensitive material from her narrative). We wrote about her case like all the rest, at a time when we thought she, too, would carry a pseudonym, and we obtained permission from her only after we had put the book together and sent it to her for review.

We are grateful to the therapists and other hospital personnel who did the actual caretaking of the patients in question. Without their dedication and hard work, these cases would not be available. We are also in debt to the late Dexter M. Bullard, Sr., the patriarch of Chestnut Lodge, whose wisdom and foresight ensured the proper documentation of these activities over the years.

Other contributors, both direct and by example, are many. Dr. Bert Nayfack of the Chestnut Lodge medical staff deserves special mention. He and THM studied a unique subgroup of schizophrenic patients from the overall Chestnut Lodge Follow-up Study, patients with a history of extensive chronicity and institutionalization of at least 10 years' duration. This project studied those who underwent a late onset functional improvement as opposed to those who did not. Many of the treatment or process variables that emerged overlapped with and enriched those presented here.

We acknowledge our debt to the team of individuals who carried out the "mother" follow-up study, which set the stage for the playing forth of these individual stories. Dr. Renee Marshel and Victoria Solsberry, M.S.W. helped THM with the follow-up interviews and Allison Benesch, M.S.W., laboriously reconstructed each patient's anamnesis for rating and rediagnosis. Ms. Polly Curry kept us sane and on track during that early frenetic harvest of data.

More contemporary kudos go to our research coordinator, Ms. Linda Berman, for her talents in translating our scribbles into readable text and for her careful editing. Ms. Eve Shapiro at the American Psychiatric Press added the final editorial touches to the piece.

We cannot end without acknowledging a large debt to our patients and teachers. Our patients continually inform us about mental disability and the multiple ways of coping with its aberrations. Our mentors have taught us to see the disability of schizophrenia in human terms. THM is especially indebted to the late Elvin Semrad, M.D., who brought love to his patients in the midst of technocratic fragmentation, and to William T. Carpenter, Jr., M.D., who taught THM to negotiate the mogul fields of scientific investigation. CJK is indebted to Lyman Wynne, M.D., and to other teachers and colleagues at the University of Rochester for providing a rich, diverse, supportive environment in which to study psychiatry. Finally, we both owe special thanks to D. M. Bullard, Jr., M.D., who, as Medical Director of Chestnut Lodge, has supported our investigations unflinchingly, his eye steadfast on the goal of *lux et veritas*.

Thomas H. McGlashan
Christopher J. Keats

About the Authors

Thomas H. McGlashan, M.D. is Director of Research at Chestnut Lodge, Research Professor of Psychiatry at the University of Maryland School of Medicine, Instructor at the Washington Psychoanalytic Institute, and a practicing psychotherapist and psychoanalyst.

Christopher J. Keats, M.D. received his B.A. from Harvard College and his M.D. from Temple University. A long-time interest in epistemology drew him to Chestnut Lodge and to the Washington Psychoanalytic Institute, where work with patients provides an anchor in the sea of speculation.

Part One:

The Cases

Case Study Rationale and Method

George, a hospitalized schizophrenic patient, never got out of bed. Psychological tests suggested that George isolated himself from others to protect them from his aggression. He stayed in bed to avoid fights with nurses and patients. Even when he was out of bed, he frequently lay down at the door of the dining room, or on the path outside, no matter what the weather.

Three years later, George walked off the hospital grounds at 7:00 a.m. to go to his job in a printing shop. This seemed a miracle to those who knew him. What had happened? How can we understand this development? In a verbatim transcript of George's case conference, his third psychotherapist, Dr. Henry Mitchell, said he was keen on establishing a positive relatedness with his patient at the inception of their work together. Accordingly, Dr. Mitchell considered it top priority that, whatever occurred in their four hours together each week, the interaction should be fun. As a result, Dr. Mitchell and George spent a great deal of time playing catch or billiards, drawing pictures, or reading novels. Out of this a dialogue developed, and a relationship.

Could all this have been the cause of George's transformation? Perhaps. It could also have been the effect of some other, less apparent process, such as a late onset spontaneous remission. Cause and effect can never be clarified from this perspective. Nevertheless, we feel it is valuable and interesting to note that, as part of George's change, he and his therapist successfully forged a relationship: not a "working relationship" or a "therapeutic alliance" in the classical sense, but a relationship that *was*.

Curious about such phenomena, we found ourselves beginning to read the records of other patients like George with the diagnosis of schizophrenia. We became so engrossed, in fact, that we decided to do a "study," and finally to write a book about our findings. This is that book. It is based upon the idea that the study of individual cases can still teach us something about schizophrenia and something about its treatment.

The number of persons diagnosed as suffering from chronic schizophrenia who are later completely cured is probably *very* small, although a larger number can be helped to live with their illness with some degree of independence and comfort. Therefore, it is noteworthy if someone improves radically; there can be something important to learn from the study of even a single case. Likewise, it is important to track closely the quality and vicissitudes of the doctor–patient relationship (here termed the "process") in those who fail to improve, or who deteriorate despite treatment efforts. With a careful clinical eye, and some luck, we may discern patterns in treatment process over time, patterns that discriminate between cases in which there is improvement and those in which there is deterioration.

These process patterns, if valid, can serve as useful predictors of likely treatment success or failure. Conversely, knowledge concerning outcome can inform the study of process by infusing it with direction, value, or valence. From a prior follow-up study (McGlashan 1984a, 1984b), we knew the long-term outcome of over 150 schizophrenic patients from our institution. Since we could identify specific good or poor outcome cases, it was possible to work backwards and study their associated treatment processes.

This book is also prompted by the existence of rich archives documenting a unique historical "experiment" in the study and treatment of schizophrenia. This experiment was the translation of psychoanalytic treatment principles into psychoanalytically oriented psychotherapy for severely ill psychotic patients. The psychotherapeutic approach with patients like George was pioneered, at the gathering of World War II and in the following three decades, by a number of outstanding clinicians collected under one roof by Dexter M. Bullard, M.D., the Medical Director of Chestnut Lodge. A few whose work became more widely known include Donald Burnham, John Cameron, Mabel and Robert Cohen, Frieda Fromm-Reichmann, Robert Gibson, John Kafka, Ping-Nie Pao, Margaret and David Rioch, Clarence Schulz, Harold Searles, and Otto Will. These individuals were informed by their studies in psychoanalysis and by the thinking of Harry Stack Sullivan, who gave seminars at Chestnut Lodge at the invitation of Dr. Bullard.

Much of the ongoing clinical work of the Chestnut Lodge staff, including everyone mentioned above, is recorded in extensive clinical histories, treatment process notes (both psychotherapeutic and nursing), and discharge summaries. Furthermore, each patient's treatment is reviewed regularly at clinical case conferences where the patient's therapist presents the ongoing psychotherapeutic work in the presence of his or her colleagues. Verbatim transcripts of *all* of these conferences are available, going back to the early 1940s— a rich clinical legacy, indeed.

Our book uses material from a period of American psychiatry in which practitioners devoted themselves to the study of interpersonal processes in a special way. For some therapists at Chestnut Lodge then, the *only* focus was on psychotherapeutic relatedness. One obvious disadvantage to using case material from this period is that we now live in an era when much more is known not only about the biological aberrations and treatments of schizophrenia, but also about what other psychosocial treatments can provide. George, in fact, is a "modern" patient who is making progress partly through the use of medication and partly through involvement in an especially active rehabilitation program. But George, as all before and after him, is also an individual human being, with complex desires and fears. In short, many of the issues which so preoccupied the therapists of the 1950s and 1960s have not gone away and will not, so that the study of treatment which took place in that unique era is of abiding interest to us all.

The individual treatment stories of patients like George at Chestnut Lodge may have special interest because the hospital is a place where patients and therapists are afforded the opportunity to come to know each other over a period of years. This is a setting in which one can develop with a patient a deepening sense of what a patient really thinks and feels. Such understandings are regularly achieved in psychoanalyses with neurotic patients. However, with patients who, like George, stay in bed to avoid fighting with their human brethren, there are special difficulties in the therapeutic work. These difficulties tend to abide intensely in the interpersonal sphere; that is, they pertain to the relationship between doctor and patient and are not easily resolved by traditional technical maneuvers such as interpreting resistance. Traditional theories and categories, in fact, frequently do not apply—hence our need to return to the primary clinical data with a naive perspective. Furthermore, now as in times past, we still have the treatment failures among us. Some patients have not benefited from brief hospitalizations, outpatient programs, and regimens of medication. The very existence of this group of chronic mental patients implies that we do not know what is necessary or sufficient to effect a cure. Chestnut Lodge has admitted many patients for whom current treatment strategies are demonstrably ineffective. A spirit of investigation therefore continues to characterize the institution's therapeutic approach, along with adherence to the long established primacy of the interpersonal relationship. We feel such relationships can still be mutative, and their study remains an endeavor of top priority.

We hope to create a typology of process that may prove useful to clinicians treating patients with schizophrenic disorders. With a knowledge of processes linked to both good and poor outcome, the clinician will be able to determine whether he or she is on track in the treatment effort and to chart a new course if necessary. We also hope to define something transmissible about the psychotherapy of schizophrenia, thereby enabling more persons to learn skills which tended to be shrouded in mystery and to be linked with the vertiginous persona of the mad-genius psychotherapist, whose skills were innate, unique, and impossible to learn.

Our method has been to study how, in selected instances, psychotherapeutic work was conducted over a long period and with what results, again over a long period. We are reviewing long-term treatment and long-term outcome of specific severely disturbed patients, some of whom did well, and some of whom did not.

In the instance of George, for example, a nodal point in therapy involved the discovery that he loved horse racing and had a talent for picking winners. Staff soon vied for the duty of escorting him to the track, and George took on a new image to those who cared for him. We are trying to integrate such vignettes into our understanding of what was going on in treatment in a way that might not be possible if we stayed with more "countable" phenomena such as number of treatment hours received, or types of interpretations given.

This kind of integration, we hope, will offer something new for research into schizophrenia, for research into psychotherapy, and for the practice of psychotherapy of persons with schizophrenic disorders.

SCHIZOPHRENIA AND PSYCHOTHERAPY RESEARCH

No one raised in the philosophical climate of twentieth century rationalism can accept mere testimony as valid; there needs to be scientific study. Yet nothing is more difficult than to apply experimental technique to meaningful questions about the human condition. Those who, following scientific principles, investigate only the reliably observable may well miss what goes on beneath the surface. There remains the lurking suspicion that what is being measured is not as important as what is essentially unmeasurable.

The study of psychotherapy and its outcome has been plagued in particular by disagreement as to what one is trying to achieve. What, in fact, constitutes a good result? Some of the concerns about how to define quality outcome seem like splitting hairs when we are studying the schizophrenic disorders. These patients are so ill that it would be fairly easy to reach consensus about improvement. For example, if, at the behest of hallucinated voices, a man puts his hand in the fire, or masturbates at the pulpit, or walks in the center of the highway, he has a readily observable problem; if he stops hearing voices and stops doing these things he is better, at least at a first approximation. Even a quality enthusiast might admit that such easily countable things as time spent out of institutions do reflect something important about outcome, since it is likely that very severely ill people would be in the hospital rather than out. Of course there are exceptions, but again as a first approximation, the man working the night shift at the Post Office, albeit with few social engagements and idiosyncratic thoughts, is doing better than the seclusion room patient who needs intensive nursing care for his personal hygiene. It is impossible to escape the conclusion that given an adequate description of the schizophrenic patient and his situation, objective assessments of outcome *can* be made.

It is also impossible to escape the feeling, when reading the empirical literature on outcome and the treatment of schizophrenia, that psychotherapy is the wrong tool for the job. The overall outcome of schizophrenic patients in brief or long-term psychotherapy versus other therapies has differed very little in controlled prospective studies. When psychotherapy alone was compared with medication alone, or with medication and psychotherapy together, the treatments involving medications were overwhelmingly the most successful. Beverly Gomes-Schwartz provided a review of individual psychotherapy of schizophrenia and concluded that "the results of the major studies of psychoanalytically oriented therapy are sobering. There is very little to indicate that the average schizophrenic accomplishes a great deal in much of the psychotherapy that is currently practiced" (Gomes-Schwartz 1984, p.324).

Follow-up studies have also lent little support to belief in the efficacy of psychotherapy with schizophrenia. Many of John Rosen's patients, for example, who seemed in the short run to have improved from "direct analysis," were severely compromised many years later (Horwitz et al. 1958). The Chestnut Lodge Study showed that two of three schizophrenic patients were only marginally better or had been continuously ill at the time of follow-up (McGlashan 1984b). Michael Stone's work at Columbia's Psychiatric Institute revealed that for the schizophrenic group receiving individual psychotherapy three times per week, the results were virtually the same as those at Chestnut Lodge: a decided majority was doing poorly at the final evaluation. This group of schizophrenic patients, in contrast to those at Chestnut Lodge, included many who were not chronically ill; prognostically, they were a better sample, yet the outcome was still abysmal (Stone 1986).

The total picture from research, as far as psychotherapy of schizophrenia is concerned, is of one unimpressive result after another. This has been the case for short-term psychotherapy, long-term psychotherapy, insight-oriented therapy, supportive-adaptive therapy, psychoanalytic psychotherapy, client-centered Rogerian therapy, and direct analysis. It has been true whether the therapists were experienced or inexperienced, whether the patients' illnesses were acute or chronic, and whether they were inpatients or outpatients. Psychotherapy alone was not effective. This conclusion was reached based on studies from the 1960s and 1970s, and was so impressive that psychotherapy stopped being used. As Gomes-Schwartz (1984) reminds us, while as recently as 1968 it was considered unethical not to include psychotherapy in a treatment program, it is now widely believed to be unethical to offer psychotherapy without drug treatment.

On the other hand, research support for some sort of interpersonal intervention comes from two directions. Psychosocial treatments directed at the schizophrenic patient and his or her family seem to have demonstrable effects. Hogarty and his colleagues in Pittsburgh (Hogarty et al. 1986) replicated work showing that schizophrenic patients who returned home to families in which there were high levels of criticism and emotional overinvolvement suffered an increased rate of relapse. Psychoeducational family therapy that helped families lower these levels proved effective in reducing manifest psychopathology and rehospitalization rates. Hogarty compared four groups of schizophrenic patients: one treated with drug alone, the second treated with drug and family therapy, the third treated with drug and social skills training, and the fourth treated with drug, family therapy, and social skills training. Over the same time period, the relapse rates in these three groups were 41 percent, 19 percent, 20 percent, and 0 percent, respectively.

Although patients in these studies maintained reduced levels of florid symptomatology, they often continued to lead constricted lives without social contacts or employment. To this extent, the magnitude of the result was diminished. Yet for the first time, a powerful, replicable effect on a core outcome measure was shown to result from a social interaction, something previous studies of psychotherapy had never been able to demonstrate.

The other direction from which support for psychotherapy has come is the sweeping review of Smith and colleagues (1980), which showed that psychotherapy, broadly defined, was efficacious and contributed more to outcome than could be accounted for by the passage of time. Eysenck (1952) had challenged researchers to show that their interventions produced results over the gradual improvement that could in many cases be expected from the natural history of the illness. Smith and associates (1980) answered this challenge, albeit chiefly for a very mixed population of outpatients. Their work also showed that no particular technique was superior; behavior modification, psychoanalysis, once a week psychotherapy, and many others, were equally efficacious. While Smith and colleagues did not extend their work to psychotherapy of schizophrenia specifically, their results provided evidence for the value of psychotherapy in general.

Three broad conclusions can be drawn from the empirical literature. One, several forms of individual psychotherapy with schizophrenia are ineffective or no more effective than more expedient alternatives. Two, there is broad evidence that psychotherapy as an endeavor is worthwhile. Three, recent work shows that certain psychosocial interventions can demonstrably affect some schizophrenic patients. It seems, therefore, that reports of the demise of psychotherapy of schizophrenia may be premature. Perhaps only particular forms of it are moribund while other forms hold more promise.

The standard prospective research design calls for the application of psychotherapy and a different treatment to separate patient groups with the same diagnosis. Outcome is measured, usually after completion of treatment, and the group results compared. Among the requirements for a good empirical test is the need for competing therapies to be explicit, identifiable, consistent, and distinguishable. Because of these requirements, studies in the last decade have relied increasingly on the use of "manuals" to standardize the types of therapy being compared. From a research perspective, this is an ideal strategy. What if, however, the optimal form of psychotherapy for schizophrenia is an approach that uses the widest variety of techniques imaginable, both from one patient to another, or with the same patient over time? It would be difficult to design a valid study of this kind of psychotherapy. In fact, this type of broadly defined, individually tailored psychotherapy has never been tested.

We decided to approach this problem from a new angle. In the past, outcome has been the *dependent* variable, conferring validity on one or another of the treatments in question. We decided to make outcome the *independent* variable in the research equation. Psychotherapy would be the question mark, the dependent variable. Instead of studying one or another kind of psychotherapeutic intervention prospectively we simply began at the end, knowing the outcome. We then looked back and asked what the human interaction was like, and whether it could be described.

Most importantly, we worked from examples to theory. We started with what actually happened, rather than with some idea about what should have happened. We do not present a point of view with the aim of substantiating it but instead we move from the specific to the general. Instead of asking whether the conduct of therapy in a specific case conformed to standards prescribed by a particular school of thought or manual of technique, we asked, quite simply, what *did* happen in the therapist–patient dyad? Our knowledge of outcome gave a valence to the quality of the therapeutic work. We knew in advance whether the work was associated with success or failure and we purposefully allowed this to bias our review of the process.

Relative to current psychotherapy research, what we tried doing was so traditional as to be radical; we returned to case history and narrative before devising theory. As emphasized, we *assumed* outcome was related to process (as well as to natural history). We assumed that if there was a good outcome, something in the process of treatment was good as well. What, for example, enabled George to stop lying on the sidewalk and apply for work? Something of great interest occurred, and we searched to find out what it was. We were forced to look at the patient's illness, and the psychotherapeutic process, since those were the data available to us. We also believed there should be a correlation between these factors and outcome, and that the events of the process could be clearly described if not objectively measured.

METHOD

Extensive patient histories, verbatim transcriptions of ongoing case conferences, and results of long-term follow-up inquiries constitute the data for our present work. During the Chestnut Lodge Follow-up Study (McGlashan 1984a, 1984b), the case histories had been submitted for recategorization under *DSM-III* criteria, and the patients we considered were those suffering from schizophrenic disorders. The 163 schizophrenic patients from this original follow-up study were inpatients at Chestnut Lodge for at least 3 months, and discharged between the years 1950 and 1975. They received individual psychotherapy four times per week and, in addition to being assigned a psychoanalytically oriented therapist, they received care from an administrative psychiatrist who made decisions about their life in the hospital milieu. Patients in the study were assessed by telephone or during face-to-face interviews (with the patients themselves or with relatives) an average of 15 years after they were discharged.

Our method for the present study was to select charts of patients for whom there was especially definitive follow-up material, of equal mix, male and female, and of both good and poor outcome. We selected 10 patients on this basis and reviewed their hospital charts. It was necessary, in writing an account of each patient's past history, hospital course, and posthospital adjustment, to be selective. The assessment of any skew these selections imparted to the project is difficult to make. We are both psychoanalytically trained psychiatrists who believe symptoms arise from intrapsychic conflict, and that difficulties can also occur because of organic deficit or problems in the development of psychic structure. If we had a different orientation, believing, for example, that something like date of birth was crucial in determining outcome, then that information would have received a salient place in our review. Instead, it was uniformly omitted, as were many other details. Of course, our selections were made from a set of data already influenced by the original authors of the charted material. Their own biases can be inferred from the fact that they worked at a psychoanalytic hospital at a time when psychoanalytic principles were applied in the long-term treatment of severely disturbed individuals, and neuroleptic medications were beginning to be introduced.

We owe a debt, of course, to those doctors and nurses. They did the work and compiled the original records. They might vociferously dispute the decisions we made in the retelling, not to mention the speculations we made about what was happening in the treatment. We studied the narratives in series, over the course of several years, and generated hypotheses about what was going on. The format in which we present the material should now allow the reader to participate in this process as well.

The narratives themselves do not always seem particularly complete. This, however, gave us another level of interaction to observe:

the seeming completeness or incompleteness of the record itself became a point of interest. No effort was made to smooth out gaps in the record, even when they were egregious. In a sense, the written record of treatment, rather than the patient, was the object of study. We assumed that whether the record held together, whether it contained much or little data, whether the record gave rise to dynamic speculations, all reflected something important about the doctor–patient relationship.

We have necessarily taken a broad perspective; the data simply did not allow a close focus on the give and take within each therapy hour. In much of the analytic and psychotherapy research literature, scrutiny centers upon specific interchanges between doctor and patient. We were looking instead at the gestalt of the work, the ambience of the dyad, and we were trying to understand the ingredients of a "good relationship."

In the following chapters we describe 4 patients of the 10 we studied: 2 men, 2 women; 2 good outcomes, 2 poor outcomes. Except for Joanne Greenberg, who gave us permission, and her therapist, Dr. Fromm-Reichmann, who is deceased, the names of most staff members and all patients have been changed to protect confidentiality.

Ben

Ben, single, white, 21 years old, entered Chestnut Lodge in the early 1960s. His overt psychiatric illness began while he was attending college in his hometown, and followed two losses: his girlfriend Amy died mysteriously (Ben's mother thought she committed suicide following a rejection from Ben), and the maternal grandmother died shortly thereafter. That winter Ben became depressed, could not concentrate, and missed classes. He complained that no one understood him and that the people around him were phony.

Then, on a day in mid-April, Ben's mother sent him on an errand. He never returned, and there were several reconstructions of what happened. According to mother's version, he knocked on a stranger's door and announced he had cancer and syphilis. The stranger, frightened, called the police, who detained Ben for observation and then sent him to a nearby general hospital. In another version, Ben knocked at the door of Amy's house and expressed hostility toward her father. The hospital record version said Ben attempted suicide by inhaling carbon monoxide from a running car following a bout of heavy drinking during which he was frightened when a man made homosexual advances. Ben himself said he had attempted suicide but did not say how.

By all accounts, it seems that Ben suffered an acute psychosis. He behaved like an infant at the general hospital, and after two weeks was transferred to a private psychiatric hospital where he stayed for three months, hallucinating and delusional. He believed other people felt he was stupid, and he worried about being homosexual. A few weeks after admission, Ben spoke of his desire to kill himself and surrendered a small pocket knife to the nurse. He told her he planned to jump out the window, and he was put on extra observation and bigger doses of Thorazine. He had a dream of being tortured by a Nazi officer who squeezed Ben's testicles with his hands and pressed them to his knee. The Nazi officer was linked in Ben's associations to his therapist, who wondered if Ben was having homosexual fantasies about him. Shortly afterwards, Ben's panic and excitement in the doctor's office necessitated the use of physical restraint. Thorazine was increased to nearly 2,000 mg daily. A trial of electroconvulsive therapy (ECT) was considered. Ben continued to be depressed and suicidal. He was in a constant state of panic with persecutory delusions and auditory hallucinations of his name being called. He thought his therapist would either kill him or try to seduce him. The hospital staff insisted Ben be given ECT, and his mother therefore transferred him to another hospital, where he remained for three months before coming to Chestnut Lodge. The staff at the new hospital had also decided ECT was indicated. Their diagnosis was schizophrenic reaction, chronic, undifferentiated type.

Ben was firstborn. Although delivered at full term, his posterior presentation made the birth difficult and painful. When Ben was 10 months old, his father left for a year in the Army and his mother moved to her parents' home but "couldn't stand it," and returned to her apartment after 2 months.

There is little information about weaning, bowel training, or other events from early childhood. Ben's mother was perhaps too distraught to attend to the details of his life; for whatever reasons she did not remember his developmental steps. She did recall that Ben resisted going to nursery school when he was three by crying and having temper tantrums. Ben himself remembered a recurrent nightmare from this time in which there was a "war," expressed as "an explosion of colors."

The birth of a sister, Jane, when Ben was six years old, marked a kind of watershed, for afterward he showed increased reticence and conformity. He never complained and always did as he was told. Jane, however, created turmoil with incessant demands. Mother and father worked, leaving the children with a housekeeper, Anna, an English spinster in her fifties. The children saw little of their parents for the next four years, which may have been just as well, since Ben's father was a harsh disciplinarian who hit Ben with a strap, or slapped his face, or twisted his arm, and Ben's mother was an inhibited person with many anxieties. Anna, on the other hand, managed the household warmly and competently. Ben's mother, seeing this, eventually became jealous of the housekeeper, and fired her. Compounding the loss, Ben's father contracted a fatal illness and died 6 months later, when Ben was 10 years old.

Ben, a loner and marginal student in elementary school, entered junior high school with excess emotional baggage. This situation darkened upon mother's remarriage when Ben was 13; the marriage was annulled one month later. Ben suffered a period of depression during which he stayed in his room and did not play with peers. Aware that something was wrong, his mother sent him to the doctor, but after three months at a mental health outpatient clinic, Ben stopped going. He said he was not depressed but bored and "wrathful" toward society. Still, he remained quite self-conscious and vulnerable. Looking at himself in the mirror, for example, unable to part his hair in just the way he wanted, he broke out in tears.

Ben did mediocre work in high school and had no close friends. He did not date and characterized himself as a "baby" sexually. His one area of accomplishment was athletics; he played football and tennis. Involvement in sports did not improve his social life, however. In his senior year he became withdrawn, had difficulty sleeping, and refused to go to school. He entered therapy with a psychologist. During the six months they worked together, Ben returned to school, graduated, and won acceptance to college.

Ben experienced adolescence as a period of despair, loneliness, and estrangement. At college things improved somewhat. Ben continued to be active in sports and became the coeditor of the campus newspaper. He lived in a dormitory but moved home for the summer, where he worked as a busboy in a restaurant. Relations with male peers were always superficial, but now Ben's involvement with women went from no involvement to sudden, very intense and jealous affairs; first with Amy, with whom he enjoyed heavy petting, and then briefly with Doris, with whom he had sexual intercourse. Then came Amy's unfortunate death and the beginning of Ben's overt psychotic illness.

Ben came to Chestnut Lodge by ambulance, heavily sedated with Thorazine, 800 mg per day, which he had received regularly for a few days prior to admission. Drowsy and mute, Ben was unresponsive even in his facial expression. Despite his muteness, he did demonstrate hostility and anger. He came within inches of other people and stared in a threatening way. He pinched girls on their breasts and buttocks, and made homosexual advances toward some of the aides. He bragged that his genitals were longer and larger than anyone else's.

On psychological testing at admission, Ben scored a full scale Intelligence Quotient (IQ) of 108. Although he was talking by this time, he was not very cooperative. He became disorganized when performing perceptual motor tasks, which led to speculation that his poor grade school performance was due to minimal brain dysfunction. On projective tests, Ben offered little fantasy material, and gave the impression of deliberate withholding, as if he were teasing. He gave depressive associations to two Thematic Aperception Test (TAT) pictures showing a younger man with an elderly man and woman. He said the old man looked like his grandfather, but he was clearly reluctant to elaborate.

The psychologist concluded that Ben was an excited, unstable, psychotic young man whose central problems revolved around his reactions to the loss of significant people. The test showed that Ben had profound anxiety about the integrity of his body, his genitals in particular. He was concerned about impulse control, especially aggressive impulses, with fear of destructive consequences to himself and others. Independence was construed as an aggressive act which would trigger counteraggression. Ben appeared to be striving to return to a safer level of relationship, regressing to a position of preadolescent dependency, at least in relation to women.

He presented little evidence of systematized delusions or any consistent thought disorder, but he seemed to have grossly distorted ideas about himself and his relationship to others. The diagnosis was schizophrenia, catatonic, in partial remission.

The therapist chosen for Ben was Dr. Schwarz, a young man recently launched on his studies at the Psychoanalytic Institute, who took Ben as one of his first cases at Chestnut Lodge. He believed the reactive nature of Ben's illness (i.e., in response to losses of various kinds), the lack of chronicity, Ben's past ability to contain and limit symptoms, and his relatively good functioning at college and with girlfriends, were good prognostic signs. Against these positive factors was a background of inadequate personality development, which, if not changed by therapy, might cause future problems.

None of these ideas helped much in Ben's first session with Dr. Schwarz. Ben was brought to the office by an aide. The therapist stepped into the hall and said, "I'm Dr. Schwarz." They shook hands. Ben came in, and Dr. Schwarz said he could sit wherever he liked, or lie on the couch.

In retrospect, regarding early use of the couch, Dr. Schwarz said, "Just why I told him this is not clear to me, but I suspect it was partly due to my apprehension and partly due to my theory at the time of how the couch was to be used."

Ben immediately sprawled on the couch in a tremulous freeze. He maintained this position for a few minutes, and then gradually brought his left hand over his genitals, and then his right hand.

Dr. Schwarz continued his account of the first session: "I told him I was going to be his doctor. Soon he got up and began to explore the office. He opened the door and read the nameplates, 'Dr. Schwarz, Dr. Billings' (we were sharing an office then). He returned to lie on the couch, then rose, walked over to the desk and began knocking my pipes onto the floor in a slow, tentative fashion.

"'Don't do that!' I said. He put the pipes back in place and came over to sit beside me. He stared at me and I said, in slow cadence in pace with his slow movements, 'I sense you are in deep trouble.'

"He put out his right hand for me to take and then his left, crossing it over the right, and we sat holding hands. He then rose, walked to the door, and gave it a hard kick. He looked quite menacing at this moment. He returned and we held hands again, the same as before. Next, he lay on the couch and soon there was deep snoring. He slept for 40 minutes and I woke him and said time was up and asked if he had any questions about the hospital.

"No," he said.

"I told him the schedule, we shook hands, and he left."

Thus was born a relationship which might seem to have had an inauspicious beginning.

The beginning was equally difficult for the ward administrator, Dr. Simmons. Thorazine was reduced from 800 mg per day to nothing over the course of Ben's first two or three weeks in the hospital. Ben appeared in the nude on the sun porch with an erection, and propositioned both men and women. He ran his hands over the women, and approached closer than normal distance when speaking, all of which felt more irritating than frightening to staff. Whenever staff intervened, Ben portrayed what he was doing as a joke, and promised to stop. If a substitute activity were offered, he took part, but when it was over, he returned to making the same advances as before.

Therapy sessions with Dr. Schwarz soon took on a repetitive pattern. Ben began by saying something off-putting, such as, "Well, have you got laid recently?" Then he asked other questions, which the therapist might answer. Dr. Schwarz occasionally commented or asked a question of his own, in the middle of which Ben would suddenly say, "Can I go to sleep?"

Dr. Schwarz would say it was up to him. Ben invariably fell asleep, woke up at the end of the session, shook hands, and said "Have a nice day."

"You too, Ben," said Dr. Schwarz.

The repetitive sameness became familiar territory for patient and therapist, a place where Ben could repeatedly attack (with intrusive, disrespectful questions), withdraw (into sleep), and make reparation (shake hands). Dr. Schwarz recalled what the psychological test said about Ben's problem controlling aggressive impulses and his fear of their destructive consequences to himself and others. Ben was enacting this problem in the transference.

In another session Ben asked, "How the fuck are you?" He then lay on the couch and said he telephoned his mother. One of Ben's delusional beliefs was that she was held prisoner in a different section of the hospital. He was relieved to find she was at the other end of the phone, alive and in good health. Ben added, "I think I'll go to sleep."

"Why do that?" Dr. Schwarz asked.

"I'm paying good money."

"Yes. Why sleep through something you're paying good money for?"

Ben obediently remained awake, and at the end of the session he broke wind and said, "What do you think that was?"

The therapist was silent.

"Come on, you snivelling idiot, what do you think that was?"

"I think it was a fart."

"Well, yes, but what do you think of it?"

"Maybe B plus."

Ben burst out laughing and said, "Are you sure it's not an A minus?"

Another time Ben was sleeping, and the therapist had nearly reached his limit of tolerance. He thought to himself, "If the little son of a bitch wants to fight, we'll fight!" He realized he would like to slam Ben against the door, swing him onto the couch, and announce that the analysis was about to begin. Two sessions later, Ben said, "I might become violent. What will you do?"

"Defend myself," said Dr. Schwarz.

"That sounds reasonable," Ben said.

By the beginning of the third month after admission, Ben did require restraint. He was placed in cold wet sheet pack twice daily, primarily because he was molesting women. Dr. Schwarz saw him in the pack, and would hold his cigarettes or give him coffee. For five or six days, Ben yelled as loudly as possible, sometimes spewing profanity, but often screaming incoherently. Dr. Schwarz held his ears because the noise was so loud.

"What's wrong?" Ben asked.

"So much noise. But go ahead and scream if you want to."

"I'll let you know when I'm about to start, OK?"

"Fine," said Dr. Schwarz.

From then on he would say "now" or "ready," before beginning the earsplitting shrieks.

By the end of the third month, Ben showed an emerging capacity for self-observation. He said he had been disoriented and thought he was in hell when he came to the hospital. Now he believed the cold wet sheet pack would make his penis grow larger. He said his main problem was that his penis was too big.

For the next three months, Ben stayed in bed during his hours. When Dr. Schwarz appeared on the unit, Ben immediately lay down and fell asleep. When not asleep, he often read for the entire hour. By the end of this period, his behavior outside the hours was more conventional, and he obtained the privileges of walking by himself on hospital grounds, and of working part-time at the patient-run store.

The reason for the change in Ben's behavior, according to the head nurse, was that he had been moved to a room shared with another patient. Shortly after the move, Ben stopped behaving and speaking obscenely. He related to his new roommate as to a father or a big brother. Ben's manner was that of an obsequious little boy. He was more verbal, but his sentences were brief and the words simple. The subject matter changed constantly. He rushed onto the unit saying "Guess what I just did!" or "Guess what I just saw!" or presenting the staff with a cut finger. The staff felt warmly toward Ben, and aides stopped what they were doing to listen to him and take care of him. Ben still blustered, but presented himself in such a way as to make clear that it *was* bluster, and nothing more.

Now, his sexual assaults could be reduced to humor very rapidly. For example, he grabbed an occupational therapist around the chest and she screamed, "Hold it!" This became a joke throughout the hospital.

The nursing staff noticed that Ben took an interest in other patients who needed assistance, and that he often volunteered to walk with those who needed escort. The patients liked him, sensing his warmth.

Ben came by his warmth and somewhat manic quality partly through identification with his mother. Once when she came to see him she entered the social worker's office loaded down with Playboy magazines, miniature chocolate men, and chewing gum, all in a little bag, and she raved to the social worker about how clever it was of her to think of putting everything in the bag as she had done.

Then Ben came in and they pounded each other on the back like two buddies meeting.

In June, six months after admission, Ben brought these qualities to the softball field. He bragged that he could hit the ball 500 feet, and exaggerated the number of his home runs. At practice he was full of talk until the opposing team arrived, and then his teammates told him to put a lid on it.

Dr. Schwarz realized the defensive aspect of Ben's grandiosity. He told Ben it must be difficult to have to be perfect all the time and he wondered if this led to depression when Ben failed to meet goals which were impossible by their nature to fulfill. At first, despite this intervention, Ben continued to present himself as a potential international hero to all within earshot. Soon, however, a less lofty view of himself emerged. He told Dr. Schwarz of a woman who could run the 100 yard dash in 10.4 seconds and admitted he could not do it in less than 11 seconds himself. By October, Ben had become modest in speech, and whereas in the past he walked naked around the room, he was now careful to keep himself dressed. He lost weight on a diet of breakfast cereal, and began to look less like an oversized little boy.

By November, Ben spoke of outpatiency, and reviewed his experiences in a way that suggested he was capable of perspective. For instance, he said, "What the hell do you think my life has been like? My father died when I was 10, my mother's a wreck, and my grandmother was impossible to live with." Then he smiled and added, "She was stubborn. So am I." Ben seemed ready to manage living outside the hospital, although he was still in need of treatment, and a few weeks later, he became an outpatient. On the same day, he bought an automobile. "You must know I'm really in love with cars," he told Dr. Schwarz.

Another action Ben took upon being discharged from the hospital was to start a relationship with a married patient, Mrs. Jones, who had been quite destructive to herself and others in the past. Within two months, however, he renounced Mrs. Jones. In a January session, Ben spoke for the first time of masturbation. He then reported a dream in which he was in a car with a four-speed gear shift. He said, "It's very strange, I wasn't anxious. Somehow I was able to manipulate the gears. I was able to shift." He added that he hadn't the foggiest idea what the dream meant. Dr. Schwarz told Ben the dream meant Ben was thinking of shifting from one woman to another. He did not take up Ben's reference to masturbation, nor the fact that Ben had often questioned Dr. Schwarz about his car and its four-speed gear shift. At that time, Ben could only drive an automatic shift, and Dr. Schwarz did not want to wound his self-esteem.

Ben's treatment came to an end. He did not ruminate about termination. In one final note the therapist said that Ben remembered almost all of what happened to him during his period of acute psychosis. Dr. Schwarz hoped Ben would move beyond remembering to a more abstract curiosity about his life and eventually to an integration of the psychotic experience.

What became of these hopes? Although no account exists of the process of treatment from the time of the gearshift dream to the final termination, we do possess a record of outcome. The follow-up interviewer contacted Ben in person 15 years after treatment began.

Ben was a stocky, pleasant looking 36-year-old man with glasses. He dressed appropriately, and from his demeanor his intelligence seemed above average. He started the interview by saying he hoped his participation in the follow-up study would help mankind, and then he questioned the method by which his address was obtained. He repeatedly sought assurance about confidentiality.

Ben told the interviewer that upon leaving Chestnut Lodge, he pursued and earned a degree in education at a nearby college. He taught elementary school on the Eastern Shore for three months, but the teachers and kids began to "bother" him; work became "a hassle." Ben did not or could not specify further what this meant. He quit teaching and traveled to Quebec, where he enrolled in a Yoga course that lasted the entire summer. To make ends meet, he delivered newspapers or sold cars part-time.

In the fall, Ben traveled to Colorado. He described this period, which lasted three or four months, as "like a transition in my life; it was as if I was leaving my childhood and becoming a grown-up." He taught yoga for money and also volunteered as a yoga instructor at a psychiatric clinic. "I just hung around and talked to people," he said. On a whim, he decided to return East and had a very good experience driving back cross-country. Then, for reasons not clear to himself, he settled in the town where Chestnut Lodge is located. "When I came around here," he said, "I felt like I was reborn in a sense. I started to feel better and my life started working better ever since I was in here, and so I was drawn back to this area." At that time, he was not formally employed, but "doing some writing and really enjoying life." He had a girlfriend, Ruby.

Ruby and Ben were married by a justice of the peace after a six-week courtship. Ruby worked as a paralegal in a nearby town so they went there to live. Ben had a six-month stint as a part-time teacher's aide at a school for emotionally disturbed children. Then he returned to car sales, but found the job unethical and quit. He sold advertising copy to a newspaper for nearly a year and later took two department store sales jobs. At the time of follow-up, Ben had been working for three years on commission as a shoe salesman in a department store. He saw the reward as mostly financial. "What I get out of it is money, and I like some of the people that I work with and I like some of the customers some of the time," he said. "I enjoy sociability and the chance to talk; at other times I want to be reclusive, really alone. I still need to be like that."

At follow-up, Ben's family included two children, a son in kindergarten and a daughter 18 months old. Ben and his wife together earned $35,000 per year. Socially they were close with a divorced woman who was one of their neighbors. Ben also hiked or played tennis with male friends, but did not feel close to any of them, with the possible exception of Ralph. Ben said that to others Ralph would look like a friend, "but there are always two levels of everything. What things look like from the outside is not always the same as what is going on inside." Ralph did not work at the same store, but when he and Ben had time off together, they went to a mall or went swimming.

Ben enjoyed a good relationship with his father-in-law, a retired carpenter, who took an interest in Ben and made furniture for him. He made a beautiful cradle for the baby and a bunk bed for Eddy, the kindergartener.

As for his own family, Ben was not on speaking terms with his sister because he believed she treated their mother poorly. Ben thought his former problems were caused by family tensions. "My grandmother and my mother didn't get along much, and I was caught in the middle. All kinds of stuff was going on after my father died. That is one thing that kept me from really studying or doing well in school or anything." Ben felt that he was changed by therapy. "In my soul now I feel like a poet. I feel happy. I look at the snow, I feel happy. I just see things and I feel happy in life. Especially when I see my kids, you know; I look at Eddy and I think, gee, if it wasn't for me pulling through and at least surviving, then he and I wouldn't be here."

Ben denied suicidal thoughts, serious depression, or symptoms of thought disorder such as paranoid thinking or hallucinations. He suffered, however, from an ulcer which was diagnosed one year after his discharge. He also believed some unconscious anxiety caused him to grind his teeth. He wore a mouthguard at night to protect them. He noted there were times he was happy: "alive and healthy, my body functioning; I'm gonna sell so many shoes and I'm gonna meet so many people; I feel real good." At other times he felt he was not doing enough with his mind and body, not living up to his potential. Ben did not believe his happy periods were anything like the manic agitation he had in the hospital, nor that his down periods were anything like the pain of psychosis. He remembered what it was like at the time when "just trying to find something good about yourself was such a struggle. You just wanted to stay in bed all day or die. I never feel like that now. Sometimes, when I feel real bad I just want to escape, but that is just a fantasy, and I realize I can't do that."

In response to relatively unstructured questions, Ben became anxious and somewhat disorganized. He would start rambling about poetry, reincarnation, or philosophy, apparently in an effort to rationalize his difficulties, whenever he told the interviewer something about himself that was negatively tinged. For example, the interviewer asked Ben who he thought was responsible for making the major decisions in his life.

"Me," he said.

"Like what?" asked the interviewer.

"Like what kind of a car to buy. Well in a way, Ruby influences me a lot. Like about the children; I really didn't want a second baby much. Then we tried to have another one. Sometimes I am resentful about that because I think it made life more complicated. Sometimes I don't feel so positive about life and I think, gosh, why would I want to bring another life into the world? When you are married you can't just do everything on your own; you have to decide where you are going to live, what kind of car you are going to buy, what you are going to spend your money on. You know what, people don't have that much power in life anyway. I mean you are like a flow of things anyway, I mean you are born and you are going to die at a certain time and you are just in here and you have illusions of freedom in a lot of things."

In general, Ben related cooperatively to the interviewer, but he envied her position as a mental health professional, and in order to defend himself against awareness of this envy, he sexualized their relationship. He flirted with her and insinuated they could have an affair, since it was his day off.

The interviewer was impressed that Ben had managed to hold a job for three years and to marry and father children despite ongoing paranoid concerns, despite intense envy of those he felt made more of their lives than he, and despite conflicts over dependency, intimacy, and responsibility. Ben practiced yoga as a way of "centering" himself and as a means of "controlling" himself. For many years he was a vegetarian, and he continued to pay particular attention to being in good physical shape. The emphasis he placed on being physically strong suggested a concern about being cohesive and whole.

Ben was intensely dependent on his wife, and perhaps because of this dependency, sex with her was not totally satisfying. He had occasional affairs about which he said, "It probably is better for the marriage not to play around, in terms of energy, or money, or of hurting the other person. Because if you are going to sleep with someone, I mean I'm gonna love the person. I'm not going to sleep with someone just to sleep with someone. So it is not going to go anywhere. It would probably be a futile thing to do. Plus there is guilt, too, even though rationally you say it is okay."

Ben had never been rehospitalized, nor had he been placed on psychoactive medication. He did see a psychotherapist briefly on his return from Colorado and felt there was something positive gained in the relationship.

The interviewer asked Ben what things came to mind about his experience at Chestnut Lodge.

"I think about sports," he said. "I think about playing tennis with people, or playing softball, or some of the people I got to know. I think about getting better, I think about sunny days and spring, like all of a sudden this grey shadow lifted and I was starting to feel better, and I think about cold wet sheet packs. I had those for a long time. I think about some of the doctors; I think really warm stuff about some of the doctors that tried to help me. I think about money, how much money I spent here. I think, boy, it would be nice to have all that money again, but I think I have more positive than negative thoughts about this place."

"Can you say what was the most therapeutic experience you had here?"

"It was probably getting away from my [home] environment and just taking the drugs away."

Ben said the least therapeutic experience was being put in cold wet sheet pack, but added, "Cold wet sheet pack probably was good, because it forced me to meditate and be still. That is what yoga does, it helps you to sit still and just watch your thoughts; you realize none of them are going to overpower you. I remember I used to smoke cigarettes in the pack and people would hold them for me, or they would give me drinks. People took care of me while I was immobile. Maybe it made me feel like a baby or something, in a warm environment. You know I had some nice friends here, like girlfriends from here, at the time. They were nice relationships."

The interviewer asked Ben what sort of match he made with his therapist.

"I don't know," Ben said, "I was in bad shape when I got here. I think he was a good man, but I was pretty resistant to him. I don't think it would have been different with anyone else unless you could get somebody like Carl Jung or something, but I wasn't even willing, or able, to talk to some wise old man, even a terrific father figure or grandfather figure. I guess we were as good a match as any. I remember spending a lot of time talking about cars with him. He took me to a sporting event once. We went to a basketball game and he really took an interest in me as a person. I don't know whether that was part of the therapy or not, probably it was, but he seemed to care about me, not because of his career or something, but he listened real well. He was a good therapist."

The interviewer felt that the time when Ben returned East marked a watershed for him. Before then, although he had finished college, he led an essentially nomadic existence with no strong attachment to any occupation or person, as if his sense of self depended on solitude and isolation. Oddly enough, it may have been among other "drifters" in Colorado that Ben somehow found an identity, and gained enough self-cohesion to be ready to relate. Quickly, he found his wife-to-be: Ruby, a solid, motherly person. The whirlwind speed of courtship suggested that Ben was especially primed for marriage. If his needs were in the direction of overdependency, at least he was able to find someone who was essentially good for him. Ruby had a job, was apparently stable, and ready to share *her* life. It sounded as if she complemented him well. Although Ben fantasized about "taking off" when "things became too complicated," he did not do so. Sex was not all he hoped for with Ruby, and Ben had an occasional affair, but he also demonstrated a capacity for enjoyment and playfulness with his wife. Sometimes, Ben said, they had sex right in the middle of a fight; then they screamed at each other while doing it. "It's really funny," Ben said. "We do all kinds of funny things while having sex, like singing 'Ode to Joy' or putting records on."

This vignette demonstrated to the interviewer that Ben could tolerate a wide range of affects within his relationships, suggesting there had been shifts in Ben's capacity for object relations over time. In high school, for example, he was a lonely person and never dated. In college, his relationships were characterized by idealization and overinvestment, and he was unable to cope with object loss. At the time of follow-up, Ben's strategies were more flexible, and he had a more realistic, less idealized view of people.

Asked by the interviewer to describe how he dealt with frustration, Ben said, "Yesterday I got real mad. I was thinking of going out for coffee and all of a sudden someone returned a pair of shoes and my boss told me to clear the shelf, all at the same time. I just endured it. I figured I'd wait until after work and then I'd handle it. I knew I had something to do later so I thought about that. I projected myself into the future. I have a sense of humor about stuff now. What is the sense of getting upset about a small thing? Not that I let people walk all over me. I want to be treated fairly, and not be a doormat, but not be overly aggressive either. I still do yoga. I did a yoga exercise and it is really a healthy thing for me. It centers me, it puts me in the moment, it makes me feel very good about myself and about life that I have this skill and I can center myself. That helps me, to know that I have this place in myself that I can get to."

This quote demonstrated to the interviewer that Ben could take distance, and see humor in the situation. At the same time he also needed yoga, a narcissistic preoccupation, to construct a palpable sense of self.

Generally, Ben was more satisfied with his identity as a parent and husband than with his work identity. He said he sold shoes only to support his family; if ever there was a reason for him to return to therapy, it would be to work on employment goals. "I have the ability as a salesperson, which is okay," he said. "But I think I should have been given more guidance on what I was going to do for the rest of my life."

Chapter
— 3 —

Betty

Betty was a 21-year-old, single Jewish female transferred to Chestnut Lodge from a hospital in another state. There, her diagnosis was paranoid schizophrenia.

Betty was first overtly ill in her freshman year of college. She returned home, increasingly withdrawn and isolated. Preoccupied by paranoid delusions, chiefly about her father, she underwent a variety of treatments in and out of hospitals before being referred to Chestnut Lodge.

Actually, Betty had always seemed in some way different from normal children. It could be said that her illness had no clear onset but began in her earliest years. Mother described Betty as having been particularly sensitive, even at age two, to what people said to her and to her environment. Mother was not more specific than this about Betty's sensitivity as a toddler, but she did say that later, in elementary school, Betty refused new clothes for fear that the poor children in class would feel badly. Moreover, in fourth grade Betty deliberately held back from doing her best to avoid being seen as the teacher's pet. A general practitioner was consulted about Betty's behavior, and he said she would outgrow it.

Betty was an only child conceived accidentally during the first year of her parent's marriage. Labor and delivery were uncomplicated except for the presence of a nuchal cord, which the mother said, "the doctor worked out quickly," so that it did not cause any apparent problems. Betty was breast fed, with supplemental bottles, for six and one-half months. The feedings went well, except for what mother called "the usual teething problems," and Betty seemed healthy. There is no record of how the early developmental landmarks were negotiated.

Betty's father was in business on his own, and prospered for the first five or six years after her birth. Then came the Great Depression, and demand for his product fell precipitously, so the business had to be given up. The parents also relinquished their apartment; all three now shared a room at the maternal grandparents' house. Betty's father had enough money to buy food but was unable to work for about a year. That summer, the mother's menstrual period was delayed. Believing she was pregnant, and not wanting another child because of the family's impoverished circumstances, she took an ergot preparation and became quite ill. Her period began abruptly and flowed heavily. She became dizzy and thought she was dying. She retreated to bed for prolonged spans of time. The ergot pills also brought on colitis, which weakened her further. Whereas previously she had no trouble with her menses, from then on Betty's mother re-experienced problems at the time of her periods, which were heavy, and she frequently returned to bed because of dizziness, extreme exhaustion, and weakness. Gradually she developed these symptoms even between periods. Thus mother had a mysterious and incapacitating illness which began when Betty was about six and lasted until Betty was sixteen, when mother recovered almost overnight.

"I wouldn't be a bit surprised if some of my illness was caused from fear," mother said. "I think I got over a lot of it when Betty became involved with her own problems." During the illness she also had thyroid trouble and strong palpitations. "I saw quite a few doctors, but I don't think any of them did anything that helped," she said.

The psychiatrist who admitted Betty to Chestnut Lodge had the impression that mother's illness must have been a dominating factor in Betty's early personality development. He felt that Betty's mother had used her illness to exert a large degree of control over her environment and to command a great deal of attention and nursing care, which must have pushed Betty far out of the usual child's role.

Indeed, as a child Betty never played freely, was ill at ease with strangers, and had few friends. Academically she did well, and this strength brought her some prominence as valedictorian of her class in junior high school. She was interested in sports and reading, but markedly disinterested in boys. She even severed relations with her few girlfriends if they made a show of interest in the opposite sex.

Entrance into high school was marked by some decline in academic performance. Betty was shy about reciting in class and was occasionally truant. She did well scholastically in her final year but was remembered by the principal as a lethargic student. Nevertheless her performance earned her admission to a top women's college. She matriculated after a summer at home during which she showed little social interest but read a great deal. She had become increasingly antagonistic toward both parents, and said things that made her mother think something was wrong.

"It began during her—I guess you call it 'pooberty'?—she tended to slam doors and be at odds with my husband all the time," Betty's mother said. But mother felt this was probably a normal phase. Then, just before Betty went to college, the two went shopping for Betty's wardrobe. Betty made some vague remarks about not being comfortable. She said she was going away and never coming home again. "I didn't know what that meant," her mother said. "I didn't understand what made her say that. She said she didn't like the women in our area." Indeed, Betty wanted her parents to move to another location in their town where she considered the women to be "smarter."

It seems likely, in retrospect, that Betty was suffering from separation anxiety. She was worried that if she left home she might never return, perhaps because she would find the women at college somehow smarter than the women around home. In addition, mother and daughter were not communicating very well. Conversation was often difficult because of the rather idiosyncratic way in which Betty expressed herself. "I thought all the things she didn't like would iron themselves out in the course of her being at college," Betty's mother said. "She went willingly enough, but the first night she called up and said she wanted to come home."

Betty did not come home, however, not then and not even for Thanksgiving. When she did return home for Christmas, her mother felt things were going all right. She recalled that Betty did not say much and spent a lot of her holiday going to the theatre.

Any complacency about the situation was premature, as Betty proved in January. The college housemother called Betty's parents to tell them Betty had left impulsively. Her schoolwork was not the problem. Betty had performed satisfactorily from an academic point of view, although her professors had noted her shyness and sensitivity. The college authorities assumed she must have emotional difficulties.

Betty returned home and her parents sent her to a psychiatrist. The problem was that Betty spent all day in her room. She said nothing to her parents, toward whom she showed only resentment.

This same resentment soon became focused on a succession of psychiatrists. She saw three in four years, terminating with each for obscure reasons. One of the doctors, feeling that she had an Oedipal disturbance, endorsed her seemingly outrageous request that her father move away from home. For two years, Betty's father took an apartment. Mother met him for dinner after work three evenings a week, and spent Saturday and Sunday with him. The fact that her parents went along with this arrangement showed the extent to which Betty ran their lives, or indicated a wide split in their relationship.

By the fourth year at home, Betty was disturbed, disdainful, hostile, and arrogant. She was agitated and prone to verbal outbursts. She collected a year's editions of *The New York Times* in her room, believing the articles contained covert messages to her from the British royal family. She had auditory and visual hallucinations and grandiose, persecutory delusions. Betty's hostility toward her father was based on her belief that he "desired her carnally." Because she failed to improve, her parents finally accepted the recommendation that she be taken to the local hospital.

On admission there in the 1950s she was described as a markedly hirsute, misshapen young woman, withdrawn, uninterested in activities, evasive, with flat, cold affect, and loosely associated thoughts. A psychological test indicated psychotic illness of long standing. Betty appeared to have only sporadic contact with reality, and a sexual orientation on the preadolescent level with some suggestion of homosexual interest. The gynecologist prescribed hormonal therapy for Betty's hirsutism. Betty herself said, "My body is so hairy it's ugly. I haven't washed in months. I've been in an apartment with my mother but I wouldn't call it living with her."

At that hospital, Betty received nine electroconvulsive treatments and several insulin coma treatments. After the first shock treatment she stopped speaking of her parents as Mr. and Mrs. Johnson and instead began to call them father and mother again. This seemed to indicate progress since she had previously been very cold toward them. Her father, in particular, had been the target of her resentment because she felt he could do a lot of damage to her, particularly through her "vaginal tract." Betty maintained that mother "never gave proper birth" to her, but said she experienced a rebirth the year prior to hospitalization, after which she no longer felt sick. She now claimed to have many plans and dreams. When asked what these were, she said calmly and emphatically, "You know there is one place where I would like to work, where I could do good work: Buckingham Palace. I've always thought I was Princess Elizabeth."

Betty stayed at the hospital for six months, during which time she had three therapists. She requested reassignment after one week with the first, and after two months the second left the hospital. This seemed unfortunate in retrospect, because a surprisingly good rapport had been reached. The second doctor felt Betty could use psychoanalysis, and therefore suggested a transfer to Chestnut Lodge. This recommendation was acted upon when the third physician felt that he and Betty had reached an impasse in treatment.

When Betty arrived at Chestnut Lodge, she was a moderately attractive, appealing young woman who at first volunteered nothing and then mimicked the admitting psychiatrist, referring to him in the third person. She paced slowly, and after making a few sarcastic remarks she lapsed into vague ruminations saying she could only speak freely with friends and even then might not be able to because of "the situation."

One week later psychological testing showed her IQ to be in the low superior range. On the Rorschach, there was no overt psychosis, but there was evidence for schizoid withdrawal and disintegration of the higher mental processes which strongly suggested a psychotic process. The test revealed that Betty's contacts with the external world were tentative and precarious. She seemed to be afraid of her own aggression and could find no acceptable outlets for negative feelings. She was unsure about her assets as a woman and reluctant to identify herself with any feminine role. Betty commented at the end of the Rorschach that she had seen many more things when she took the test before, but this time she was tired so she had not said much.

Dr. Judith Williams, who performed the testing, thought Betty had a good prognosis, based on her unimpaired intellectual functioning and relatively undisturbed Rorschach.

With this preamble, Betty began individual therapy with Dr. Emily Norris. In the first session, Betty continued her pacing. "I used to fight my parents," she said. "I'm fighting the hospital and I'm fighting you. You're of use to me if I can fight you." Predictably, Betty soon complained about her doctor's personality. She attacked Dr. Norris as hopeless, helpless, and useless. Dr. Norris understood this as a projection but nevertheless acknowledged that these accusations shook her confidence in herself.

In addition, the patient and therapist never had a clear contract to work together and there was considerable early sparring over this issue. One day Betty said she had come only because she had to and she did not really want to get acquainted. Dr. Norris called the aides to take Betty back to the ward. Afterwards, Dr. Norris repented, feeling this had been hostile and rejecting. The next day Betty sent a message: "Tell her I have nothing to say to her. Ask if she is interested in seeing me anyway." Dr. Norris, encouraged, answered in the affirmative, and Betty came to the hour, which they passed largely in silence. Toward the end of the hour, Betty told her therapist the session was not as bad as the harrowing thoughts she had just prior to her hour, but she would not reveal what these thoughts were. "You wouldn't understand," she said. "Your personality is such that you create obstacles."

This sort of criticism made quite an impact on Dr. Norris, who admitted at a case conference that Betty had touched on personal conflicts having to do with Dr. Norris' relationship with her own mother. "I could not keep my mind on Betty," Dr. Norris said. "I was so preoccupied that whenever I had Betty's chart in front of me I couldn't read it. I became so uncomfortable that I couldn't see her. Sometimes I canceled hours and sometimes I came late. I became increasingly depressed." Meanwhile, Betty was saying things such as, "Sometimes I feel I understand you better than you understand yourself. I feel you don't really want to learn about yourself. You put obstacles in the way." The treatment situation seemed to be reversed.

Despite these problems, one achievement in therapy was that Betty's attitude toward her parents mellowed. She now complained that she felt all alone in the world. "This isn't living," she said. "You can hardly call this existence, me hanging around here like this. I'm half dead, more than half dead." Colleagues to whom Dr. Norris presented her work believed that a reason for this change was that Betty had displaced her antagonistic feelings away from her parents and onto the hospital and her therapist. Everyone was impressed by the friendly interaction Betty now had with her parents whenever they came to visit. This warmth had been entirely lacking in the recent past. The ward administrator confirmed that Betty's hostility was indeed diverted to the hospital. "She has dealt with me and most of the other personnel by writing us off," he said. "She spent 20 minutes telling me what a thick head I was. I got up and started to leave. She said, 'Oh, don't go yet. I may be able to say something to you.' "

One question raised at a case conference was whether Dr. Norris was merely the recipient of projections or whether the feelings she had were genuinely her own. A doctor speculated that Betty would try to make Dr. Norris sick just the way she felt she made her mother sick in the past, that this was her way of dealing with women. Eventually, Dr. Norris reported she had come to grips with her personal troubles and felt more comfortable with Betty. In part, this change came about in the process of discussing Betty with a small group of peers. Now, when Betty said, "The way you can be useful to me is to accomplish nothing," Dr. Norris relaxed. She no longer worried whether anything was accomplished, and Betty dropped the issue. Any silences which developed between Betty and her therapist were now passed more comfortably.

Despite this new ease in their relationship, their treatment situation ceased six months after it began. There was no record of exactly why this occurred. From the conference notes, it seemed Dr. Norris and her colleagues had a fair notion about what was going on, and Dr. Norris even appeared able to apply this knowledge in her work with Betty, so it is somewhat of a mystery why they stopped seeing each other.

Betty did not see an individual therapist again for nearly four years. Instead, she joined group therapy with three other female patients under Dr. Rhonda Stein and Dr. Trudy Woodhall. These cotherapists were augmented by a third, Dr. David Thorpe, who later took over Dr. Woodhall's position. Dr. Thorpe was the only one to write down anything of what happened in the group and he did this only sporadically, so there is no continuous account of the group therapy treatment. Fortunately, Betty's hospital record also included reports from her psychiatric administrator and the unit staff.

The nursing report, for example, written 15 months after group treatment began, said that Betty ate and slept well, dressed herself, and cared for her own appearance. She tended to stay by herself, but would come out to watch television with the group, and enjoyed a birthday party for her on the ward at which she cut and served her own cake.

A problem with family finances was brought to the staff's attention by Betty's father, who wrote one year after her admission requesting a reduction in rate. The hospital offered to lower the monthly fee by 25 percent, but even so, Betty's father said he could not afford another year of inpatiency. Despite misgivings that Betty was ready to make the transition to outpatiency, a concerted effort to move her out was being made in order to prolong her stay at Chestnut Lodge. These efforts were communicated directly to Betty, and her group therapy leaders felt that she was relieved. At least she did not say "no" to these efforts and the group leaders felt it would be too much to ask of her to say yes, that she wanted to stay.

Betty's administrator began preparing for the inevitable. He told the social worker to help Betty find living quarters off the hospital grounds. Betty complained that she could not handle the difficulties, that it was too complicated for her to move. Staff members recalled that Betty had trouble moving from one room to another *on* the unit. She had been offered a room by herself, which at first she seemed eager to take. When the time came for the change, however, she found endless reasons why the room was inadequate.

Despite the delays, Betty did become a day patient by the first of the year. Just prior to leaving the hospital she was more reticent than ever to divulge her problems or distorted thoughts in group. After the move, she came to the hospital only for her group therapy sessions and for meals. She seemed very lonely. Then the administrator saw an interesting change. In the course of several brief talks with Betty, she seemed friendlier toward him than on previous occasions. He learned she was making tentative contacts with another woman, also a day patient. Confronted with potential *anomie*, Betty was rallying to new levels of relatedness. Dr. Thorpe noted this change, too. Even though Betty did not say much in the group, she was cheerful. She laughed frequently and was more amiable with people in and around the hospital.

By the second month of day patiency, Betty had unpacked her things and was beginning to take care of her room. Altogether, she survived the experience better than any of the staff had felt was likely. Her behavior was distant but acceptable. She told her administrator, "I am doing the best I can. I don't want anyone to think I ought to do better, because I can't. I won't give out any information about what I am doing." The administrator felt that Betty was indeed trying very hard. He continued to see her frequently but their conversations were usually limited to his asking if there was anything he could do for her, and her telling him no.

For the most part, Betty remained aloof from others. She sat on the unit during the day and read, observing but not mixing. She was so withdrawn that everyone was quite startled if she said hello. She said even less to staff than she said to patients. Once, however, something disturbed her in group. She tried to leave the session, but Dr. Thorpe blocked the way. She was furious with him and afterwards complained to the administrator that Dr. Thorpe had assaulted her "feloniously." The administrator was pleased Betty had sought him out. It was the first time she showed him any need for help.

An intriguing change occurred when Dr. Rhonda Stein left the group three years after Betty joined. Betty was upset by this loss. She had been doing well and was assuming a more active role in the group. When Dr. Stein left, Betty gave up this role. She was surprised she missed Dr. Stein and tried to deny it, proclaiming a new philosophy of looking on the bright side of things. She said she was indifferent to Dr. Stein's leaving except that it left her with Dr. Thorpe, who was inconsiderate. Dr. Thorpe himself noted that Betty had a number of delusional ideas. The group confronted her about her lack of bathing and lack of attention to her hair and clothes. After this she tended to bathe more often and look more attractive.

The next year, Betty received a substantial reduction in her day patient fee, which allowed her to continue in treatment. She was relieved, and began to express herself more freely. Though couched in denial, she now revealed the intensity of her own feelings. For example, Betty told Dr. Thorpe he was a crude, aggressive, assaultive, overanxious, impolite, and generally thoughtless person. Worse, she said, he was a "tie-less lout." She denied any positive feeling for him and compared him unfavorably with her father.

She was quite sexually preoccupied, with Dr. Thorpe and beyond. Betty complained to the group members that a student nurse had tried to molest her. As she spoke it became clear that the person had not touched Betty, but the very fact that she had made a movement toward her was enough for Betty to think it was a homosexual attack. She wanted the student fired and permanently barred from nursing. Or, she said, the student should be put in cold wet sheet pack, taken to the Main Building, and psychoanalyzed. Betty herself laughed, along with everyone in the group.

A few months later, the group moved to a new room. An awful silence set in that lasted for two weeks. Then Betty turned on a heater, saying she had been frozen to the bone for two weeks and that the damp and cold in the "ice house" was unbearable. She said Dr. Thorpe was a bum compared to Drs. Stein and Woodhall. "All you had to do was call maintenance to get the heat working," she said. "You just sat there." Another of the women linked the talk about heat with sex, and everyone became more lively except Betty, who lapsed into silence again.

Dr. Thorpe reported in June that Betty seemed only a little brighter. "I can't find the answer with her," he said. "No approach works. She is always here, though, so apparently she gets something out of it." The administrator, on the other hand, had an optimistic perspective. "Betty sat in the front row at the patient play," he said. "Although she made no direct contacts with anyone, she clearly enjoyed herself. She came spontaneously into my office to ask about a dental appointment. She is slowly learning to live a well organized life outside the hospital."

In July, a woman was temporarily assigned to work with Dr. Thorpe in the group as a cotherapist. Betty became more and more angry at this person, obviously jealous of her relationship with Dr.

Thorpe. Betty's outbursts betrayed the intensity of feelings that she otherwise steadfastly denied. Dr. Thorpe tried all sorts of ways to draw her out. He even told the group of a dream he had about her, and Betty was pleased but did not respond. This led Dr. Thorpe to say Betty was like Achilles sulking in his tent. In fact, Dr. Thorpe saw her as the key person in the group. He believed she exercised power when she really wanted love, and told her so. He linked this to the anger she expressed toward her father, but she again made no response. At times Betty could realize the absurdity of her denials and could be kidded into smiling, but even then, she would turn her face to the wall and with great effort control any expression.

Betty's pattern of social interaction remained unchanged. In the fall of that year, she read the paper and did crossword puzzles at the Center, a place on the hospital grounds where other patients tended to congregate. Surreptitiously, but with evident enjoyment, she watched the activity around her. She did not start conversations, and answered only briefly if approached.

A new administrator, Dr. Fawcett, was assigned in September. He saw Betty regularly, but she was shy or silent in response to his greeting, and she never turned to him for help as she had to her previous administrator.

Early in the next year, Betty came to the Center almost every day. She spent most of her time in front of the television, apparently engrossed in what was on the screen, and uninvolved with those around her. On one occasion, the activities therapist observed Betty literally climb into a cupboard to avoid another person seeing her.

A second psychological assessment was made at this time. Betty's performance on the test was more constricted than it had been previously. This suggested to Dr. Williams, the psychologist, that she was more blocked and more depressed than she had been four years ago. Dr. Williams considered it likely that Betty was undergoing progressive withdrawal. On the basis of this new test, she made a diagnosis of schizophrenic psychosis with withdrawal and depression as prominent features. She felt the prognosis was less favorable than before because of greater impoverishment in the content of Betty's thinking.

That same month, Dr. Thorpe sent Betty to talk with Dr. Nathan Beasely, the director of psychotherapy, to see if he could elicit any information from her concerning her present treatment and future plans. Dr. Thorpe felt that as the only day patient in the group and in many ways its least overtly disturbed member, Betty was not deriving maximum benefit from her treatment. After consultation, the decision was made that Betty would again receive individual therapy, at first on a once-a-week basis while she terminated with the group.

That August, in his monthly progress note, the administrator said, "Dr. Thorpe will be the one to continue seeing Betty in individual therapy." He added, as if on another topic, "Her father is too protective and too involved in her affairs." An argument could be made, of course, that Dr. Thorpe himself had become very protective and involved in taking Betty out of the group, like a cowboy cutting a special horse from the herd. Having been chosen in this way, perhaps Betty needed fewer defenses against loss. Whatever the reason, by November, Dr. Thorpe reported that Betty's capacity to relate to him had greatly improved even though her dealings with others remained distant and distorted.

Despite this seemingly auspicious report, after a little more than a year, during which there was no written record of treatment, Dr. Thorpe stopped seeing Betty because of "increased administrative duties." He added, at a later time, that he did not feel her treatment with him was going anywhere.

Dr. Richard Xeno began to work with her in individual psychotherapy four times per week. No psychoactive medications were prescribed by him or anyone else at any time during her treatment at Chestnut Lodge.

Although Betty always came to her sessions, she volunteered no information of any sort. If Dr. Xeno spoke, she listened but said nothing. If Dr. Xeno was quiet, Betty stared at him, which eventually prompted him to say *something*, again with no response. Once Dr. Xeno learned that Betty called her parents long distance to ask them to phone her landlady, Mrs. Ashford, to make Mrs. Ashford give her an extra blanket. Dr. Xeno brought this up with Betty, who only smiled. When Dr. Xeno tried to summarize Betty's therapy, and asked what feelings she had toward him, Betty simply listened and acted amused.

Dr. Xeno felt he was knocking his head against the wall so he decided to sit silently just as Betty was doing. This was not easy for him, however. He began to read aloud to Betty and then to himself. When his initial misgivings gave way, he became quite engrossed in what he was reading. Betty welcomed this. She seemed less stiff, and moved around the room, looking at books on the shelf. Often she returned to the same book and apparently made progress with reading it.

About this time Dr. Xeno heard reports from nurses and colleagues that at first he did not believe. He heard that Betty was asserting herself more, learning how to play bridge, and how to dance. He inquired further, found that indeed all these things were happening, and felt that something must be going right. Betty now made trips home to see her parents, though she never told Dr. Xeno anything about them. But it was clear that she was doing more than ever.

Soon thereafter, Betty announced her plan to stop working with Dr. Xeno, saying only that she was tired of treatment. She claimed she found talking with Dr. Xeno too difficult because he was "serious." When pressed by the director of psychotherapy, she admitted it was a problem for her that she thought too frequently of Dr. Xeno. He was on her mind even outside the sessions.

In his own discussions with Dr. Beasely, Dr. Xeno said he liked Betty. He never felt sure where he stood with her, however. Nothing about the doctor–patient relationship had ever been explicit between them. She had told him she did not see how he could make so many mistakes and she was sure that he disliked her. He wondered if Betty needed to undo a growing attachment to him by moving physically and emotionally toward her parents. Why she sought distance at just that time was unclear, but he believed it had to do with the previous disruption of her good relationship with Dr. Thorpe. She was probably frightened of repeated abandonment. Her wish to terminate therapy was a reflection of her attraction to Dr. Xeno and her fear of it.

Dr. Beasely told Betty that she contributed to many misunderstandings because she rarely, if ever, expressed herself. Dr. Beasely also told Betty she was a powerful person who controlled others by silence and, in particular, controlled the therapist by the threat that if he did anything wrong she would leave him. Betty greeted this interpretation with apparent relish, happy to know that her power was recognized.

Although she wished to go home immediately, she agreed to stay in the local area as an "administrative" patient for an indefinite period. She had no assigned therapist but met frequently with Dr. Beasely, Dr. Fawcett, the administrator, and Mrs. Byrd, the social worker. On one occasion in the last year of treatment, Betty went home to her parents and refused to return until a new apartment was obtained for her. The administrator and social worker at first insisted that Betty be involved in this process, but after several weeks of silence from her, Mrs. Byrd found Betty a new apartment and she agreed to come back.

Betty made her final break with the Lodge two years after she had begun work with Dr. Xeno. For the last few months before she left, she seemed quite improved. She visited the hospital frequently, played cards, wore lipstick and attractive clothing, and took care of her shopping and banking. Her parents collaborated in the final discharge plan. Betty would go home and live with them.

Despite her apparent gains, not everyone agreed that Betty was doing well. Mrs. Byrd judged that when Betty left the hospital, she was suffering continuous, severe impairment. Dr. Xeno, however, felt she might do well. He noted that she was often able to get her way, and that she managed day patiency with less difficulty than had been expected.

What happened to Betty after she left the hospital was never available in much detail. Two years after she was discharged, Betty's father responded to an early follow-up questionnaire. He considered her to be improved compared to the way she was before she came to Chestnut Lodge. Her physical health was excellent. She took care of herself medically and dentally, and attended to her personal hygiene, going for electrolysis and to the beauty parlor on her own. She was overweight, at 150 pounds. She had received neither psychotherapy nor psychoactive medication, and seemed to be enjoying life. Her interests, however, were restricted to country hiking, and to sports such as rowing, in which she could participate without other people being involved. She enjoyed shopping for food for the home, and did this about once a week. Her social life was limited to outings with her parents or by herself: she played bridge with them, so long as they did not leave the house, and would venture forth to restaurants with them, or to movies by herself, once or twice a month. Basically, her father said, she led the life of a stay-at-home with her activities confined to what she could do with the immediate family. Saliently, he noted, she got along better with him and with her mother than she had in the past. She refused to consider any kind of employment. A few months after Betty's father returned this questionnaire, Betty herself wrote to the hospital. She addressed her letter to the medical director, and asked that he send a note to her dentist stating that he would pay all of her dental bills. She asked that this note be written on personal stationery, and that the medical director allege he was a friend of hers so that the dentist would not get the idea that she had ever been a mental patient. Betty's letter was written in a perfect hand and there was no sign of thought disorder in the syntax. Nevertheless, her request of the medical director that he pay all her dental bills was clearly inappropriate, and she revealed frankly delusional thinking when she asked, on the next page, that the medical director go to the police about Dr. Thorpe.

She said he had tried to kill her. She also demanded her parents' money back for her stay at Chestnut Lodge. Nothing further was heard from Betty.

Twenty years later, her father returned another follow-up questionnaire, stating again that Betty had never in the interim been admitted to a mental hospital nor been employed. She continued to live with her parents, and never met with friends. Her father said she seemed satisfied and happy with this arrangement. He said Betty experienced few symptoms, but that they were so severe that they significantly interfered with her life. He did not characterize these symptoms in any way but he said there had been essentially no period of normal functioning since she returned home. Betty, he said, lived the life of a recluse. He said that she was bright, even of superior intelligence, and possessed a very forceful personality, but that she would not leave the building under any circumstances other than to go with her parents when they were on vacation. He added that, "because of the circumstances described, it is *most important* that you *do not correspond* any further."

Chapter

— 4 —

Joanne

Joanne was 16 years old when she was admitted to Chestnut Lodge. She had been in treatment since the age of nine, but this was her first time in the hospital. For two years, her symptoms had included obesity, compulsive eating, and ideas of persecution. Psychotic symptoms precipitated admission; Joanne ate nonedible substances, hallucinated, and was socially isolated, with her own private language and religion.

Joanne was the first child in a Jewish immigrant family. Her father was a lobbyist, and her mother was a professional artist who suffered several bouts of depression for which she received no treatment. No other member of the family had a history of mental illness, with the possible exception of an uncle, whose oddities included being a vegetarian.

Joanne's birth was uncomplicated. Labor and delivery were normal, and there were no feeding problems. Joanne walked and talked early. She was a very good child who never cried. The outstanding single difficulty was that Joanne was enuretic. Her father, especially, scolded her for this. Joanne remembered her father saying "We have no use for a pants-wetting stinker in this house."

When Joanne was three, a brother was stillborn. Joanne felt her father's difficulties with her were due to his resentment over not having a son. She remembered father's temper as terrifically frightening. Once, at the time when Hitler invaded Czechoslovakia, father sat at breakfast and had a tantrum over the stab in the back Hitler gave the League of Nations and the Czechs. Joanne understood only that her father was mad about some "stab in the back," and thought the Czechs were the checks on the table cloth on the breakfast table. Later, this memory was mixed up with father's warnings about rapists, so that Joanne thought a "stab in the back" was something which came from a man in a dark alley and had something to do with Czechs.

Later, Joanne learned that when the baby was stillborn, her mother and father left for two weeks so mother could recover. Joanne was told that she lay in her crib, paralyzed with apathy, and took little food. She dimly remembered something terrible had happened, and when mother came back, Joanne greeted her with a tremendous shriek. Moreover, just at this time, Joanne's paternal grandfather died, and her father went to Europe for six months to settle the estate. Joanne's fear of being abandoned persisted, and was later a factor in the transference with her therapist at Chestnut Lodge.

In the early years, the maternal grandfather and grandmother were in the home frequently, as well as the maternal aunt, uncle, and two cousins. The grandfather demanded perfection from everyone, and unfavorably compared Joanne's mother to the aunt. On the other hand, the cousins, who were slightly older than Joanne, became close friends of hers, and these two cousins and the aunt helped to provide the good experiences which were a factor in Joanne's eventual outcome.

When Joanne was five, sister Betsy was born. Joanne felt all attention being taken away from her. Alone in the nursery with the new baby, Joanne was seized by impulse. She picked Betsy up with the idea of throwing her out the window. For a moment she struggled, but then put Betsy back in the crib. Mother, hearing the baby cry, had concern only for what might be wrong with the little one. Joanne of course felt *she* was the one who needed help; she had gone through the experience of a murderous impulse which, only by the grace of God, she had thwarted at the last minute.

On another occasion Joanne saw Betsy nursing at mother's breast. She had never seen or heard about that before. Frightened, she cried to father, "Betsy is eating Mommy up." Ignoring Joanne's distress, Father said, "Well, I said not to go into that room. Who let you go in there?"

Joanne's enuresis was finally discovered to be based on a structural deficit, an abnormal urethral opening. Joanne never forgave her parents for being critical of her even after it was clear that the urinary incontinence was not under her control. Furthermore, she had to undergo a cystoscopy and two operations, which she could have borne except for a piece of deception. She was told that her doll, not herself, would be operated on. Joanne did not know whether it was worse to be subject to deceit or worse that the adults would really think she was so dumb that she would believe it. Years afterwards, she developed an olfactory hallucination, so that when things were going "foul," everything smelled of ether.

From ages six to nine, Joanne was sent to camp, very much against her will. She did not play freely with other children, and she feared everything when away from home. In this case, Joanne had reason to be afraid; the camp was very anti-Semitic. Joanne did not tell her parents because she felt they would not believe her. She went through this agony until her uncle sent his children and saw the extent of the discrimination. From then on, Joanne did not have to go.

Clearly, there was poor communication between Joanne and her parents. Despite alleged closeness with mother, with whom Joanne shared a chummy preadolescent relationship in some areas, Joanne could never tell her mother the real problems. Whenever she complained of something, her parents said it was her fault. Eventually she stopped confiding in them.

At age nine, Joanne moved with her family from Albany to Syracuse to live with the aunt, uncle, and cousins. Overall, this was a happy time because Joanne liked her aunt and cousins. However, she began to put on weight. She told herself, "No one would want to look at such a girl." When she looked into the mirror there seemed to be two people, whom she called "she" and "her." Joanne had trouble experiencing these two as one. She thought she was not only fat and ugly in body but also ugly in mind because she felt mean. She did not want to be mean, she said, "it just came out" of her.

Food was an important issue. Mother had always been preoccupied with Joanne's food intake because she herself had a weight problem. Joanne never was allowed to eat all she wanted. Before age nine she did occasionally receive forbidden things such as chocolate pudding, but afterwards everything not on Joanne's diet was under lock and key. Then Joanne began to eat things such as unprepared Jello and raw staple foods.

Joanne became increasingly disturbed. She was clinging, unhappy, worried, tearful, and dependent. She had a great fear of approaching anything new. She bit her nails, sucked her thumb, picked her nose, ground her teeth, and complained of her eyes going out of focus. She had a constant need for praise and affection. She was dependent on her mother, and envious of mother's artistic talent. She was so jealous that father actually suggested his wife give up painting.

Joanne's school adjustment was difficult through all grade levels, even though she had a vocabulary and command of language not often seen in adults. If she showed any of her considerable giftedness, reciting her own or others' poetry, or showing her paintings, she felt the teachers and classmates laughed at her.

She was choosy of friends and tended to pick underdogs, members of minority races, or people with physical defects. Actually, she preferred adult company. Speaking of her peers, Joanne said, "What do I have to do—split infinitives to get along with them?"

Although neither of her parents saw anything in Joanne's behavior to convince them she needed psychiatric help, the school authorities felt differently. Psychological testing revealed Joanne's superior intellectual capacities. The report said that while Joanne was "clever" and had an excellent memory, her achievements were not commensurate with her capacities because of her failure to organize her thinking constructively. The report said that much of Joanne's originality was strained and affected, and represented a striving to be different. Joanne was not creative in the sense of producing something from her own imagination; she was simply a keen observer of unusual aspects of reality. Emotionally Joanne was said to be immature, with an inner life dominated by strong instinctual drives which were expressed in aggressive, highly competitive activities. Her affective responses were repressed, projected, or denied. She was easily disturbed by emotionally stimulating situations, and obsessional defenses were mounted against serious loss of rational control. When she did express feelings, it was in an egocentric form accompanied by strong anxiety. Therapy was recommended to relieve the basic insecurity and sense of inadequacy underlying Joanne's defensive aggression and ambition.

Joanne saw Dr. Sorenson for six months. Therapy was discontinued when Joanne asked her mother if she, Joanne, was a delinquent. Her mother believed it would be better for Joanne to stop therapy than to think this was so.

Joanne withdrew increasingly to her room. Her father opened the door to spy on her. To keep him from reading the poetry she wrote, Joanne invented a language of her own. She called it "Irian." It had roots from Spanish, French, English, and Russian, and she spoke it fluently. When her father saw something written in Irian in English letters, Joanne took a further step and invented symbols, like Chinese or Japanese, in which to write. She also developed a religion with gods and goddesses and seven worlds. She felt everyone she met inhabited one or another of these worlds. It was unclear whether people could move between worlds, or whether people from different worlds could understand each other.

When Joanne was 12, her family moved back to Albany. This meant separation from the beloved aunt and cousins. Mother wanted to surprise the girls and fix a lovely room with pink and blue for them. These, she felt, were the nicest colors for young girls. Later, in therapy, Joanne said, "I hated pink but nothing could be done. Here it was, all fixed, and mother thought she had done a nice thing for us, and so we had to have the room."

Joanne now obtained relief from anxiety in several ways. She bought sweets, retreated to the semidark living room, and gorged herself. She crawled way inside herself where nobody could disturb her. Often abdominal pain would take her mind off psychological distress, or she would put herself in a trance. She complained of stomach aches a great deal, and was taken to a number of internists who said it was just her imagination.

Because of weight gain, the basal metabolic rate was assessed. Thyroid medication (unspecified) was administered, with no effect.

Joanne was transferred to a special school for talented artistic children, where her adjustment was even worse than it had been at previous schools she attended. Before, she had received good marks in English and history, although she was termed "too precocious." Now she was unable to work; she spent all of her time daydreaming. She received poor marks in conduct for being critical of her teachers and jealous of other children. Her failure to adjust at the new school was one reason her parents again sought psychiatric help for her.

She saw Dr. Remington, and in his letter to Chestnut Lodge, he said Joanne seemed friendly and communicative but frightened and depressed. There was a 20-point spread between her Verbal IQ score of 131 and Performance IQ score of 111. The Full Scale IQ score was 123. Joanne achieved these scores despite serious psychological disturbance. She had nightmares of deaths, murders, attacks, accidents, sexual assaults, operations, and mutilations. She reported feelings of depersonalization and derealization. At times, she seemed disoriented. There were visual, auditory, tactile, and olfactory hallucinations, episodes of bulimia, and other gastrointestinal symptoms. Despite all this, Joanne wore a mask of gaiety and few around her realized her distress. When her functioning in school and in music became compromised, she took refuge in poetry, singing, and piano playing when alone.

Nevertheless, Dr. Remington said, Joanne maintained excellent contact with him. There were improvements in social adaptation, but no control of the overeating or the bouts of abdominal pain. Frantic and panicked, Joanne made abortive attempts to cut her wrists. She also fantasized slashing her body. While Joanne spent part of the summer alone at a mountain inn, where she had a good time and was less disturbed, school remained a severe threat and, in view of the overall situation, Dr. Remington felt Joanne needed residential treatment. He thought the general picture was of a schizophrenic process. The prognosis was favorable because of Joanne's many resources.

So at last the family made the decision to put Joanne in the hospital and she came to Chestnut Lodge. She was tall but overweight at 200 pounds. She had long, straggly blonde hair, bitten-off fingernails, and unbrushed teeth. She could not allow people to walk behind her on the street and had to wait for them to pass before going on. She burned herself with cigarettes whenever anxiety increased, and pulled skin from various parts of her body, especially her heels. Nevertheless she was in reasonably good contact. While she had a private language, she could speak without thought disorder in normal English to her therapist and other caretakers.

As part of the initial evaluation, Joanne was seen by Dr. Burdette, an expert in the treatment of obesity and eating disorders. Dr. Burdette concluded that Joanne used food to prevent panic. Dr. Burdette felt that for Joanne, food had a symbolic, magical significance which explained why she ate inedible objects, now including movie tickets, corners of concert programs, and small amounts of string. Dr. Burdette said the complaint of never having enough food was common in obese patients and could be translated to mean never getting enough love. In Joanne's case, Dr. Burdette noted, her father was largely uninvolved; Joanne was close to her mother but keenly competitive with her. Dr. Burdette felt Joanne had needed to express her individuality in artistic development, but also to stay clear of direct competition with mother. The alternation of self-deprecation with grandiosity that Joanne displayed was, according to Dr. Burdette, frequently seen in obese patients. Joanne's need to possess some extraordinary talent derived from the requirement to compensate for the extraordinary handicap of feeling ugly. Dr. Burdette knew Joanne equated fat with ugliness and dirt. It required courage for her to take a bath or look into a mirror, because then Joanne could not hide her ugliness from herself. She could not bear to face company, anticipating how others would hate and despise her. Eventually, convinced of her own inner worthlessness, she believed no one would like her even if she reduced the weight.

Dr. Burdette suggested that Joanne's eating habits not become the focus of a struggle between her and the staff. Dr. Burdette said that the capacity to lose weight or the daydream of doing so represented an important "potential of power" for obese patients. She advised that Joanne be permitted to regulate her own food intake, thereby indulging Joanne's need to be in control in this most personal way.

Another part of the admission evaluation was repeated psychological testing. Now, the Full Scale IQ score was 119. As in the previous protocol, performance on verbal subtests was superior. However, despite high verbal scores, Joanne was hampered in carrying out ideas that she was readily able to conceive. For example, she drew imaginary lines in one complicated block design to clarify where the division of the blocks should come. After showing this initial intelligent grasp of the problem, her performance became so slow that her score waned to average. There were striking gaps in Joanne's general information in some areas and very sophisticated knowledge in others. She thought, for instance, that there were three pints in a quart, and she did not know on what day of February George Washington's birthday fell.

On the Bender Visual Motor Gestalt Test, Joanne placed all the figures in irregular order. She rotated the card on which the original drawings were reproduced by 90 degrees, and copied them in this new orientation, showing her need to do things her own way. Her figures showed a conflict between expansive and constricting tendencies, as if Joanne did not know whether she were aggressive and impulsive or frightened and withdrawn.

On the Rorschach Test, Joanne was unable to grasp a broad, overall view, but instead fastened attention on small detail. She disregarded logical order, as if her personal needs were so pressing that the more usually accepted systematic ways of thinking had to be set aside. She lost sight of the fact she was interpreting ink blots and spoke as if the splotches really *were* something which she must find out. This confusion suggested a loss of ability to distinguish reality from reverie. Defenses against anxiety included intellectualization and making fun. Whistling to herself was a sign of tension. Among her responses, "widow" and "murder" appeared frequently. Joanne identified with "wild sows turned up for the spit, their legs tied together," and with a "wounded, wild, female pig." There was evidence that she struggled with fears of violence and unconscious murderous impulses. She found phallic shapes ugly and disturbing. About one she said, "This is a hooded lamprey, a thing that preys on fish, and *that*, on the end, is the device for sucking out the blood from the fish's stomach." On the other hand, "a fountain with white spray" (often interpreted as a phallic symbol) was seen as "the prettiest thing in the test." Here was a strong suggestion of ambivalence toward men. All the frightening, aggressive, evil, or disagreeable figures were male, whereas the female ones were either suffering or neutral. Joanne's emotional life was strongly imbued with violence. Yet she also had softer, more adaptive, and responsive attitudes. Severe repressive processes limited her inner creativity, her ability to synthesize, and her capacity for relating to others, but still Joanne had liveliness, imagination, and enthusiasm, all of which suggested a favorable prognosis.

Joanne's speech did not often betray formal thought disorder. She was coherent and logical, even if her ideas were somewhat idiosyncratic. For example, in response to one inkblot, Joanne said, "A nice lady reading to her baby. On the other side it is not a lady with a baby but a widow with her crown—her veil." On inquiry, Joanne said, "Here the baby is gone, she has a black veil and that makes her a widow, but if it were white I could still make her a widow, I would just say she was a Chinese widow."

The content of Joanne's responses to the Mosaic Test was concrete but also full of symbolism. From the point of view of composition, her productions were loosely organized. Only the first was bilaterally symmetrical. The others made no pretensions to symmetry and seemed rather to follow the course of Joanne's associations. The more Joanne "let herself go" in producing personally meaningful symbols, the less integrated was their total gestalt. It was as if she would *either* organize and synthesize *or* produce emotionally significant material, but she could not do both. In making designs, Joanne used all the shapes and colors, indicating that her emotional and intellectual experience had not become as limited or constricted as that of many chronic patients.

The psychologist who performed the test said Joanne's protocol gave quite clear indications of a schizophrenic disorder with paranoid trends. Nevertheless, she went on, the psychotic signs were not all-pervasive; she assumed there would be fairly large areas of normal function.

With this background, the treatment began, the course of which was recorded at case conferences over four years. The therapist, Dr. Frieda Fromm-Reichmann, noted many day-to-day developments and much of her own thinking as the work progressed. Dr. Fromm-Reichmann's immediate goal was to relieve Joanne of early wariness, while at the same time allowing suspicion to be expressed; and to demonstrate that the therapist was not god-like, but instead fallible, human, liable to err, and open to correction. Establishing the right kind of relationship was the first priority in treating someone like Joanne. It was not that Dr. Fromm-Reichmann was so much better than others, but that she might be able to understand, and Joanne could correct her if she did not.

Dr. Fromm-Reichmann was committed to allowing Joanne to change at her own pace. Specifically, she would not ask Joanne to give up maladaptive defenses until better responses could be set in place. On the question of weight, for example, Dr. Fromm-Reichmann told other members of the treatment team, "The weight loss would help, but I have great doubts about the actions to get her to come to the weight loss, unless she really wanted them. Therefore I think we should wait until she says something, and she may, because she suffers from her looks, but on the other hand she needs to look the way she does."

Initially, Joanne seemed happy with the understanding shown by her therapist; for her it was a new experience not always to be criticized. She came to the doctor's office and slouched around, smoking a pipe.

This lasted a month, and then tension developed in the following way. The unit nurse began to call Dr. Fromm-Reichmann to ask whether Joanne had a session that day and, if so, when. Dr. Fromm-Reichmann asked Joanne why the nurse was getting involved, why Joanne herself could not keep in mind when to come to the sessions? Joanne did not like being questioned. She said this proved Dr. Fromm-Reichmann was just as demanding as everyone else. Joanne stopped smoking her pipe and did not feel so much at ease. She became more reserved.

Dr. Fromm-Reichmann asked Joanne to write down important events in her life, since it was difficult to keep all of the events straight. Joanne agreed, but left looking subdued. The next day, Dr. Fromm-Reichmann asked if she had worked on the project. Joanne said, "No," and explained that it reminded her of the school principal insisting she do her assignments, and how terrible it was when she couldn't do them because she was preoccupied.

"Well, what the heck, why didn't you say so?," Dr. Fromm-Reichmann asked.

"I was afraid you would be angry."

"There you are all wrong and you know it," Dr. Fromm-Reichmann said.

"But that's how people are," Joanne said.

Dr. Fromm-Reichmann told Joanne she was mistaken, that in fact there were more people like Dr. Fromm-Reichmann than otherwise.

"I don't believe it," Joanne said.

"That's one of our jobs, that through working with me you learn to see that," Dr. Fromm-Reichmann said.

To show Joanne that people could be different, Dr. Fromm-Reichmann expressed herself without the conventional sweetness Joanne's mother used to bridge over differences. Dr. Fromm-Reichmann showed that people could be quite spontaneous without having temper tantrums like Joanne's father, and quite friendly without mother's saccharine quality.

Also, Dr. Fromm-Reichmann actively supported Joanne's resentment about the deception practiced on her at the time of surgery (when she was told that the doll, and not her, would undergo the operation), and about her parents' poor understanding of her struggles with murderous impulses towards her sister, and about her parents' ignorance of anti-Semitic attitudes at camp. Joanne said she also resented the way her father treated her like a possession; for example, he never left the children alone in their rooms. Dr. Fromm-Reichmann sometimes playfully acted the part of father hunting all over the house for his children, calling Joanne or her sister first to get his slippers, second the newspaper, and third something from the icebox. The result was that Joanne's interest never flagged. Dr. Fromm-Reichmann's technique of active intervention limited Joanne's tendency to wander, pontificate, and intellectualize. She began to talk more and more about how she actually felt.

Nevertheless, Joanne clung to her other defenses: her privacy, her abdominal pains, and her trances. She worried lest Dr. Fromm-Reichmann try to take these away.

"Yes," Dr. Fromm-Reichmann said. "I hope I will, sooner or later, but not before you are ready. Then it won't be me taking these away, but you not needing them, being ready to give them up. No one can take these away before you are able to live without them." Joanne smiled in relief.

She shared more about her private world, the Irian gods and the spheres they inhabited. Dr. Fromm-Reichmann interpreted Joanne's withdrawal into this fantasy realm as a reflection of her need for privacy, but she also listened to the material as a metaphorical expression of Joanne's thinking about current, everyday issues. Sometimes Dr. Fromm-Reichmann used the material for her own purposes. Once, for example, Joanne expressed how confused she felt. She told Dr. Fromm-Reichmann not to ask questions, because that made things worse. Joanne said, "Yesterday from two to four I was confused and today I am confused again." Finally Dr. Fromm-Reichmann suggested that Joanne ask Antilobia, the chief Irian god, whether he would permit letting Dr. Fromm-Reichmann in on the secret of the confusion.

"Nobody ever told me such a thing," Joanne said. "I will try, but it will take a lot of concentration."

The next session Joanne said, "I tried it. It was very hard. I was interrupted because other patients came in, or I was preoccupied with the stab in the back or the ether smell, but finally I got it and Antilobia said, 'Well, even though she seems all right and even though she seems to be from the sixth world it can't be done.' 'Why?' I asked. 'Because nobody can share anybody else's experiences!' "

"Of course not," Dr. Fromm-Reichmann said. "I think he's quite right, or you who talk to him are quite right. But I want to intensely participate in the experience while I am observing it and come as near it as I can, so I can help you understand it."

Again Joanne seemed relieved.

While Dr. Fromm-Reichmann could enter Joanne's fantasy world, she consistently tried to align the material into its correct relation with reality. For example, Joanne said that her father talked so much about rape, it was no wonder she was frightened to death. Dr. Fromm-Reichmann said father's ideas about rape were not realistic; rape indeed occurred, but only about one millionth as frequently as her father would have her believe.

"By the way," Dr. Fromm-Reichmann added, "you know this already, without my telling you."

"How do I know it?" Joanne asked. "Whenever I walk at night, I am sure someone follows me, and I am all the more certain because when I speed up, he speeds up, and when I slow down, he slows down."

Dr. Fromm-Reichmann maintained that Joanne knew some of her fear was a distortion, and Joanne was persuaded ultimately to agree.

During the first year of treatment, Joanne told Dr. Fromm-Reichmann of an upsetting incident on the hospital ward. There was a melee in which pillows were torn and feathers strewn all over the living room. Joanne fought with Miss G., and Miss M. romped through the feathers.

"For once I was destructive, whereas everybody constantly wants me to be creative," Joanne said. "For once I really shared experiences with two other people, destructiveness with Miss G. and feathers with Miss M. But I know it was terrible, and now they will hate me."

I shouldn't have done it, but I am a mean, ugly, fat, louse-covered creature, and now everything is over." Joanne began to cry. "I haven't cried in such a long time. I have only teared, or cried to the inside. It helps a little. Can I have a Kleenex?"

Dr. Fromm-Reichmann, wishing to give Joanne the idea that appropriate help and attention should be given readily, said, "I am a big fool not to offer you Kleenex to begin with; I should have seen you needed one."

"Last night," Joanne said, "I think I did that [the melee] because . . ."

"I don't think you know why," Dr. Fromm-Reichmann interrupted. "You told me before about an 'it' inside you that makes you do things. I think this time the 'it' made you do it, and you should not believe that you yourself did it."

Joanne agreed nothing could be done about her impulsive acts until she understood the 'it' that was behind them. Here, Dr. Fromm-Reichmann was essentially encouraging the emergence of a self-observing capacity. Later Dr. Fromm-Reichmann felt Joanne was ready to see that her impulsivity was an attempt to ward off anxiety. Dr. Fromm-Reichmann did not use the word "anxiety" because it was too abstract. Instead, Dr. Fromm-Reichmann said much of what Joanne did was because of fear; Joanne was afraid of many things, but her impulsive actions kept her from being aware of this.

Dr. Fromm-Reichmann, in fact, suspected a connection between Joanne's anxiety about Dr. Fromm-Reichmann's vacation and Joanne's impulsive acts, since they occurred the same day the doctor announced her plans. Dr. Fromm-Reichmann was given the opportunity to bring this up when Joanne complained she had been abandoned by her therapist, Dr. Remington, before coming to Chestnut Lodge.

"You know he did not abandon you," Dr. Fromm-Reichmann said. "You, your mother, and he all decided hospitalization would be wiser for your condition."

"But I was afraid you would abandon me too. And here you go for a vacation." This was the specific anxiety being warded off by Joanne's impulsive pillow-shredding behavior on the unit. Joanne felt she "had it coming to her"; she felt abandonment was inevitable because she was such a worthless creature.

One sign of Antilobia's interdiction against talking with Dr. Fromm-Reichmann was the "ether smell." At first, Dr. Fromm-Reichmann had no idea what Joanne meant by the "ether smell," but this became clear later. Again, a vacation issue catalyzed the discovery. Dr. Fromm-Reichmann had been away at Christmas time, but told

Joanne she planned to be in the hospital on Christmas Day, and would be glad to see Joanne then, since she knew this was a hard time for any patient and particularly for Joanne.

Joanne said, "There's the big man with the ether gun."

"What's that?" Dr. Fromm-Reichmann said.

It turned out "the man with the ether gun" was the anesthesiologist at the operation on Joanne's urethra. The idea of "the man with the ether gun" now stood for the deception of being told the operation would be on her doll, not on her. Joanne believed Dr. Fromm-Reichmann was practicing a similar deception in offering an hour on Christmas.

Joanne was always alert to deception and especially so in her relationship with mother. The official myth was that mother was very understanding, full of love, and only wanted to do what was right by Joanne. Joanne knew that her mother could also be quite unempathetic, especially if her vanity had been hurt. On another level, however, Joanne could not afford to realize this. She could not dare to see mother's shortcomings, because, beleaguered at school and without close friends, mother's support had to be maintained at all costs. Gradually, Dr. Fromm-Reichmann helped Joanne to tolerate awareness of mother's failures as well as to appreciate her virtues.

Once Joanne's mother sent Dr. Fromm-Reichmann a huge box of exquisitely rich, unique cookies. These were sent via Joanne.

"There you have my mother," Joanne said. "She gives these to everybody. She knows that she and I are not supposed to eat them, but I have to hear 10 times a day how delighted other people are with them."

Nevertheless, Joanne was obviously pleased that Dr. Fromm-Reichmann admired what her mother had made; her mother was not all that bad.

At another time, Joanne wrote some poems, which her mother liked and promised to have typed by the secretary. The poems came back with the lines set the wrong way, and the punctuation changed.

"She expects thanks for this!" Joanne said.

Dr. Fromm-Reichmann told Joanne to send the poems back and tell her mother how disappointed she was that her mother had not felt the poems should be printed in the same way as they had been written out. At first, Joanne was frightened by this suggestion, but Dr. Fromm-Reichmann eventually taught her to understand that real relationships can only be established when such objections are made.

Next came material about Joanne's overeating and obesity. Joanne admitted she ate whenever she was anxious. In the beginning, however, overeating was a form of rebellion against mother, who was very upset about it. While they were talking about this, Joanne suddenly told Dr. Fromm-Reichmann that the gods were trying to say something.

"Whenever the gods are trying to talk to you," Dr. Fromm-Reichmann said, "you really mean something in you has an idea, but you don't dare give yourself credit for it. So when you talk about the gods, I know it is you."

What the gods had told Joanne was that "wet" and "weight" were related concepts. Now she recalled that when she had been at camp she had urinated on a towel on the floor of the dressing room. The other girls were disgusted and told her to clean it out as quickly as possible. She had to lift the towel, which was terrifically heavy, and she was humiliated. The humiliation was as much about "weight" as about "wet." Joanne now saw, together with Dr. Fromm-Reichmann, that wetting her pants and being overweight were similar: each was humiliating, and each made her parents upset. Joanne said that being wet was the terrible weight of her childhood.

Dr. Fromm-Reichmann interpreted the link between humiliation and rebellion. "You felt rebellious toward the grown-ups all your life, but that felt dangerous to you so you turned it around and inflicted the suffering on yourself."

This made sense to Joanne and she began referring to her mother as "mamma" instead of "fit-fat" or "the duchess of fat," which she had called her before.

At the end of the first year, Joanne seemed quite invested in treatment, and there were already signs of improvement. In the beginning she had engaged in bouts of mild self-mutilation. She said hurting herself distracted her from her gut pain and emotional pain. These mutilations had stopped for several months. Also, Joanne stopped eating extra food and nonedible substances. There was less talk of confusion, and less writing in Irian. Joanne spoke more freely to Dr. Fromm-Reichmann about hallucinations, panic spells, and nightmares, all of which were still present. One indication that the hallucinations had diminished was that Joanne no longer needed her radio so much. "It is not necessary now to kill other things in me with the noise of the radio," she said.

Furthermore, many of Joanne's interpersonal difficulties had disappeared. In the beginning, insolent and presumptuous behavior had alternated with self-deprecation. Joanne's precocity could irritate, and she had a never-ending series of complaints about the nurses. Now, she might complain, but in a joking way, and she learned to get along with patients and others.

She continued, however, to feel misunderstood and to think she would be rejected and abandoned. She feared not being able to live up to others' standards. She anticipated losing her singing voice and losing her ability to write poetry. She was so sensitive to criticism that, whenever she felt blamed, she became mean, which tended to make her less popular. She lived in fear of shame.

When she felt rejected, Joanne countered her suicidal feelings by holding imaginary conversations with flowers and trees. The "heart tree" was her favorite, but it would talk only if she treated it with the high regard it deserved. Joanne had a lively exchange even with clouds; communion with nature helped her when she felt neglected.

Since Joanne was concerned about losing her ability to sing or write, Dr. Fromm-Reichmann occasionally entered a "practical relationship" with Joanne. She asked Joanne to show her a poem, or to sing and play the piano. Then Dr. Fromm-Reichmann said, "Now we both know what it [the singing, poetry, etc.] is like. Even though I enjoy it, we can't spend too much time on it, and I am sure the artistic quality won't be lost." Joanne was relieved.

Another source of relief, in addition to Dr. Fromm-Reichmann's willingness to participate in a real relationship, was her sensitivity to nuance. For instance, she and Joanne once again sought to understand the reasons for Joanne's often-expressed confusion. If a session time was changed, if the couch was in a slightly different place, if Dr. Fromm-Reichmann's dog was not present, or if Dr. Fromm-Reichmann did not seem alert, Joanne claimed to be confused. It was clear she said she was "confused" when in fact she was upset.

"You know I had great confusion when I worked with Dr. Remington too," Joanne said, trying to reassure Dr. Fromm-Reichmann that she was not the only person guilty of confusing her. Dr. Fromm-Reichmann should not worry that she was unique in causing the problem. Instead of doggedly pursuing the formal issue at hand— that is, Joanne's confusion—Dr. Fromm-Reichmann became alert to the here-and-now issue of Joanne's need to be reassuring. She saw that in her zeal to understand Joanne's confusion she came across as overly concerned. She also saw that the intent of Joanne's last statement was to comfort the therapist. She told Joanne this; Joanne agreed, and then relaxed with a sense of being understood.

At the second case conference, after the first 1½ years of work, Dr. Fromm-Reichmann reviewed Joanne's progress. She said the work should go even more quickly, given Joanne's involvement and verbal capacity.

Dr. Franklin, the administrative psychiatrist, worried that Dr. Fromm-Reichmann was reenacting mother's position by admiring the patient and taking pleasure in Joanne's creations. As was typical in these conferences, each doctor had a different view, and there was little effort to arrive at consensus. A staff doctor, Dr. Peter Fordham, said Dr. Fromm-Reichmann should take up Joanne's stated reason for not getting better, namely that it would mean returning to an impossible school situation. Dr. Fordham said the problems about school should be addressed, and new issues might then be exposed which would explain Joanne's current social behavior.

Dr. Fromm-Reichmann said that her own worries about Joanne's rate of progress arose while reading a report from New York City, describing success with early deinstitutionalization. The work was done in 1949. Eight of 10 severely psychotic patients, sent from the hospital as soon as the acute disturbance was over, were able to hold jobs and to go on with their treatment. One of these patients had in fact been supervised by Dr. Fromm-Reichmann, and had made excellent progress. No one, Dr. Fromm-Reichmann said, claimed that these people were well at the time of discharge—ongoing treatment was necessary—but significant periods of rehospitalization had been avoided. Dr. Fromm-Reichmann wondered if this sort of program might be considered for Joanne.

Dr. Elizabeth Corbin, another staff doctor, asked whether New York City offered more resources for such patients than Rockville or Washington.

"I wouldn't know," said Dr. Fromm-Reichmann.

"They are very selective with their patients up there," Dr. Fordham said, referring to the institution that had written the report.

"I would think it would be easier for Joanne to live in Rockville than in New York, because it's still very hard for her to handle the practicalities of life," Dr. Fromm-Reichmann said.

"There's a peculiar attachment patients get to this hospital," Dr. Corbin said. "I'm not sure it's so healthy. I've heard many doctors say they have private patients who are very sick and yet make it, never needing to be in the hospital. The same kind of patient here gets tied to this place and begins to slash wrists or call you at two in the morning to a degree you wouldn't expect."

Returning to the criticism that she reenacted mother's position, Dr. Fromm-Reichmann admitted that in her attempt to look at Joanne's assets, she might have fueled Joanne's fantasy about being special. In a session soon after the conference, Joanne herself brought up some of the negative aspects of being special, and asked for help in giving this up. Joanne even became dubious about the benefit of having a private world. There were two or three weeks of good therapeutic progress, interrupted by another of Dr. Fromm-Reichmann's vacations.

When Dr. Fromm-Reichmann returned, she found Joanne had become a very defiant adolescent. All along, the factor of adolescence had made it difficult for Dr. Fromm-Reichmann to judge the effectiveness of therapy, since Joanne was at an age when she could change and grow without treatment. Also, in deference to Joanne's adolescence and expected age-related mistrust of authority, Dr. Fromm-Reichmann had avoided being didactic and, for example, had used play techniques to some extent in the therapy.

Now, however, Joanne complained that her interim therapist, Dr. Ward, had been terrible. The complaints were endless, and Dr. Fromm-Reichmann knew Dr. Ward's competence was not the real issue. First of all, as Dr. Fromm-Reichmann told her, Joanne was not equipped to know whether or not Dr. Ward was good. Second, Joanne's judgment ran counter to that of most other patients. Finally, Joanne said what really had upset her: Dr. Fromm-Reichmann had promised to talk with Dr. Ward before she left but had not done so. Dr. Ward therefore represented this betrayal and had become Joanne's scapegoat. Dr. Fromm-Reichmann readily admitted her mistake. She said that Joanne was right to be upset and that she should have done what she promised. Joanne replied no one had ever talked to her that way, meaning no one had ever admitted an error and told her she was right.

"So long as you tell people what you have to say in such an indirect manner," said Dr. Fromm-Reichmann "it's no wonder that you are misunderstood. Who has the time to spend three full hours until the truth comes out?" (Joanne had spent three sessions complaining about Dr. Ward.) Although Dr. Fromm-Reichmann was quick to point out ways in which she and most people were different from what Joanne expected, Dr. Fromm-Reichmann also tried to make Joanne aware of her own contribution to empathic failures in communication.

A specific example of Joanne's indirect communication was the imaginary world of Iria. Dr. Fromm-Reichmann told Joanne that Iria did not exist but that the use Joanne made of it was real enough. By describing events in Iria, Joanne articulated thoughts and anxieties, the expression of which was otherwise forbidden.

Gradually Joanne accepted that believing in Iria contributed to unhappiness rather than happiness, and saw how the Irian gods encouraged her self-destructive tendencies, such as "penances," during which she was not allowed to eat. However, as often happened when Joanne gave up symptoms, she became transiently upset, burned herself, and had to be sent to the "disturbed unit."

Dr. Fromm-Reichmann remained calm. She said that no one who had been using crutches for so long could walk suddenly without them.

Shortly before relinquishing Iria for good, Joanne burned herself one more time. Dr. Fromm-Reichmann asked Joanne why she did this. Joanne could now give a series of responses with increasingly specific focus. At first she said, "I am so ugly, fat, and mean that I might just as well make myself more ugly, fat, and mean." This gave way to "I don't know where to go with my intense feelings of anxiety and need for action and so I turn it against myself." Finally, "I have so much passion and I can't have men." Here at last was a problem that anyone could understand.

But Joanne said to Dr. Fromm-Reichmann, "Don't believe that Iria has gone. I still talk to Gloria."

"Who is Gloria?" Dr. Fromm-Reichmann asked.

"Gloria is my name in Irian."

"Well," said Dr. Fromm-Reichmann, "I didn't think it had gone. But one of these days I suppose you will throw Gloria out the window and see that she can go through the window without the window being opened and that there is no spot on the ground where she lands and then you will realize she was your creation."

For three days in a row Joanne said Gloria was still with her but on the fourth day she told Dr. Fromm-Reichmann, "You were right. She has gone. No signs of her."

Gradually, over several weeks, as if somehow related to shedding Gloria, Joanne started to lose weight. She returned to the "normal girl" problem of not having a boyfriend. She told Dr. Fromm-Reichmann, "I have lost so much weight, why do no men ever look at me?"

"Look at yourself in the mirror. Why should they? You don't take care of yourself at all and look attractive, even though you could."

Joanne tolerated this feedback and made constructive use of it. She got a permanent wave in her hair, bought some nice clothes, and from that point enjoyed taking care of herself.

More changes now occurred in Joanne's external life. By the middle of the second year, she started school, first with a tutor, taking up where she had left off in the second year of high school. This decision was made with the support of the medical director of the hospital; Dr. Fromm-Reichmann stayed out of the decision-making in order not to be another pushy authority figure. In addition to attending school, and instead of writing poetry or singing, as her ambitious parents wanted her to do, Joanne now happily busied herself with ironing, sewing, and laundering. Joanne also involved herself in social groups outside the hospital. She went to local churches, saying she was Jewish, but asking nevertheless if she could sing in the choir. She became a regular member of several choirs. In therapy hours she talked about school, difficulties with people, and other older problems which continued to need work.

Joanne's course pursued a saw-toothed pattern, although the general direction was up. For example, in a period of therapeutic advance, Joanne reported harboring a secret fantasy about being a Japanese American who was neither understood by the Americans nor the Japanese. This person was tortured with enemas and finally died. Joanne's associations linked this fantasy to Joanne's father giving her enemas when she was a child. She then realized she was defending herself against feelings of closeness with father by making herself feel the experience was very horrible. Having made this revelation, Joanne suffered a clinical setback. "I can't go to school," she said. "I went yesterday, I couldn't hear a word. I couldn't follow; it was just like the old times and it is impossible. I guess I will have to stop it again. I even feel I should start mutilating myself again." Dr. Fromm-Reichmann linked the onset of Joanne's recurrent symptoms to the disclosure of her private fantasy in the previous session. When this linkage was made, Joanne returned to school in a few days and was able to concentrate.

Another hurdle was successfully negotiated when, within a few months of beginning school, Joanne began to feel depressed and thought about quitting. At first, she had been the center of attention at the hospital because of her accomplishments. Dr. Fromm-Reichmann clarified that her sad feelings came from a loss of specialness. Once Joanne saw this, she was able to bear this loss and to continue school.

Joanne's improvement was reflected in further psychological testing. The chief change seemed to be in the direction of less childish naivete, less emphasis on very personal fantasies, and a more simple, factual approach to situations. There was also decreased restlessness and anxiety. Joanne now thought easily along more generally accepted lines. One question raised on the basis of this test was whether the increased comfort, stability, and realism had been bought at the price of impoverishment of imagination and vividness of experience. The psychologist illustrated the change by giving Joanne's response to the same ink blot on two different sittings. On the first occasion, Joanne said, "It is the horse of the

Apocalypse. He is running, his heart beats and there is a hooded rider on him, probably in the dark. The rest is whirling." On the second test, she simply stated, "There is a horse and a rider." The psychologist reported that, overall, the test results had not changed greatly since those of two years ago. She saw this as basically positive since in her experience large changes often indicated instability while small changes were more compatible with steady growth.

Colleagues of Dr. Fromm-Reichmann's could see Joanne's improvement, but raised the question as to whether Joanne's masochism was not a defense against hostility, and whether aggressive feelings could not be identified and interpreted in Joanne's relationship with Dr. Fromm-Reichmann.

"Each time I side with the nurses or side with other patients, she gets good and mad at me," Dr. Fromm-Reichmann said.

"But then she harms herself," Dr. Franklin said. "She hurts herself and not her analyst. She reverts to her own masochistic way of doing things. I wonder if she has worked out the tendency to lie to herself and to everyone else about her wish to hurt the person she wants to be with."

"Let's put it this way," said Dr. Fromm-Reichmann, "No, she has not yet worked it out, but she knows about it. It's on the record."

At this point Dr. Fordham said he was sure everyone recognized there had been a remarkable change in Joanne and that this change could not be considered anything but a good result of treatment. On the other hand, he went on, the question arose as to whether there were something incomplete.

"My only fear," said Dr. Fordham, "is that she tells you only what she can bear to face, and she does not tell you what is unacceptable to her. There may be a lot of that."

"We'll see," said Dr. Fromm-Reichmann. "I hope I would not call it a day without the patient being aware of that kind of thing and bringing it into treatment."

Dr. Fromm-Reichmann did not call it a day, but instead she and Joanne kept at it for three more years. Finally, Dr. Fromm-Reichmann brought up the question of termination. There was an immediate, intense flare-up of Joanne's symptoms that Dr. Fromm-Reichmann interpreted as an expression of Joanne's very strong dependency needs. These needs had three sources: first, Joanne's overdependence on mother; second, the new dependence on the analyst with whom Joanne had gone through so much; and third, dependence on the analyst because she did not yet have a steady boyfriend. Dr. Fromm-Reichmann and Joanne worked on these issues for several weeks with one symptom after another coming and going. "Practically everything seemed to come back," Dr. Fromm-Reichmann said in her final report to the staff. In the end, Joanne could accept and integrate her need for the relationship with Dr. Fromm-Reichmann, so that later, when she did have a steady boyfriend, she was able to tell him about her hospitalization. His reaction to this surprised her.

"Now I understand why you have so much insight," he said. "I always thought a girl of 20 couldn't have that insight. Now I understand it." This response made their friendship a very close one.

Four and one-half years after admission, Joanne was an outstanding student in creative writing at a local university. She was well groomed, had boyfriends, kept her own apartment without help, and gave dinner parties for her professors and fellow students.

One last psychological test helped document these changes. Not only was there marked improvement compared to the two previous protocols, but Joanne's increase in emotional stability came this time without a loss of richness and liveliness. Compared to the rather prosaic quality of the second test, Joanne now showed much greater freedom of imagination and fantasy. Compared to the restless, frightened, and sometimes macabre quality of the first test, she now demonstrated a more serene and pleasantly humorous approach to life. The aspect of the test which still suggested pathology was her manner of organizing the visual field and her small but recognizable tendency to distort perception.

Dr. Fromm-Reichmann felt that something quite unusual had occurred. Never in her previous experience had she treated anyone initially diagnosed as schizophrenic who had made such a complete recovery. In her last case presentation she provided examples of Joanne's "normal girl" thinking and behavior from recent hours.

"My professor is very satisfied with my poetry," Joanne said. "He said something very nice: 'I hope this will make you real humble, Joanne. I think you are the best student in my creative writing class in the last 20 years.' Indeed, it made me humble! He offered to show my poems and my fairy tale to a literary critic. He wanted to publish them in a magazine. I told him I definitely did not want this to happen. He was surprised, and wondered how a girl who is offered such a chance could refuse. I did not tell the professor, but I can tell you, I did not want to be known as 'that girl Joanne whose poetry is published.' The boys would be scared and I would get no dates. I know that I can do good poetry, but I feel that I have missed out on normal teenage experiences, and I have to try to make up for it. I don't know yet how I will do in that area, and it is more important to me now."

Later, Joanne reported that one of the literature classes took place at a local hospital so that nurses and Red Cross workers could participate. "I usually bring sandwiches for the professors, and they take care of my transportation," she said. "They complimented me on my homemade bread and said they would like to learn how the rest of my cooking is. My girlfriend and I had them in for supper the other night, and that was so good, because it made the relationship real and we had a wonderful conversation. It took care of my crush for the English professor. I am not less interested in him now, but it has no longer the quality of a crush so this supper party was really a good idea."

And again, on the subject of poetry: Joanne had made a home visit, and her father asked her to write a poem. She did so, but, as she reported to Dr. Fromm-Reichmann, it highlighted a problem about which she needed to do more work; that is, her compliance. "You know what I should have done?" Joanne asked. "I should have told my father, 'My professor tells me I do real good poetry. Would you say to a real poet, go in the next room and do a poem for us?' Do you believe he would have understood that asking me to show how 'special' I am is actually not a sign of respect for me? It's like the story you used to tell of a father who called his grown-up son 'my darling goldfish' and kissed and hugged him, and had to be told that that would be no way to make it possible for his son to have a real mutual adult relationship with him." Dr. Fromm-Reichmann and Joanne shared a good laugh.

Now, after five years of work, they could reflect on their time together and see what Joanne had found useful. She mentioned several interactions in particular. Once, after 2½ years of treatment, Joanne had left the hospital and lived in an apartment nearby. Shortly afterwards she became terribly upset, and had to be readmitted. She had burned herself again, and was so given over to the idea of self-mutilation that she was put in cold wet sheet pack. Dr. Fromm-Reichmann saw her and in their conversation it became clear that self-injury was an inverted expression of negative feelings about Dr. Fromm-Reichmann. She interpreted this to Joanne, against considerable resistance.

"I fought that idea with all I was worth," Joanne said, looking back. "It didn't make sense to me, but I realized later you were perfectly right. I did not want to think you could be so important to me; that I could harm myself because of feelings toward you. After that time, I did not do any more burning. But God, was I mad at you for suggesting what seemed to me such nonsense!" Joanne left the hospital again after only a few days of working intensely with Dr. Fromm-Reichmann on these issues.

A very important turning point came when Joanne realized Dr. Fromm-Reichmann was genuinely worried about her symptom of burning herself. Joanne wondered why Dr. Fromm-Reichmann thought the problem was so important. Dr. Fromm-Reichmann said, "You are an attractive young girl and if you get well and your arms are full of scars, that will be too bad." It took Joanne a long time to believe Dr. Fromm-Reichmann meant what she said.

Joanne said it was helpful that Dr. Fromm-Reichmann always insisted the treatment was a collaboration. This collaborative attitude could be seen in the resolution of Joanne's skin-pulling. She was still doing it even when she otherwise appeared completely well. At night she came home, took off her shoes, and pulled skin. Dr. Fromm-Reichmann made many guesses as to why but they were all wrong. Finally, in the course of discussion, Joanne said, "I am suddenly terribly frightened, as anxious as I was in the worst time of my illness." They went back over what they had been talking about to see if they could discover what triggered this feeling. It turned out the feeling occurred when Dr. Fromm-Reichmann used the word "change."

Joanne said, "Change is terribly frightening because I think time and time again, how can I understand that this college girl, Joanne, is the same person who was crazy on the fourth floor? I lack a sense of continuity. Oh!"

"What? asked Dr. Fromm-Reichmann.

"You know what?" Joanne asked. "That is the skin-pulling. Nobody sees it. I can practically pass for well yet I have a severe symptom. So I am still sick. That safeguards against the dangers of change and gives me a sense of continuity."

Its function understood, the symptom disappeared.

Joanne mentioned one further interchange as having been particularly useful. It was Dr. Fromm-Reichmann's remark to the effect that, even if Joanne recovered, life would not be a rose garden, but that she hoped Joanne would be strong enough to stand the times when it wasn't and enjoy the times when it was.

"I didn't believe you then," Joanne said. "I was quite sure that if I really got well, it would be a rose garden all the way. But the fact that you said it and obviously believed it gave me the feeling you really took me seriously and really had confidence in me as a human being. And that's why it meant so much even though I didn't believe a word. I am a little nearer to believing it now although even now I am reasonably happy, but I can understand it may not always be that way."

Approximately 30 years later, Dr. Thomas McGlashan, the principal investigator of the Chestnut Lodge Follow-Up Study, contacted Joanne by telephone. She told him how things had been.

After leaving Chestnut Lodge, Joanne attended a local university and continued to see Dr. Fromm-Reichmann as a private patient. Sessions continued for a year or two at decreasing frequency, so that in the end she saw Dr. Fromm-Reichmann every six months. As Dr. Fromm-Reichmann told Joanne, "Your activities in life will begin to be more important than our meetings. Soon you're just not going to want to fit them in." That, according to Joanne, was exactly what happened. After termination with Dr. Fromm-Reichmann, Joanne did not reenter psychotherapy. She never took psychoactive medication and was never readmitted to a hospital.

Joanne attended college, studied and worked hard, and fell in love. She was engaged, and jilted, and fell in love again. One summer she went to Europe; another she worked on a Navajo reservation. She was assistant to the superintendent of Navajo schools, and herded horses. Back at college, she studied anthropology and English and sang in a choir.

Following graduation, Joanne married, then honeymooned in Europe, traveling to the places her husband had been during World War II. They journeyed for eight months abroad before returning to the United States and settling in New Mexico.

Joanne's husband worked as a psychotherapist on the crisis team of a mental health center. He had retired one year before Joanne had been contacted for follow-up. Joanne said he might go into making fine instruments. This had been his hobby for three years.

The eldest of her two sons, now 21, had been quite a handful. "Some kids are more difficult than others," Joanne said. "I think he had a learning disability, but nobody knew it at the time. Everyone at school knew my first name. I was at school more often than I was home. But I think he's found his place in the world and he is coming around." He was now in Kansas City making electronic music, working with Moog synthesizers. From a recording of his mother playing one of the dulcimers his father built, he could make a product that sounded like the Mormon Tabernacle Choir. Joanne felt he was turning a corner.

"When did you start to feel he was out of the woods?" Dr. McGlashan asked.

"Well, this is Thursday," Joanne said, laughing. "You know, it's a process. I started to feel better about him the last couple of years. He is slowly harmonizing his expectations of the world with the realities thereof. That takes a long time for anybody, but it seemed to me it took a longer time for him because his dreams were so immodest."

The 19-year-old son, on the other hand, was doing well. "I'm whacko about that kid; always have been," Joanne said. "He is a gentle, loving, kind, witty young man, who works as a bill collector." He was living about 13 miles away from home, and saving for college. He had a roommate, and was supporting himself entirely, but was still in close touch with his family. "He was up here last night," Joanne said, "filling his face with pie."

The early years had not been easy. When Joanne was a young mother, she had cabin fever, living in a very small house with two squalling kids and no help. During this time Joanne experienced, for only a few minutes, feelings like those she had during her mental illness. "That was a message to me about the difference between problems and symptoms," Joanne said. "I was confusing my feelings about being all cooped up with the two kids with what being crazy was like. Realizing the difference was extremely valuable." No matter how bad cabin fever seemed to be, it was nowhere near so bad as the mental illness from which she had emerged. Joanne said there was one further time, again lasting only a few minutes, in which she felt the terror, the disorientation, and the feeling of unreality, which had characterized her psychosis in the hospital. The circumstances in which this episode arose were unclear. These were the only times since leaving Chestnut Lodge that Joanne experienced anything like mental illness, and it was important to her to highlight the distinction between these episodes and usual, everyday miseries. Joanne admitted she had had depressions, but said they didn't last long and seemed related to circumstance.

Although Joanne may have felt oppressed by cabin fever in the past, now she enjoyed being relatively isolated. For example, it was snowing when the follow-up interviewer contacted her by phone. She exclaimed, "We're socked in like I don't know what. . .like a flea in a pillow!" There was pleasure in being socked in, and a sense of being pitted against the elements. In her struggle with the elements, Joanne was now "second banana" in the local fire and rescue squad. "It all got started this way," Joanne said. "A woman called up and asked if I realized nobody was around here during the day, and suggested we train on the fire trucks so if something happened we could hold out until the guys got here. I said OK and before we knew it, we were pressing to join the department. That precipitated a huge blow-up in the male establishment. But we got training and really liked it. Then they put in a new interstate and the whole district doubled in population and before we knew it, we were playing big ball. I can't tell you how many hours we go out. I've done some three-day fires, but fire and rescue is like raisins in a rice pudding. It's a big surprise when you get one."

Joanne's verbal ability permitted further adaptations: she was a writer, a teacher of English etymology, and a tutor of writing and of Hebrew. One of her books described her experience at Chestnut Lodge. This book, *I Never Promised You a Rose Garden,* became a national bestseller and was made into a popular movie.

Joanne had been writing since she moved to New Mexico. Altogether she had written eight books. "I never planned much," Joanne said. "Life just came along and suggested things."

She was asked to estimate the amount of time she spent on each of her various occupations.

"Teaching is twice a week for two hours a shift. Writing is seven days a week, one hour. That does not include typing up the written work, which takes another two hours a week. Tutoring is eight hours a week. I have three Hebrew students and a writing student. Then one afternoon a week I have a secretary come. As for fire and rescue, last year I answered 142 calls."

All this left Joanne and her husband financially well off. "We don't have a wet bar, or a hot tub, but we make a lot of money," Joanne said.

Joanne saw friends and relatives frequently. She made little discrimination between work and leisure, because she enjoyed time spent in both pursuits. Those with whom she worked and those she taught often became social friends.

Joanne belonged to the League of Women Voters and the National Association for the Deaf. She made up one-fifth of the sisterhood of a small Jewish congregation she called Beth Evergreen. She helped with the dinners and refreshments. "All the old biddy skills," Joanne said. "We're the old biddies who stand around and serve hot coffee after the service."

Concerning her involvement with the National Association for the Deaf, Joanne said, "My husband used to be a counselor for State Rehabilitation with a deaf clientele. I learned sign language because deaf people showed up here on Sunday, it was simple as that. I became interested in the deaf community. Five or six years later, I wrote *In This Sign*. Because of *Rose Garden* I have been asked to speak at various mental health services for the deaf in three states, including, finally, New Mexico. It's amazing: Unless you're an expert from out of state, they don't listen to you."

It took 10 years for Joanne to get enough distance from her experience at Chestnut Lodge to be able to write about it. At first, she wrote under a pseudonym, but later the secret got out and she was asked to talk at various places. She felt this was a chance to integrate the past with the present. But, as Joanne said, it "got kind of old, being a professional ex-nut. I only do it now when they let me talk about the deaf. I get to do what I want with the experience; then it's okay."

Joanne had done much thinking about her time at Chestnut Lodge and was able to say more about what she felt had been helpful. She appreciated it enormously if a doctor or nurse had taken time to talk with her. Dr. Hawkins, for example, who was new at the hospital, had come to visit occasionally, "just to shoot the breeze." The people Joanne had liked shared one thing in common: "It was a kind of matter-of-factness," Joanne said. "An ordinariness. They looked across at me—not up or down at me, but across at me."

Another comfort to Joanne came when her illness was acknowledged. "When the doctor said, 'You are terribly sick,' the feeling was of profound relief, like an arrow hitting the target right in the middle. Relief and satisfaction. And then, of course, fear and terror. But relief and satisfaction came first. For years and years, people had been saying things like, 'You know, you ought to fix yourself up a little. Go out more, get a social life.' Well, that's like telling a legless person to run in the Olympics. Then somebody said to me, 'Forget all that crap. None of that is it. You're very ill and you have to be away.' You know, I count that as one of the three big times in my life. The other two were: 'Joanne, I love you,' and 'Mrs. Greenberg, you have a son.' I remember it with tremendous gratitude and happiness."

This simple statement that something was wrong had been the necessary first step in getting well. Subsequent advances were mostly small accomplishments, not epiphanies. "But then there was a day," Joanne said, "a certain moment when I was sitting on the radiator on the fourth floor, when I suddenly had a revelation or a mystical conjunction of some kind, and became aware of being alive. I was aware that I was alive and wanted to live. I really took off pretty much after that. I was not working against anyone after that." The reason for this revelation remained a mystery. Joanne felt Dr. Fromm-Reichmann had somehow contributed to it. "I was enlisted very early by Dr. Fromm-Reichmann in my own life," Joanne said. "Our collaboration was the model for how I now live. I don't have much trouble with authority because I see things basically as collaborative. This began with my collaboration with Dr. Fromm-Reichmann, with whom I worked against the illness."

Joanne felt relief that Dr. Fromm-Reichmann was not frightened of her, and did not force anything on her before she was ready for it. "She didn't tell me what the dynamics were," Joanne said. "She let me gain insight on my own, as a sort of reward."

"The situation was this way," Joanne went on. "I was pretty far gone from age 8 or 9. Reality and I had divorced, and from age 9 on it was a matter of trying to scrape the rags of semblance over me to hide what was there. There was no meaning and without meaning there was no learning. You can't weigh anything if you don't have gravity; up was as good as down."

This situation was not susceptible to immediate correction. Joanne saw Dr. Fromm-Reichmann four times a week for three years in the hospital and another year and a half outside. Change was often subtle. The chief thing, Joanne said, was that Dr. Fromm-Reichmann taught Joanne to trust the method, to trust primarily the collaboration, rather than trust the person, Dr. Fromm-Reichmann. That came later. Whenever disagreements arose, each was free to tell the other that she had blown the whole thing, or that there had been a misinterpretation.

Joanne also said she suffered antitherapeutic experiences at the hospital. "Most of it was people," she said. "You can't always get the best people. Some staff members were sicker than the patients. How are you going to help that? That's the way it is. Anytime when people have authority over others, those in authority will blow it sometimes and the others will feel misused."

"Once while I was at the Lodge, there was a severe blood shortage. They had blood trucks going all around the state looking for donors. The staff was allowed to donate but none of the patients were. I felt very excluded. The first day out of the hospital, I went to Washington and donated blood. That probably accounted for a tremendous rise in mental illness—all the crazy blood I donated! All the patients felt that way—purposeless and useless. Some hospitals force their patients to do things so they will feel useful. To me, that's not good either. It is a terrible thing to be mentally ill, one of the worst things that can happen."

One type of "force" used at Chestnut Lodge was cold wet sheet packs. For these, Joanne had nothing but praise. "I'm for them, strongly," she said. "They are a nonaddictive, very helpful method of producing relaxation. In cold wet sheet pack, I had my first experience of what it was like to be sane, in which I could look down into my mind and see what I thought. Sedative tubs, on the other hand, did me no good at all, except get me clean." For Joanne, the most helpful thing about pack was the sense of being held. "There's no place to go," she said. "You could fight all day. You could try to thrash around and kick your feet and wave your arms, but you weren't going to budge an inch. Did you know the American Indians break horses that way? They don't wrap them up in sheets, of course. They immobilize them by holding them. Everybody just holds them until they cannot move at all, whatsoever, for a certain space of time. Then the horses can be ridden.

"The cold wet sheet packs are like being held by many, many hands, but very impersonally, so there is no cost. It was like being held in arms without the price of commitment."

Joanne's experience in pack of "looking down into her mind," was the precursor to her later method of decision-making, called the "bare test." Joanne used this test whenever she had to make a difficult choice. Lying down, she considered the choice in its barest essentials, "just letting the thing wash over" her. She would then find out what she really believed, and it was often a surprise to her.

Joanne learned a capacity for productive introspection in the cold wet sheet pack, and the experience at Chestnut Lodge may also have contributed to her ability to take on different social roles. She was a wife and mother, an old biddy in Beth Evergreen, a social reformer, a performer on the lecture circuit, a fire and rescue leader, a teacher, and a writer. Such a varied group of occupations is unusual in anyone, and phenomenal in a person who once suffered from severe mental illness. Joanne had an enviable comfort with interpersonal relationships. The "three big events" in her life were all transactional. "You are ill," "Joanne, I love you," and "Mrs. Greenberg, you have a son," all involved dealings with other people and were qualitatively different from an experience such as, for example, the exhilaration of climbing a mountain.

The one thing Joanne indicated she would like to exclude from interpersonal relations was competition. In some ways, of course, she was quite a successful competitor, but she claimed not to have a grain of competitiveness in her. "I have a lot of friends who love football," she said. "But I think there ought to be a ball for each team. I think tennis is something that gives waste of time new meaning. One reason the craft of writing is so appealing is that you don't compete with anybody but yourself."

Joanne used the "Lewis Carroll method" of writing, in which you start at the beginning, go on to the end, and then stop. She said the flow of creativity in her was fairly steady, but she emphasized the part self-discipline played. She did not subscribe to the "divine muse" theory. "In order to write, you have to start," she said. "Then you have to go on doing it, and when you come to the end, you read it over and see what you've got. One hour a day, times thirty years."

One striking feature of the follow-up was the facility with which Joanne presented herself. There was something engaging and charming about her, and it was evident that Joanne had a self, or selves, to present, which was a level well beyond that achieved by most patients in the cohort under review.

Throughout the interview, Joanne displayed a resilience, sense of humor, and pleasure in life which bore the stamp of health. The mixture of playfulness and reverence with which Joanne greeted experience bespoke a capacity for joy and concern.

"Do you vacation? Have fun?" Dr. McGlashan asked.

"I don't segregate things into play and work," Joanne said. "I go skiing. I talk with friends. That's play. On the other hand, skiing is not play. It's a form of prayer. It's what God does on Saturday afternoons. I know, because I saw him on the slopes."

Chapter
— 5 —

Mark

Mark Jones came to Chestnut Lodge when he was 26 years old. He was graduated from a military college, but had four psychiatric hospitalizations before coming to Chestnut Lodge. Mark's mother said his illness began four years earlier, when he gave each family member $20 as a Christmas present. This was very unusual generosity for him, and marked a change in his behavior. He had not been the same since.

At that time, Mark was working for his father as an electrical engineer at the family-owned machine shop. All was well until Mark's brother, home from the war, received a better job at the shop than Mark's. Mark lost interest in the work. He stayed in bed, irritable and demanding, with sex always on his mind. Preoccupied with women, he asked his mother, "What would you do if a girl turned you down?" Soon he began taking long drives in the country with no destination. Often, accompanied by younger brothers or sisters, he drove extremely fast.

One day, Mark disappeared in the car and was gone for a week. The family received a call from a hospital in another state. Mark had smashed his car into a truck. The truck driver said Mark's car was veering down the road from side to side (even though he had not been drinking alcohol).

When Mark recovered sufficiently to be moved, he was taken home, but his behavior deteriorated. He piled things up in the house in a bizarre manner, picked flowers and stuck them in posts along the street, and seemed so confused that his family took him to the local mental hospital.

On admission he was oddly dressed. He saluted when entering and leaving the room. His speech was hesitant, and answers to questions were silly or absurd. He had no insight into his illness, and he showed poor judgment. He gave illogical and unusual responses to the Rorschach consistent with the diagnosis of schizophrenic reaction, catatonic type. After 26 electroconvulsive treatments, 33 insulin coma treatments, and "considerable" psychotherapy, there was little progress. Mark would not get out of bed, would not eat, would not open his eyes, and would not speak. At times he was restless and assaultive.

The family was advised that he needed long-term hospitalization away from the home, and Mark was transferred to a second facility, where he received 79 insulin coma treatments and 15 electroconvulsive treatments. He read newspapers and watched television, but there was little change in his condition overall at discharge five months after admission. He did not follow the recommendation to enter outpatient treatment. Mark lived with his family but did not return to work. His personality gradually changed; he became hostile toward a younger sister and increasingly restless. One night he called a taxi at 2:00 a.m. When the taxi driver discovered—after driving Mark to many places—that he had no money, he took Mark to the police station. Mark's psychiatric illness was impossible to overlook, and he returned to the hospital. His speech was rambling and illogical, his mood was inappropriate, and he had auditory hallucinations. He said he felt he was being observed by Russians. Sex troubled him. He thought nurses at previous hospitals made sexual advances toward him. Over the next three months he received 26 electroconvulsive treatments. Despite gradual improvement, Mark did not take a normal interest in his surroundings. Much effort was required to involve him in activities; for the most part he was seclusive. The hospitalization ended when Mark refused to return to the ward after a ride with his family.

At home Mark was cooperative at first, but later became recalcitrant. His mother made a reservation for readmission several times, but Mark refused to return to the hospital, and the family was reluctant to use force. That summer, he lived with his married sister and enrolled in a geology course at the university. He was sent to the psychiatrist when he laughed out loud in class for no apparent reason. This precipitated a fourth hospitalization, about which we have no record. There must have been little progress, however, because after several months Mark was referred to Chestnut Lodge.

Mark came from a large family. All of the children were delivered at home. Mrs. Jones felt marvelous during the pregnancies, and labors were easy. Frances was the eldest child, 29 years old at the time of Mark's admission to Chestnut Lodge. She was married, and had one daughter. She was named after her father's twin brother, Frank. Bertrand, 28, a graduate electrical engineer, married, with one child, was his father's namesake. Mark, 26, was next. There followed Sylvia, Beatrice, Jan (a son), Paul, Gloria, Jill, and Reginald. All were doing well except Paul, 20 years old, still in high school. His mother described him as "a most interesting somebody." No one saw any need for psychiatric counseling for him.

A maternal uncle had been treated for mental illness of undefined type at the Veterans Administration hospital. After recovery, he went to live with his wife's relatives in the north and did well. The paternal grandfather was alcoholic. No one else in the family suffered from psychiatric illness.

Mark's father was an inventor turned industrialist. He had not finished high school but placed a high value on education for his children, with whom he was very strict. Bertrand was the only one of them who was not in nearly constant struggle with him.

Mother was long-suffering. Although she was fully occupied keeping house and caring for babies, she made herself available to her husband in every way possible. She taught herself to type and did clerical work for him at the office. The crowded house was noisy and disorderly, which was one reason the father so frequently escaped to the factory. Following their fifth child, Mark's parents went to the doctor to discuss birth control. They did not have an appointment, so they had to wait. After a long time, they gave up, and decided to take whatever children came to them.

Mother's sister, Georgia Fay, just out of business school, came to live with the family and worked for Mark's father at the office. She took over Mrs. Jones's secretarial duties, and "moved in on her" in other ways. Now it was Ms. Fay who stayed late for dictation after everyone else had left the shop, which aroused the suspicions of even the minister.

The night of Mark's birth, Mr. Jones had been away on business for several weeks. After a long drive home, he fell asleep. When labor began, Mrs. Jones was unable to wake him. She finally succeeded, and he dashed for the doctor. Delivery proceeded smoothly. Mark was a pretty baby. He nursed for two or three months and then took the bottle. He cried frequently, and had no appetite. His mother tried to get him to drink a raw egg in his milk. She worried about his eating until he was three and then gave up, figuring worry would do no good. Mark developed normally, except that he was slow getting his teeth. Mother did not recall his response to the birth of his siblings or how he got on with them. Years later, recalling those times, Mark wrote, "I lived my early years with a nurse by the name of Rose. She amused us with children's games and we sat at the front windows of the small white house and watched the streetcars go by."

When he was old enough to walk, Mark was struck by a car and received a slight head injury. It was the scene father made with the woman driver that mother remembered in particular. Mark's own recollection was as follows: "Right after my sister Sylvia was born, I was hit by an automobile in front of the house. I can remember lying in the gutter, a bloody ball. I was evidently not hurt to any extent, and no doubt the driver of the car was not blamed as I had no doubt jumped from behind a parked car." Mark associated the accident to the time his sister was born. He specifically did not remember what his mother saliently recalled, namely the blame father placed on the driver. Blame belonged, in Mark's memory, to the child who darted into the traffic. This assignment of blame to himself may have been Mark's way of resolving a perceived disagreement between his parents. He was very sensitive to their quarrels, once dropping a shoe downstairs when the decibel level rose.

As for other medical problems, Mark had whooping cough and measles. He broke his arm when he was 6, and had a ruptured appendix when he was 12. The appendicitis came on silently. The cleaning woman was the first to notice that Mark was pale. Father rushed him to the hospital and stayed to watch the surgery. Once the operation was over, however, the pressures of work prevented his returning to visit Mark during the week-long recovery period.

The children attended the same elementary school, junior high, and high school. Mark was a good student except for nearly failing German in the 10th grade. His German teacher found that Mark was busy with a backyard chicken-raising project. On Easter his mother had given him three baby chicks. When they grew up, he sold them to raise money for an additional 100 chickens, which he kept at first in the bathroom because there was no other place for them. All his time was spent building chicken houses and fences. The German teacher took a supportive interest in this project, and Mark's grades improved immediately. Mark also excelled in swimming, but not in other sports, possibly because he wore thick glasses. He had no close friends and never dated. His father opposed any of the boys going to dances at the recreation center across the street. He did not involve himself in the boys' sex education, or any of their other interests, because he was too busy with work. Mark attended military college and performed adequately. Little information was available about his college years.

The onset of Mark's illness was insidious. The presence of early delusional thinking was revealed in his own later account of childhood: "My father spent much of his time at work and we were left to play. The family business consisted of the design and manufacture of machinery. I remember a tobacco machine from which my brother and I manufactured our own cigarettes with small amounts of tobacco sheddings. My relationship toward my father was one of respect and little closeness. It was during this time that I had an early respect for Jesus Christ through the church and desired to emulate him later on to the extent of eliminating war and preserving the peace, a goal which was inspired by the wishes of two women who I do not know the names of. Next was to be an outstanding industrialist."

Thought disorder was already apparent. By Mark's retrospective account, it may have been present even before the move to the house where he raised the chickens (thus sometime before the 10th grade): "During life on Fourth Avenue also came to mind the thought of the atom bomb or some bomb which one man could use to control millions under threat of death. I determined to exceed the greatest man of the world or even to be the greatest in the universe *no doubt as opposition to someone else* (emphasis added) who decided to be just one other human being creature in the universe. Control of this one atom bomb would not control the world for in destroying others would destroy himself. I determined in gaining peace to emulate Christ as he coming again and the other religions *with sisters and brothers as helpmates* (emphasis added), then gain peace for the world in gaining one world, then set up ruling power for the world and universe."

The italicized sections suggest that Mark had been dealing with conflict with his father and his siblings, and that resolution of this conflict took a paranoid, grandiose turn long before there were overt signs of illness.

Mark went to work for his father in the summer of his 22nd year. Bertrand was already in military service, and Mark would have been drafted after college but for the fact that his father requested his deferment. Mother was uncertain whether this was ever discussed with Mark or how he felt about it. She did hear Mark complain from time to time that his father was running his life. His father saw it differently. Mark had been refused a commission at military college because of poor vision, yet on graduation, the draft board classified him as 1-A. His father was furious. His son was officer material, and if he was refused because of his eyes, then he should not be a private, either. Father raised such a fuss with the draft board that they made Mark's status 4-F. Although Father was sure Mark did not know he had done this, Mark was the one who had brought his 1-A classification to his father's attention and seemed to expect him to do something about it.

Mark himself said, "My brother was drafted into the Army because of the Korean War and I was left with my father to work at the business. This consisted a good bit of installing a new power system and cleaning up for the installation of new machinery for the added volume of war-born business. Our main order consisted of 40,000 rings for the Army, parts for a cannon. My job consisted of getting these into production, which was done by buying a semiautomatic machine to finish these parts in one operation from blanks. Later my brother returned from Army duty. I was left with little to do as war business slowed and I took some time off. It was during this time I was said to have gotten sick." This account saliently omitted the difficult feelings aroused by Bertrand's return home. Denial clearly served an important defensive function, and was a characteristic of Mark's symptomatology when he was at Chestnut Lodge.

When he entered Chestnut Lodge, Mark was a prematurely greying 26-year-old of medium height, slightly overweight, and markedly nearsighted. He refused to get out of the car, saying he wanted to see his sister, who lived in a nearby town, to talk things over. Brother Bertrand brought in the suitcases and was mistaken at first for the patient. He, too, was hesitant and shy. Dr. Thomas Ricardo, the administrative psychiatrist, went out to the car to talk with Mark, and in the face of his resistance, allowed him to go to his sister's. This trip took an hour, and afterwards Mark readily agreed to be admitted.

One week later, Dr. Judith Williams performed routine psychological testing. Mark requested that his male attendant stay in the office with him. Dr. Williams saw that he was fearful. During the testing he spoke in a barely audible voice, saying almost nothing except in response to questions, but doing everything that was asked of him. He scored in the bright normal range on the intelligence test. Although his verbal score was pulled down because of trouble with abstract concepts and with concentration and attention, his performance was superior. The projective test results, in Dr. Williams' view, were clearly consistent with a schizophrenic process, probably of the paranoid type. Mark was withdrawn, apathetic, and depressed. Dr. Williams felt he could function in the real world only with tremendous effort. During the test, he was vague and focused on nonessential issues. His answers showed he was afraid that others knew disgraceful things about him for which he could be punished. Dr. Williams believed that in order to cope with his anxiety and fears of disintegration, he had limited his horizons to such an extent that he could not respond to complex social situations. The prognosis was guarded; Mark's illness was of such proportions that treatment would be long and difficult.

Dr. Gregory Norton, assigned as the therapist, was aware of this when he first met with Mark. "The main impression I got from him was that he was extremely frightened of me," Dr. Norton said. "He was very hesitant. He stood mute in the doorway and when he finally did come in it took him a long time to sit down. He seemed timorous and disturbed. He never completed a sentence, and in the early days, he didn't start many." Mark grimaced and giggled strangely. He could not make up his mind to stand or sit, to see Dr. Norton in the office, in his own room, or in the hallway of the unit. Mark shelved a new, unused encyclopedia in his room, and had a camera which he showed to Dr. Norton; apparently he was more comfortable talking about his camera than anything else. His speech was not bizarre, but it was frequently interrupted, as if his mind had flitted away, or as if what he was saying made him uneasy.

The first person with whom Mark became more open was Don Brett, the psychiatric aide initially assigned to work with him. Mark became so dependent on Don that he refused to go anywhere without him. This was striking in a person otherwise so withdrawn, and it created optimism that if Mark could become involved with Don Brett, he might also become involved with Dr. Norton.

For a time, in fact, the only person Mark spoke of in therapy was Mr. Brett. Therefore, it concerned everyone when, after two months, Mark was transferred to a unit where Mr. Brett was not working. Surprisingly, there was no ill effect: Mark's grooming, dress, and sentence structure all seemed to improve. He began to ask about hospital rules, and overcame his shyness with Dr. Norton in a way that could not have been planned for. The key seemed to be that Dr. Norton himself was new to the hospital, having just arrived from Ireland. Indeed, on first meeting, neither he nor Mark could understand the other's accent. It turned out that the fact Dr. Norton was a newcomer allowed Mark to escape the role of lowly patient and take instead the role of mentor. Mark's withdrawal was not overcome immediately, but when he really began to talk it was to advise Dr. Norton about American customs. Not too surprisingly, Mark was more comfortable giving than receiving assistance. Mutuality was a struggle, but on one happy occasion during bad weather, they helped each other out of a snowdrift.

A few months after admission Mark was telling Dr. Norton what kind of American car to buy. This made him think of trains, airplanes, and then communications devices such as telephones and radios. He spoke of roads in America and said it would be a good idea if a bridge were built from America to Europe. Dr. Norton said the two of them were trying to build a bridge together in the room. Mark agreed.

Dr. Charles Peabody, who supervised Dr. Norton's work with Mark, was impressed with this beginning. Discussing the treatment at a case conference, he said Dr. Norton received Mark's help with matter-of-fact gratitude, which in turn gave Mark status as a person who could be of use. Dr. Peabody noted that Dr. Norton showed an interest in whatever Mark brought up, rather than requiring him to stick with his personal history or problems. If Mark had some practical difficulty, Dr. Norton tried to help him to solve it right away. Dr. Peabody felt this was good, but sounded a cautionary note: Finding too quick a remedy to a problem could prevent full exploration of how the problem arose, or full exploration of Mark's feelings about the problem. Dr. Peabody felt that Mark usually swallowed his resentment, and would need the opportunity to express his anger.

Dr. Nathan Beasely, the Director of Psychotherapy, agreed. He argued, however, that the good relationship Dr. Norton was establishing with Mark would provide a basis for expressing negative feelings with greater ease. Dr. Beasely supported this approach for another reason. "I think we may be unaware how the delay between idea and action, which is the usual way analysis proceeds, can repeat something that goes on in patients' families," he said. "A great deal of anxiety develops whenever problems are unresolved between family members, and patients like Mark handle this through some psychotic mechanism, and are placed in a hospital, where often again and again they feel put off, and from this point of view, in some kind of torment. I am impressed with the usefulness of rapid action in potentially changing this picture."

Anticipating the possible later expression of Mark's anger, conference participants wondered if it had prevented therapeutic progress in the past or had disrupted treatment. "Things might go along pretty well for awhile, but I wonder what happens when he becomes dissatisfied?," Dr. Beasely asked. "What led Mark to leave the other hospitals? Was it that they had really finished therapy or did he become dissatisfied and quit?"

"I think their treatments followed an organic approach," Dr.

Norton said. "Mark was considered unresponsive to psychotherapy, and left the hospital once the organic treatment was over."

"I have another idea," Dr. Peabody said. "Mark went from his trouble in the factory to live at home, and each time he left one of the hospitals, he went home. Perhaps his mother, whose satisfactions chiefly derive from her motherly role, was not displeased that Mark came home to her. There might have been some secondary gain from the illness in this sense."

Conference participants felt that if his mother needed Mark as a dependent, then social service casework should help her develop a more mature relationship with him. One last issue discussed at this conference was that Mark's parents, although well-off, could not afford a lengthy hospitalization, and there might be need to move Mark quickly to outpatient status.

Mark's repetitive states of confusion, occurring between periods of better functioning, were the subject of discussion at a second conference eight months into treatment. The confusion was intermittent. For the most part Mark was lively, amusing, and pleasant company. He had begun to venture into town, often with student nurses. He asked Dr. Norton about graduate education; in particular, about a plan to take a correspondence course in aeronautical engineering. Hereupon, however, Mark entered the first of several confused periods, this one lasting about 10 days. He was as hesitant and withdrawn as he had been on admission. As at that time, Mark's camera provided a subject for discussion with Dr. Norton, as well as a vehicle for wider social contact: He photographed staff members and shared his pictures with them. As he emerged from this confusion, Mark peddled Japanese cigarette lighters through the hospital and turned again to his studies, telling Dr. Norton what he learned about carburetors. He bicycled with student nurses. His favorite nurse was engaged to a man whom Mark feared might become jealous. When she left, Mark became confused once again. This time his route back to coherence came via work as electrician for the patient production of *Guys and Dolls*. He also held shifts at the kiosk, the on-grounds sundries shop. Soon afterwards, however, Mark was confused yet again. Dr. Norton had missed an hour accidentally. He saw Mark the same afternoon and found him perplexed and bewildered. Four or five days later Mark had recovered.

The next time he became confused was when his parents visited. But this time, *everyone* was confused, including the staff, over facts revealed during the visit. Staff members, for example, were surprised to learn Mark had access to money no one knew about, and had bought an engagement ring for his favorite student nurse, and, most extraordinary of all, had been taking flying lessons at the airport. Dr. Ricardo was startled to find all of this occurring without his having known about it. He told Mark that being engaged was definitely out for the present, that the ring should be placed in the vault for safekeeping, and that flying lessons should be put on hold. The only thing Dr. Ricardo knew was that Mark had purchased a car, and was busy painting it. No one could ascertain the source of Mark's money.

Mark had also kept Dr. Norton in the dark about his past, his family, and many other personal issues, although he made occasional references to his father being engrossed in business. Mark said money had been given to his brother, but not to him, for taking out a pilot's license. And he talked about Gloria, the sister he visited before being admitted. He now regularly bicycled 60 miles to see her (round trip).

Whenever Dr. Norton detected transference manifestations, and linked what happened between Mark and him to what little he knew of Mark's past experiences, he drew a blank. Although Mark often "agreed" with Dr. Norton, he made no associations to confirm a single one of Dr. Norton's interpretive comments. Therefore, Dr. Norton abandoned any pretense at orthodoxy and instead drove with Mark around the countryside. Dr. Norton learned the local area, and Mark improved, so this arrangement seemed satisfactory. It all confirmed the important part that Dr. Norton felt was played by identification in the treatment. Mark adopted certain of his therapist's postures and mannerisms, and Dr. Norton was amused to hear his Irish colloquialisms spoken in Mark's southern accent. When Dr. Norton was learning to drive in America, although he did not know it at the time, Mark was learning to fly an airplane. And, later, when Dr. Norton was interested in buying a house, Mark took a course in real estate. Immediately prior to Dr. Norton's summer vacation, Mark talked about buying property at the seashore, and about yachts, and other things associated with vacations. And then, acknowledging a more specific awareness of his feelings in the relationship, he said he would feel lonely with Dr. Norton gone.

For whatever reason, Mark was doing better than ever. He now managed the kiosk, supervising other workers and keeping up the inventory. Almost as soon as Dr. Norton returned from vacation, however, the old confusion set in. Mark ascribed it to stress on the job. Dr. Peabody told Dr. Norton that, in his opinion, each time Mark became confused it was because he needed help but could not ask for it. This time, Mark was able to be direct. He asked what he could do in the kiosk to make his job easier. He wanted to open a new office and recruit more personnel. Perhaps because Mark now sought help, his confusion cleared more rapidly than in the past.

In thinking further, Dr. Peabody suggested that confusion could be Mark's defense against awareness of his need for, and attachment to, Dr. Norton. Dr. Norton's return from vacation would, of course, heighten the need for defense, and Mark's previous urge to marry the student nurse whom he knew only slightly could be interpreted as a response to conflict over his attachment to his therapist. Dr. Peabody wondered if Mark's confusion had a source in the divergent examples set by his parents. Mark's father was a capable, self-made, aggressive person, whereas his mother was quite the opposite. She turned to Mark for closeness she did not get in her marriage, which could increase his confusion. Mark felt safest in an environment with clear limits, such as the military college or at Chestnut Lodge under the firm administration of Dr. Ricardo, who said no to wedding rings and airplanes.

Everyone was impressed with Mark's capacity for secrecy and the incongruity of some of his behavior. On the one hand, he often came to his session with Dr. Norton unutterably confused, disturbed, and unable to communicate or function, and, on the other hand, he was flying a Piper Cub and earning high marks in a real estate course. In acknowledgment of Mark's genuine accomplishments, he was allowed to move to day patiency at the end of the year. He took an apartment close to the hospital and worked very hard through the entire winter, with success. He kept his job at the kiosk and made serious attempts to socialize, giving, with the help of two female patients, a party to celebrate moving out.

In the spring, Mark became dissatisfied with the kiosk and talked of finding other work. Although he reduced his time at the hospital, he remained active. He joined a new swim club in town and campaigned door-to-door to increase its membership. He also took up archery. Despite these involvements, Mark became more withdrawn. One day he shot an arrow into the bushes, and hunting for it, contracted such severe poison ivy that he did not want to be seen in public. Dr. Norton made a house call and discovered that Mark did not want to come to the hospital and was unwilling to go out for food. The poison ivy eventually cleared, but at the cost of a long isolation. Perhaps as a result of this, Mark grew closer to his family. On Thanksgiving of that year (the second since his admission) he made his first trip home, and visited home every few weeks from then on.

Meanwhile, Dr. Norton ceased driving off grounds with Mark, and insisted on meeting in the office. Dr. Norton told Mark the rides were pleasant but not terribly productive. Mark agreed, and told Dr. Norton that he, too, liked the rides but felt something was missing. What was missing, as had been predicted by Dr. Norton's colleagues at the case conferences, was any expression of angry feelings. Mark had experienced these since the time of admission, initially in response to fears that he would be taken over and "babified." Now he revealed that he had been especially uneasy because of Dr. Ricardo's name. An unpleasant acquaintance from his hometown church choir also bore that name. Thinking of that person reminded Mark of the choir itself; The choirmaster had also been unpleasant. Mark told Dr. Norton that in response to these distressing memories he had fantasized these people in a comic strip which made him grimace and giggle. Thus, a reason for Mark's past behavior fell into place. Now, when Mark giggled for no apparent cause, Dr. Norton wondered if he himself was currently the principal jackass in Mark's mental cinema. Mark laughed out loud for five minutes. He could not speak, but only nodded, indicating that this was right, Dr. Norton was the principal jackass.

One thing that bothered Mark was the very process which Dr. Norton thought so central to therapy—the process of identification. Mark said he had often been aware, back in his own room, that he was imitating Dr. Norton. He was uneasy that in doing so he was encroaching on Dr. Norton, and also that Dr. Norton was encroaching on him. Encroachment meant being taken over, having his privacy invaded. While Mark sat in his room imitating Dr. Norton, he worried that Dr. Norton would take the wrong view of it.

"What would be the wrong view of it?" Dr. Norton asked.

"That you would think I was scornful or mocking," Mark said.

Dr. Norton saw there was a great deal of mockery in much that Mark was doing. He told Mark so, and in the end both of them were more respectful to each other.

Dr. Norton thought, in retrospect, that the previous period, as pleasant and useful as it had been, was like a sentimental Disney movie. Mark had been a southern gentleman, and Dr. Norton an Irish one; the relationship improved when they ceased to mind their "p's and q's" with each other. Now, interpretations linking past and present behavior were made. For example, Mark acknowledged he had been uneasy mocking Dr. Norton because he was afraid of a reaction like his father's. He was afraid Dr. Norton would blow his top in some inappropriate and unexpected way. The stubbornness underlying Mark's confusion could now be examined, and its relation seen to mother's technique for undermining father in her passive way. Not only could Mark express anger through perplexity, but when he was perplexed he could always count on warmth from mother, so it was a behavior with powerful attractions.

Despite what the therapist regarded as progress, a new crisis developed just after Christmas in the second year of treatment. Again, there was much secrecy on Mark's part. Without telling his therapist, Mark bought a piece of land in the country. This outraged his father, who was facing a recession. Considerable pressure was placed on Mark to seek work. There was a real problem about money, and Mark was told that further day patiency for him was in jeopardy, but he tended to disbelieve this since the family had cried "wolf" on this issue so often in the past. Nevertheless, Mark began looking for a job as an electrical engineer, or in some allied field. Hospital staff members believed he might have set his sights too high. They told him to start with something more basic. Although ostensibly shy and helpless, Mark did not listen to what others had to say and went ahead on his own, doing what he wanted. He even adopted the attitude that those interviewing him for job positions were less qualified than he was, and this did not enhance his employability. Thus, he was perpetually looking for work, and never hired.

Dr. Beasely, the director of psychotherapy, wondered if the patient's very ineffectiveness was not his way of destroying the therapeutic situation. One problem, Dr. Beasely said, that prevented Mark from performing at a skilled level, was that in his therapy he had not shown the full depth of his rage. This rage could therefore be displaced in some ruinous manner to his efforts at seeking work; that is, his rage might currently be operating through the guise of ineffectiveness. There was not too much one could do, Dr. Beasely thought, when confronted with someone who was ineffective, except feel sorry for him, even if later you wanted to kick him in the pants or leave him. Therefore, Dr. Beasely felt that Mark would need to express a good deal more of his rage at Dr. Norton before he could get on with things.

Instead of this, Mark gradually became more destructive in his way of life. He spent money unwisely, remained for long periods in his room, and ate inadequately. Because Mark did not like to leave his apartment, he sent for food by mail. This was so expensive that his parents insisted he stop. An aide was dispatched to help Mark repack several kinds of hors d'oeuvres, an attache case of cheeses, a box of "Ham 'n Fixings," a delicacy box, and two "Pheasant Features" for return to the Epicure's Club. When the social worker met with Mark to help him pay the food bill and monthly installments for his encyclopedia and his piece of land, she found him indecisive and pathetic. He refused to produce his checkbook, because it was "personal."

Mark's mother and father grew increasingly concerned. They saw little progress, and were especially unhappy that Mark did not have a job. They told the hospital they would soon no longer have enough money to continue Mark's day patiency and requested his discharge to private patient status.

Dr. Norton and Dr. Thorpe, the clinical director of the hospital, were considering this request when Mark went home for the holidays in the third year of day patiency. When Mark returned to the hospital, he had stopped shaving and appeared disheveled. Dr. Norton felt this was a kind of defiance. It could also have been a call for help, as if Mark were saying that although his parents wanted him out of the hospital, he still needed to be there. Mark seemed intent on demonstrating that he was hopeless and helpless. Dr. Norton and Dr. Thorpe felt this might be the very expression of negative feelings that other colleagues had believed was so essential if Mark were to recover. They recommended continued day patiency.

At the time of Dr. Norton's next vacation, however, Mark made another home visit, from which he never returned. Mark's mother sent a letter to Dr. Norton explaining that Mark did not wish to return to Chestnut Lodge or to continue treatment privately. She said he was working again in the family business and would remain at home.

Five years later, Dr. Norton received a call from Mark. He said he was doing okay. He seemed happy with Dr. Norton's invitation to come to see him if he were bothered by anything, but did not take up the offer.

Another 15 years passed with no news, and then, as a part of the follow-up study, Mrs. Jones was contacted by telephone. She was 81 years old. Mark was at home with her and so was his now emotionally ill brother, Jan. Mrs. Jones had been a widow for 11 years. Mark's five sisters and three other brothers were married, and Mrs. Jones had 30 grandchildren and one great-grandchild.

Since Mark himself did not fill out the follow-up questionnaire sent to him by Chestnut Lodge, his mother did it for him. She indicated that after Chestnut Lodge there had been seven or more admissions to psychiatric hospitals, and that Mark had never been employed except in the family business. Mrs. Jones gave no response to questions pertaining to social activity, symptoms, or general status. "I wish Mark was capable of answering, but he is not," she wrote at the end of the questionnaire. "He has spent a lot of time in hospitals since leaving Chestnut Lodge. He comes home, does not follow the doctor's orders, and so he has to return for treatment. He has the support of his family, his friends at the church, and others. When at home he spends the greater part of his time at the family company where his three brothers are."

Later, Mrs. Jones sent a letter to the social worker who had been assigned to Mark. "Mark was doing pretty well when he left Chestnut Lodge," she wrote. "He was driving a car. His brothers tried to give him some work to do at the company. He was not able to work. As time went on, he had to get medical treatment, so he has been in and out of the hospital. He calls Fourth Avenue his home and is always glad to get back here. The church has taken a great interest in him, yet they cannot take the place of the medical help he requires."

Renee Marshel, at the time a Chestnut Lodge social worker and research interviewer, made a telephone call to the home. She asked for Mark. His mother said she would see if he would come to the phone but warned that "oftentimes he won't talk." She could not find him and believed he might be in the bathroom. She tried later to get him to come to the phone and this time he did so.

Mark denied that he had ever returned to a hospital. He said he had not had psychotherapy nor had he taken any medicines. He said he had not seen his Chestnut Lodge psychiatrist privately at any time. He had been working, he said, at the family company on a 40-hours-per-week basis, for the past 30 years. "I'm working there now," he said. He admitted he was satisfied on the job only half of the time. He assessed his competence as fair. He said he did not take alcohol or drugs, and he had not been in trouble with the law. He denied having, over the past month, any hallucinations, anxiety, or depression, but admitted that overall he was happy only a small percentage of the time. "I don't know why," he said. He seemed to feel he should be happy and did not understand why he was not. He denied any suicide attempts.

"Ever have any further schooling?" Ms. Marshel asked.

"No," Mark said.

"Where do you fall in socioeconomic class?"

"Lower class," Mark said.

"What about friends? How often do you meet with friends?"

"Yes, I have some friends. I don't meet with them too often. Every so often."

"Any close friends?"

"Yes," Mark said. "William. I've known him since Chestnut Lodge. He's someone I can talk to. I speak with him every so often."

"How satisfied are you with your relations with friends?"

"As satisfied as I could be. I don't know what else I could do. Satisfied about half of the time."

"How about with the family? Are you satisfied with them?"

"As satisfied as can be. About half of the time."

"Any social activities?"

"The Baptist Church." Mark said he attended church regularly.

Before the end of this first follow-up phone call, Ms. Marshel spoke again with Mark's mother. She said that everybody liked Mark, but when it came to close friends, there was only one, William, whom Mark had met at Chestnut Lodge. Mark would call William and they might go somewhere together every now and then. William gave a party for Mark's 50th birthday.

At the end of the call, Mark was going out the door.

"Don't forget to put your coat on," his mother shouted to him.

Ms. Marshel made a second phone call and this time spoke only with Mark's mother.

"Mark has gone off to the plant today," she said. "He walked there this morning. He's loaded with energy. His brother says what he does there is walk around, and sometimes look at magazines. This may go on for awhile, but then something will happen, like he will meddle in the machinery, and that shows he needs medical attention again.

"One of the counselors said he shouldn't be allowed over there unless he was really working, but his brothers can't treat him like that. Maybe he believes he is working. He'd certainly like to, even if he's not able to. He loves walking over there. Tonight, he'll be home by 5:30. Then he has dinner and goes to bed."

Mrs. Jones said Mark seemed in good physical health. "I don't know why he is as healthy as he is. This morning he went off in the rain without an umbrella."

She said Mark might do all right for another three or four months and then have a relapse. "He refuses to take medicines when he is not in the hospital. Then, after awhile, you know he is getting sick. He won't go to the plant and he won't go to church. He has to do all the cooking by himself, and won't accept help from me. If I ask him to turn the stove off, he ignores me. He won't talk and he hides the newspaper. He takes things from the house and puts them outdoors. He gets real hyperactive, and may walk 16 miles to the next town, like the last time. People knew there was something wrong, so they called us, and we went to get him. But he was determined to make the trip so he did it again the next day. After that, we had to get some help for him."

Help took the form of brief hospitalization. Typically, Mark would agree to take medication while he was hospitalized, and soon he would be sufficiently improved for discharge.

"He won't see a doctor between hospitalizations," his mother said. We might take him to the community mental health center, and the doctor gives him medicine, but then he won't take it."

The doctors told Mrs. Jones that an adult home would be the only alternative for him, if she felt the family could not cope.

"We found out money will not get these people well," Mrs. Jones said. "Mark responds about as well to the state hospital as if we were paying several thousand dollars a month at a private institution. The trouble is, they can't keep him there. One time we were very encouraged, about three years ago. Mark saw a young social worker who worked near our house. But the social worker left after a few months and we haven't felt so good about the situation since. He used to take Mark on trips."

Mrs. Jones was worried because at 81 years old she knew she could not always be there for Mark. "My daughter is working with the Schizophrenia Foundation," she said. "The family suffers too, you know. The Schizophrenia Foundation has speakers come to meetings. Our family is very interested in these meetings and in the whole mental health field."

Part Two:

The Synthesis

Chapter
— 6 —

Introduction to Case Critiques

The cases of Ben, Betty, Joanne, and Mark will now be critiqued. Two questions guide our conduct of this exercise. First, what does the interpersonal treatment encounter tell us about schizophrenia and about people who have the disorder? Second, what do people with schizophrenia tell us about the psychosocial treatment encounters we call psychotherapy? Our four cases can provide no more than a smattering of answers to these formidable questions, yet we feel they may at least sharpen the questions in ways that might prove stimulating.

We will resist the temptation to wander from the consulting room to the library. We wish to critique Ben, Betty, Joanne, and Mark as we meet them, face-to-face in the vortex of psychotherapeutic space. Having introduced our patients, we want to spend time with them. We do not wish to lose them through abstracted meanderings into the labyrinths of the literature. We stick with description, not explanation.

Our descriptions, nevertheless, use the academic vocabulary of two broad and venerable perspectives: the tradition of clinical psychiatry and the discipline of individual psychotherapy. The former perspective elaborates the case as a case, following the medical model of the person viewed as a carrier of illness. Although the person is not unimportant, emphasis resides with the illness and its pathogenesis, manifestations, and course. The latter perspective focuses upon what transpires when a case and a professional become implanted in a two-person *treatment* matrix. Treatment is italicized because the outcome of this interpersonal experience may, in some instances, barely justify the term. Nevertheless, treatment is the *raison d'etre* for this get-together, and whether or not it engenders change, it can usually tell us something about the person with the illness.

The clinical perspective comes first, in Chapter 7, with its primary subject matter being schizophrenia. The treatment perspective comes next in Chapters 9, 10, and 11, its major focus being the psychotherapeutic process.

Chapter
— 7 —

Schizophrenia:
One Illness or Many?

Thinking about Ben, Betty, Joanne, and Mark as cases, one is immediately struck by their startling differences. The question leaps forward: Can all these people have the same disease? Or, if schizophrenia is a single entity, then its manifestations must be multiform, indeed! Emil Kraepelin, who first described the syndrome at the turn of the 20th century, envisioned it as unitary (Kraepelin 1971). Shortly thereafter, Eugen Bleuler, to whom we owe the term schizophrenia, claimed it was a group of disorders (Bleuler 1950). Today, we have not come much further than these two pioneers. Each of these hypotheses remains plausible.

Nevertheless, a certain progress has been made: We know that we don't know. Time and experience have chipped away at theoretical certainty and replaced it with the humility of perplexity. Before, experts claimed they knew what schizophrenia was, yet nothing useful came of this enlightenment. Now, unprotected by the delusion that there is an Answer, we are in a healthier position to recognize our ignorance and to look again as pioneers.

Immediately we are struck with the heterogeneity of schizophrenia. Ben, Betty, Joanne, and Mark may all have the same disease, or they may not. We don't know. But we must proceed. Accordingly, in this chapter we will try to describe the syndrome of schizophrenia as it developed in our four cases. We will look first at the disease, both its common and its disparate elements, and second at host factors; that is, at the individuals afflicted with this disease.

THE ILLNESS: COMMON FEATURES

Since we do not know the etiology(ies) of schizophrenia, its identification has always been determined by consensus. This is basically a political process, at its best guided by dispassionate observation, at its worst subject to the enticements of fads. All four of our patients meet the criteria for one or another of the consensus definitions of schizophrenia that have emerged over the years, including the most current definitional set; that is, the *Diagnostic and Statistical Manual of Mental Disorders, Third Edition (DSM-III)* (American Psychiatric Association 1980). These require the presence, for six months or longer, of some or all of the following symptoms: hallucinations, delusions, and disordered thinking. This is called the active phase of illness. It must exist in the absence of prominent manic and/or depressive symptoms that signify affective disorder. However, this phase may be bracketed by a variety of "prodromal" or "residual" symptoms such as social isolation, peculiar behavior, poor personal hygiene, strange speech, bizarre ideas, unusual perceptions, and blunted and flat or inappropriate affect; that is, feelings that do not match the individual's prevailing ideas and thoughts. *DSM-III* criteria for schizophrenia also include deterioration of functioning, seen most frequently as derailment of or retreat from ordinary human social intercourse. Onset is typically in late adolescence, but this feature is not invariant enough to be regarded as a valid criterion.

Ben's clinical presentation was dramatic. He suddenly derailed, disappearing mysteriously one day and reappearing shortly thereafter in obvious need of help, having traversed a bizarre odyssey, the accounts of which differed with Roshomon variability. After three months of this behavior, however, it was clear that Ben was seriously ill. His psychosis included hallucinations and delusions. The former were auditory: He heard his name being called. The latter were persecutory, and probably grandiose. He believed others felt he was stupid, that his therapist would either kill him or seduce him, and he worried intensely about being homosexual. The episode of agitation in his therapist's office that led to Ben's being restrained was quite likely homosexual panic.

Ben's psychosis appeared to be a "first break"; that is, an acute psychotic breakdown which, until it lasts long enough, is labeled brief reactive psychosis or schizophreniform psychosis in *DSM-III*. By the time Ben came to Chestnut Lodge, he had been actively ill for six months, long enough to be labeled schizophrenic by *DSM-III* criteria.

Betty's disorder was well established by the time of her admission. In fact, her schizophrenia presented in ways that many would regard as prototypic. Most of the time she harbored grandiose delusions of being of royal birth and persecutory delusions of being the potential victim of her father's incestuous designs. During more intensely active phases of her illness, she experienced auditory and visual hallucinations and spoke with a stream of thought that was loosely organized. Affectively, she demonstrated the cold, flat, unmodulated feeling tone—or absence of feeling tone—that some regard as the core of the schizophrenia syndrome.

Betty's clinical picture, then, was unambiguous and long-standing. Official *DSM-III* convention requires six months of active symptoms to affix a label of schizophrenia. Unofficial convention marks the syndrome as chronic if it has been active for two years or longer. By these criteria Betty was schizophrenic and chronically so.

Joanne presented something of a diagnostic enigma. In the medical record, her disorder was labeled schizophrenia. She also met the *DSM-III* criteria for schizophrenia by virtue of ideas of persecution and hallucinatory experiences. Upon closer inspection, however, both of these symptom clusters had a "borderline" or evanescent quality. She had variable "ideas" or notions about persecution rather than firmly held delusions, or convictions that remained impervious to contrary evidence. She would, for example, feel paranoid about people walking behind her, and stop to let them pass. Once they were in front of her, she could relinquish the idea and relax. If her persecutory ideas were delusional in intensity, such a shift in reality would have no effect upon her ideations. She would remain suspicious and watchful of people, keenly scanning their behavior for "evidence" supporting her knowledge that they were out to get her. Joanne's hallucinations were extensive and involved all of her senses except taste. However, they also appeared to be highly "field dependent," meaning their presence, form, and severity were frequently influenced by ongoing real life stress. These would be regarded by some as "hysterical" hallucinations rather than as hallucinations typical of schizophrenia, which tend to be more sustained, stress-independent, and thematically repetitive.

Thus it is questionable whether Joanne had schizophrenia "proper." Nevertheless, she probably belonged within the realm of the "schizophrenia spectrum." At different times, for example, she displayed *all* the symptoms listed as *DSM-III* criteria for schizotypal personality disorder: magical thinking, bizarre fantasies, ideas of reference, social isolation, experiences of depersonalization and derealization, aloofness, suspiciousness, undue social anxiety, hypersensitivity to real or imagined criticism, and speech that was odd, overelaborate, idiosyncratic, and highly metaphorical without being loose. While her medical record does not inform a choice between "mild" schizophrenia versus "severe" schizotypal personality disorder, Joanne was nevertheless clearly compromised and in need of help.

Mark's diagnosis of schizophrenia, in contrast, was unambiguous. He displayed persistent auditory hallucinations, recurrent delusions about being observed by the Russians or being pursued sexually by nurses, and frequent illogical speech that was rambling and difficult to follow. Thought disorder was clearly apparent in his written accounts about atomic bombs and emulating Jesus Christ. His affect was frequently inappropriate to thought content; his answers to questions were described as silly or absurd. His poor judgment and lack of insight about being ill were also prominent features. These, however, may accompany any form of severe mental illness. They are not specific to schizophrenia.

Mark also demonstrated many of the prodromal and residual symptoms mentioned in *DSM-III*. Most prominent were peculiar behaviors such as piling things in his house, sticking flowers in posts along the streets, dressing oddly, saluting upon entering or leaving a room, and laughing out loud in class for no apparent reason. Mark fit the everyday assignation of "crazy." His behavior was clearly deviant, and he made no pretense of recognizing this, for example, to the point of being more secretive or even simply quiet. His bizarreness would probably evoke a twitter of nervous amusement or the chill of strangeness. An observer would be likely to respond to him with "praecoxgefuhl" (Irl 1952), that is, piloerection on the back of the neck (Havens 1986) and the thought, "Here is someone so eerie I cannot even hope to understand him."

Like Joanne, Mark displayed some of the criteria for schizotypal personality disorder from *DSM-III*. His speech was odd, he could be seclusive, and when he was with others he seemed strange due to constricted or inappropriate affect. As was not the case with Joanne, these elements bracketed a more severe and sustained derailment from normality. For Mark, schizophrenia was clearly the primary derangement, whereas for Joanne, schizotypal personality traits held center stage.

THE ILLNESS: DISPARATE FEATURES

Our four patients share the same diagnosis of schizophrenia, with the caveat already noted regarding Joanne. From this point on, diversity reigns. Cataloging their differences requires a consideration of additional parameters often used to describe mental illness. These include the onset of illness, its course up to the time of Chestnut Lodge admission, and additional phenomenological features such as associated affect states and deficits, overall severity, and the degree to which the illness disrupts interpersonal relatedness.

Onset

Descriptive features of illness onset include the time it takes for the illness to develop, the age by which the malady becomes manifest unquestionably, and the relationship of this metamorphosis to environmental stress.

Ben's schizophrenia erupted suddenly, seemingly overnight. During late adolescence he disappeared from home one day and reemerged in the hands of civil and medical authorities. For the other three patients, the beginnings of illness are impossible to pinpoint. They seemed to slide insidiously into malfunction, probably starting in their latency years, ages 7 to 11. For Joanne, aberration blossomed slowly into recognizable illness by late adolescence. It took longer for Betty to be labeled "sick," but she came from a family with either a low sensitivity for or a high tolerance of deviance. Accordingly, Betty's behavior was not identified as dysfunctional until she went to college. Mark was 22 when his family knew something was amiss. He, too, by his retrospective account, had probably been ill long before this time, but was very adept at keeping it to himself. Overall, despite variation in the rate with which their illnesses developed, all four of our patients fit Kraepelin's original description of a "praecox" or adolescent onset illness.

Ben's illness, again in contrast to the other three patients, seemed partly a reaction to specific stressful experiences—the deaths of his maternal grandmother and his girlfriend Amy. Stresses of varying kinds, in fact, loomed prominently in his narrative: separation from home for college, closeness with a new girlfriend, and concerns about being a failure in a competitive world expressed in his overcompensatory masculine braggadocio.

Joanne's life was not without stress, but the stress was not so clearly defined as it was for Ben. Her life "in general" had always been chronically stressful, and to this was added the challenge of puberty. This developmental milestone, with its surging drives for independence, sexuality, and competition, presented challenges that stopped Joanne in her tracks.

Betty seemed totally untouched by the strains of puberty, which she regarded as an oddity affecting other people, not herself. She was identified as sick in conjunction with matriculating at college, but one senses she was severely compromised long before that time. Neither developmental strain nor environmental stress, therefore, appeared to contribute to her illness onset. The foil for her seemed deeper, more fundamental. It was the universal drive to individuate from childhood and become an adult. What is a natural part of life for most people was experienced by Betty as an intolerable, even malevolent, demand.

Mark's retreat to his bedroom paralleled his brother's return from the army to assume a place of leadership in the family business. While we may readily link these two events, Mark himself would probably blink at the connection and regard *us* as crazy. And he would probably be right. His brother's return to a position of authority was undoubtedly stressful, as it would be for *anyone*, but Mark had been exposed to stresses of equal, if not greater, magnitude (e.g., college) and emerged from them seemingly nonplused. This time, however, he tripped. In his case, more than in any of the other patients', the "stress" in question seems more like the "straw that breaks the camel's back." Had it not been his brother's return from the army, something else would have happened to tip Mark over the edge, at least in retrospect. Something had changed, slowly but surely inside Mark, which ultimately stripped him of his capacity to miniaturize and contain *everyday* tension.

The often-made assertion that schizophrenia is always precipitated by stress depends upon choice of words. Close inspection reveals this to be true only if "stress" can be defined liberally enough to include anything. In our cases, the stresses associated with illness onset ranged from specific environmental events (e.g., deaths) to developmental stages (e.g., puberty), to life tasks (e.g., individuation), to everyday experience (e.g., work). The range is staggering. It suggests either that our idea about there being a relationship between illness and stress is incorrect, or that the illness is so variable virtually any relationship is possible—including *no* relationship—the more rigorously stress is defined. Another possibility is that for each individual, events assume particular importance. One person's stress is another person's everyday occurrence.

The final common path of schizophrenia is the failure of adaptation. The degree of stress that reveals this failure and the age at which it happens, in turn, tells us something about the disease. It certainly informs us about its variable severity. It may even be telling us what Bleuler first suggested, that we are dealing with different underlying illnesses or etiologies which, however, share a common expression.

Course of Illness

Stress continues to interact with the illness after its onset. In fact, it proves to be an illuminating measure about the field dependence versus independence of the illness over time. Ben's schizophrenia seemed highly "reactive," that is, sensitive to environmental events and daily interpersonal stress. Meeting in a closed room with his male psychotherapist, for example, sparked homosexual panic. Joanne's symptom formation had the same trigger sensitivity, revealed, for example, in her hallucination of ether smells in the presence of perceived hypocrisy. Schizophrenia for Betty and Mark, on the other hand, was more field independent. Imperviousness to the fluctuations of everyday stress, in fact, seemed to be an aspect of their psychopathology; that is, they were abnormally *unresponsive*. Illness for them marched to its own tune, oblivious to the surround.

The armor with which schizophrenia protects its liege subject from external stress also resists external manipulations in the form of help. A patient's response to prior treatment efforts can be particularly enlightening about the forces marshalled behind the symptomatic battlements. Usually the more field independent the illness, the more resistant it is to treatment. Before Chestnut Lodge, for example, Betty was flatly nonresponsive to a three-month hospitalization, nine electroconvulsive treatments, an unspecified number of insulin coma treatments, and six psychotherapists over a period of four years. Mark was similarly untouched by innumerable ECTs and insulin comas, and "considerable psychotherapy." Before his referral to Chestnut Lodge he drifted through four hospitalizations unaffected. There was a hint of partial responsiveness, however, in Mark's premorbid history of a turn-about in his high school German classroom performance once the teacher took an interest in his "chicken caper."

Ben's history of prior treatment responsiveness was mixed. His imperviousness to three hospitalizations and to very high doses of neuroleptics formed the basis of his referral to Chestnut Lodge as an alternative to lobotomy. In high school, on the other hand, Ben spent six months talking to a psychologist with apparent good result. He relinquished a negative stance, returned to school, and graduated. Joanne's history was also mixed. Prior to Chestnut Lodge, she entered psychotherapy with Dr. Remington. While she developed excellent contact with him, it sounds as if she responded negatively to the procedure. At first she was reported to have been scared but friendly. Later, however, she developed frequent nightmares with aggressive themes. This progressed to a proliferation of symptoms of derealization, depersonalization, blocking, and quasi-disorientation. Thus, although she was clearly affected by the psychotherapy, the direction was regressive and difficult to contain, necessitating hospitalization.

By the time they reached Chestnut Lodge, then, our four patients had established courses of illness that were strikingly different. Betty's schizophrenia was insidious in onset, largely impervious to stressful or mutative perturbations of the field, and slowly progressive. Its relentless activity ultimately rendered her continuously nonfunctional. Mark's schizophrenia was also insidious, field independent, and slowly progressive. Its activity, however, ran an intermittent course with exacerbations followed by partial, diminishing remissions. The illness seemed to be continuous, perhaps, because Mark remained anhedonic and aimless even in his "remitted" states. Ben's schizophrenia, in contrast, was acute in onset, highly field dependent, and rapidly progressive. While its explosive momentum could not be checked by vigorous treatment efforts, Ben's illness was still relatively "young" by the time he came to Chestnut Lodge. His symptoms were chronic; that is, long-standing enough to render a diagnosis of schizophrenia, but not nearly as chronic as those of Betty and Mark. Joanne's illness was more enigmatic. Her "schizophrenia" was not prominent enough to define a course. Her schizotypal manifestations, however, had a longitudinal profile characteristic of severe personality disorders; that is, early to evolve and habitual or repetitive in nature. Her progressive adaptive failures seemed not to stem from a qualitative worsening of her disorder as much as from crescendoing life demands attendant with puberty—demands that she was unprepared to handle.

Looking beyond formal diagnosis to the profiles of illness onset and early course highlights the unique aspects of schizophrenia in each individual. As a first approximation, this "cut" through the data phenomenologically appears to define different syndromes for Ben and Joanne on the one hand and for Betty and Mark on the other. Schizophrenia for the first two has an urgent, unstable, evanescent presence, whereas for the second two it is like an anchor that grows progressively larger than its ship.

Emil Kraepelin was drawn to the clarity of illness course and used it to define schizophrenia. For him the illness was a thing, the growing anchor, and the patient's course like that of the ship, chronically listing sideways or sinking. For Kraepelin, only Betty and Mark would have schizophrenia. Eugen Bleuler was not wedded to longitudinal course as the ultimate criterion of diagnostic validity. He insisted that the schizophrenias could and should include more criteria. For him the illness was also a thing, but a variable thing that could sometimes be experienced as a presence, darting forward with diabolical intent or darting backward to hide in the shadows. Bleuler would have added Ben and Joanne to Kraepelin's list of those with schizophrenia, but he would also have been careful to point out the differences.

Affect States and Deficits in the Manifest Illness

Twentieth century psychiatry has consistently distinguished schizophrenia from the other group of psychoses, the manic and depressive *affective disorders*. This division is rife with the danger of false dichotomy, especially if it results in the assumption that the schizophrenic process does not impinge on affective phenomena in the psyche. Nothing could be farther from the truth. Schizophrenia may also be regarded as an affective disorder, but one which disturbs the affective structures from a different angle. The manias and depressions produce exaggerations in the fluctuation and amplitude of feelings. The schizophrenias strike at the very source(s) of feeling. In mania one is too high and in depression one is too low, but only in schizophrenia can one be too dead.

Mark's affective presentation would probably be regarded by many as prototypic of schizophrenia. He had feelings, but they were difficult, at times virtually impossible, to identify. Sometimes affect seemed present but in the form of an ill-defined pressure, restlessness, or periodic activation without clear pleasurable or unpleasurable referents. Other times feelings seemed to disappear altogether leaving a profound blankness. At these times Mark drifted without an affective gyroscope; that is, an internally determined reckoning based on the appetitive cycle: peremptory need leading to a specific aim directed at a target leading to consummatory behavior leading to contentment. His drives or "cathexes" or investments, all basically emotional in nature, were shallow, casual, easily derailed, and highly mobile. At these times Mark was described as flat, withdrawn, uninterested, or unmotivated. He manifested what has most recently been described as the negative symptom or deficit syndrome of schizophrenia. His first symptoms of illness, for example, were of this nature: a loss of interest in work, staying in bed, muteness, and increasing nonrelatedness.

Mark was capable of experiencing and expressing some identifiable feelings. He behaved fearfully in the presence of some people, and he could laugh. Presumably he could be angry during his times of assaultiveness, although this was never documented. But Mark's repertoire of categorical affects stopped there. He seemed not to possess other feelings: joy, humor, disgust, sadness, depression, guilt, grief, envy, or gratitude. Also, the feelings he did have often failed to match the scene in which he found himself, in fantasy or in reality. This is the "inappropriate" affect of schizophrenia, the best example being Mark's laughing out loud in class for no apparent reason.

Betty's affects were like Mark's in some ways, different in others. Her repertoire was also limited. In fact it was monochromatic. Hostility alone punctuated an otherwise flat landscape, and a cold hostility at that. In this way she also presented with a deficit syndrome. In contrast to Mark, however, Betty seemed amply endowed with drive, highly aggressive drive, to be sure, but drive nevertheless. Perhaps it was one of her constitutional givens. Certainly the evidence suggests it was present early. From the age of two, for example, Betty was described as very "sensitive." In school she refused new clothes because she feared the poor children would feel badly. In fourth grade she deliberately performed poorly so as not to be seen as the teacher's pet. These are not, in our perspective, truly loving acts, but rather inhibitions based upon fears of retaliation at the hands of envious peers who, as a result of projected aggression, appeared imminently dangerous.

With Joanne, expression of affects takes a quantum leap forward. While she could be cold, aloof, and distant, such states were situation-specific, not globally pervasive. They were part of a much larger repertoire of feelings that was quite extensive and included fear, anxiety, anger, joy, humor, disgust, sadness, depression, guilt, and envy. Her deficiencies, at first, seemed limited to two affects: grief and gratitude. Needless to say she did not present with a deficit syndrome at any time. Also, while her affects were present and recognizable, they were not a prominent part of her symptomatology. She did occasionally elaborate symptoms that are sometimes associated with affective disorders, such as derealization, depersonalization, and bulimia. There were no striking or sustained mood swings, however, as far as we could tell from the record.

Of our four patients, only Ben's illness possessed distinctly affective elements. His acute psychosis was preceded by clearly documented depression with poor concentration, and a poorly documented, and questionable, suicide attempt. During his second hospitalization he surrendered a pocket knife he had sequestered to use on himself and he later threatened to jump out a window. Thus, affective psychopathology was clearly present. Whether it was of sufficient length or strength to change Mark's diagnosis to affective disorder remains a matter of judgment. Our ratings indicated that he failed to meet the necessary *DSM-III* criteria for the full syndromes of either mania or depression, whereas he did meet the full criteria for schizophrenia. Some contend that *any* affect throws into question the diagnosis of schizophrenia. We regard this view as arbitrarily narrow and based upon the assumption that the schizophrenias and the affective disorders are mutually exclusive categorical entities, an assumption that has *no* definitive supporting evidence of which we are aware.

Ben may not have been affectively disordered, but there was plenty of affect present in his psychosis. It was present not only as recognizable depression and anger, but also as heightened drive. Ben was relentlessly excited, his behavior constantly driven, his symptoms floridly proliferating. If Ben had schizophrenia, it was "positive schizophrenia," the antithesis of the negative or deficit syndrome displayed by Mark and Betty.

Our four patients, then, varied considerably in the degree to which affects formed a part of their symptomatology. They also varied in a related dimension: the degree to which they experienced *distress* either *in* their symptoms or *about* their symptoms. Joanne, for example, was decidedly uncomfortable. She was unhappy, neophobic, subject to panics, lonely, and beset by myriad longings. She did not like being ill, and worried about it. Ben's symptoms were also dysphoric: painful depression, abysmal self-image, suicidal ruminations, and panics about being homosexual or persecuted. Betty and Mark, in contrast, seemed more impervious to distress. Neither had much discomfort in their symptoms, even their persecutory delusions, and neither had any discomfort about their symptoms which they generally denied as symptoms.

Illness Severity

At first glance, the concept of illness severity seems self-evident. It means the degree to which illness has affected the individual's adaptive capacity. Closer inspection reveals it to be a rather complex and multidimensional construct. We suggest the following dimensions relate to severity, although they do not exhaust the concept:

1. *Reality Testing.* In severe schizophrenia, reality is globally erased, as is awareness of appropriate social behavior. In less severe

cases the patient remains in touch with reality in nondelusional sectors or keeps his or her delusions well sequestered or justified or rationalized. There even may be insight into the fact that the patient has an illness.

2. *Invasiveness.* The more severe the illness, the more it invades and dismantles the personality. Extremely ill patients show no will or initiative. They are passive and compliant to symptom phenomenology and, for example, may obey hallucinated commands. Less severely ill patients can sequester the illness to some extent; that is, control attention and/or their behavioral responses to signs and symptoms.

3. *Structure of the Symptomatology.* The more severe the illness, the less structure will be apparent in the symptoms elaborated. The symptom picture will be highly fragmented, disorganized, labile, fluid, and unpredictable. In less severe cases, the symptoms will be repetitive, consistent, and systematized with much secondary elaboration or liberal (even creative) weaving of reality into delusion.

4. *Maturity of Defensiveness.* Severe schizophrenia is characterized by a limited number of rigid, reflexive, externalizing defenses which put everything that is wrong or uncomfortable "out there." Denial and projection are the prototypes. Less severe schizophrenia is characterized by the presence of *more* defenses in the sense of a richer repertoire, the activation of which is less automatic, more "chosen." Suppression, reaction formation, and sublimation are examples.

5. *Primary Gain from Illness.* Primary gain may be regarded as illness efficiency, or the degree to which the illness effectively eliminates experienced dysphoria (e.g., anxiety, guilt, depression) and/or the degree to which it provides pathological gratifications, (e.g., delusional grandiosity). Gain is related to our preceding discussion about the amount of distress associated with illness. An illness that is ego dystonic and that fails to protect against dysphoria, while less efficient, is also less severe. Severity and gain, therefore, have a linear relationship.

6. *Secondary Gain from Illness.* Secondary gain refers to the pleasures attending the sick role. For some patients, the role is highly gratifying. For others it is eschewed. It is, to some extent, unrelated to illness severity *per se*, since it is possible to exploit the sick role maximally whether one's illness is mild or severe. Nevertheless, a strong secondary gain definitely makes the task of treatment harder and for this reason may be regarded as a

dimension of severity. How do our four patients line up on these dimensions of severity? Here, too, heterogeneity reigns.

Mark's schizophrenia waxed and waned. When active, it was severe. He could test reality only sparingly and had no insight that his public behavior was bizarre or that it had any impact upon other people. He seemed swamped, swept aside by an illness that was totally invasive. His symptom clusters contained little structure. They changed rather frequently and were quite fantastic with little inter- woven reality ("The Russians are observing me."). His prominent defenses were limited to pure projection, and a denial so powerful that it rendered his experiences bland—as reflected in his matter- of-fact written accounts. The primary gain of Mark's schizophrenia was the most total. He appeared to suffer little dysphoria and to revel in a delusional hegemony (recall his laughing out loud). In contrast, Mark enjoyed no secondary gain from his illness, in part because of a pervasive anhedonia and in part because he denied being sick.

Betty's schizophrenia was also severe, although probably not as severe as Mark's. Large islands of reality testing remained intact. Much of her social behavior, for example, was appropriate. Where reality testing was shaky, as around her grandiose delusions, she kept this weakness sequestered from the challenges of others. While she denied having an illness, she was in touch enough to know that others thought differently, and responded to this with appropriate secretiveness, manifest mostly as silence. Her symptoms, when ap- parent, were highly structured, consistent, and predictable. She had systematized grandiose delusions about being Princess Elizabeth and these were bolstered by messages from the newspaper. Some contact with reality was sustained even in her delusions. They were always plausible, never completely outrageous. She feared being raped by her father, not by a Martian. Her defenses were limited and primi- tive, primarily denial and projection. She used them in a particularly inflexible, repetitive fashion, over and over and over again. Perhaps she did so because they worked very well for her. Her illness was very effective, filled with massive primary gain. She seemed to suffer no obvious discomfort and perhaps enjoyed her delusional regal stat- ure. Additionally, unlike Mark, she seemed to derive a fair amount of secondary gain from being a patient. While she denied the role of patient she never challenged it or relinquished it.

Ben's schizophrenia was highly visible and disorganizing, but probably less severe than Betty's or Mark's. Ben's capacity to test reality shifted widely. Often it was profoundly lost, as with his denudative behavior or his assaultiveness. Unlike the experiences of Betty and of Mark, this loss was reversible and frequently Ben could be "brought back" to reality by setting limits or with diversions. In general, however, his psychosis had a low structure, his symptom picture fluctuating frequently and unpredictably. He could also shift rapidly between using primitive defenses such as projection (e.g., homosexual panic) or denial (grandiose self-aggrandizement), and using mature defenses such as sublimation (involving himself in activities) and altruism (caring for other patients). His repertoire of defenses, indeed, was wide. Ben seemed not, on balance, to derive either primary or secondary gain from his illness. His schizophrenia had its grandiose highs, but it was also a nightmare of persecution and self-denigration, and while Ben accepted the sick role, he did not value it. It is difficult to judge the invasiveness of Ben's schizophrenia. "Explosive" seems a better adjective, or the more colloquial "nervous breakdown." His illness, like a terrorist's bomb in a bus station, scattered bodies everywhere and created panic and terror. By the time Ben came to Chestnut Lodge, panic was still present and too disorganizing to allow an estimate of the extent of damage.

Joanne was the least severely ill of our four patients. Her reality testing was basically sound. She knew she was ill, even was relieved at some level to know it. Furthermore, she had a "friendly" relationship with reality. She often found it soothing (e.g., nature) and did not regard it with unremitting antipathy as do many patients with schizophrenia. Her symptoms were highly structured and reactive to reality. They often represented a creative effort to deal with experience, to elaborate and master environmental stress psychologically. Her world of fantasy, for example, was a retreat from the here and now, but it was also an attempt to negotiate with life via play. Most striking was the range and extent of her defensive strategies. At times, she could deny and project. She could also be obsessional. There was considerable reaction formation, especially around wishes to eat and take in. Her defenses often kept her conflicts "internalized," for example, as somatic or trance-like states. Her defensive structure was not stereotypic or reflexively automatic. Also, there was little acting out and the majority of her defenses did not severely distort her perception of the world. Her defenses supported reality testing the way dreams support sleep. It was as if Joanne were saying, "I will forget; I will postpone; I will play out in fantasy; but I will not distort what I know is real."

Joanne derived virtually no primary gain from her illness. It often failed to protect her from psychological pain. She seemed restless and uncomfortable, in fact, as if she were "trying on" different psychopathologies in search of a better fit, hence her unstable, changeable clinical picture. Secondary gain was minimal. The sick role was important to Joanne, but only in the service of securing help. She could say "I'm sick," relax, and allow herself to be cared for—all for the purpose of gathering strength for mutative work. The sick role was a medium, not an end.

Overall, Joanne's illness was extensive in its manifestations but not deep in its invasiveness. Her will and initiative remained largely intact. Only infrequently was she unable to control attention to illness percepts and distortions. Even then, however, she was usually able to control her response; that is, decide for herself and exercise choice. At times she dealt with her illness as if it were an invader. She did this by identifying with the aggressor; that is, taking pseudocontrol of her symptoms by embracing them, or seeming to create them: overeating, cutting herself, secluding herself, displaying her distress. Much of her illness and symptoms involved behaviors over which she had control. Seldom does the narrative of her illness suggest that she was a passive and compliant puppet. More often than not, she too was pulling strings.

Relatedness in the Manifest Illness

Schizophrenia not only affects an individual, it also affects that individual's ability to relate to others. The "social" repercussions of illness are obviously important, although their form and extent can vary. Some types of schizophrenia are highly *interactive*. Object hunger remains; loneliness is painful. The patient still seeks relatedness and this is reflected in the signs and symptoms of illness that are interesting and capture attention or somehow compel engagement with and by the environment. Other types of schizophrenia are *alienating*. The patient behaves in ways that provoke anxiety or disgust or rage while he or she remains unempathic with the needs and realities of others. Sometimes such alienation seems inadvertent. Often one can see an element of will in some form of *negativism*. This can range from overt negativism that resists care-taking (e.g., aggressiveness, active rebellion) to overt negativism that allows care-taking (e.g., mutism) to covert negativism (e.g., passive-aggression) to delayed negativism (e.g., making progress and then sabotaging it).

We postulate that the less interactive and the more negativistic and alienating the manifest illness, the more crippling the illness is to the patient. A schizophrenic disorder with these features, even if mild in severity, would tend to drive away needed treatment personnel and result in a dangerous thinning of the patient's social network.

Betty's illness was the most striking in this regard. Her illness seldom engaged people. In fact, it walled her off from interaction. She was overtly negativistic, indiscriminately blasting away at virtually everyone, but especially at anyone who dared to get close. She cultivated alienation and kept herself physically and personally unattractive. She was oblivious to others' needs or sensitivities, such as her father's feelings about her demands that he leave the house. Perhaps he was actually relieved to get away from her; probably more than one of the six psychotherapists she scorned prior to her admission to Chestnut Lodge breathed a sigh of relief when she walked out the door.

Mark's schizophrenia seemed geared to avoid interaction of any sort. He was not object seeking and seemed quite comfortable with isolation. The interactive potential of his illness was nil; it neither fostered relatedness nor repelled it. His symptoms captured attention by virtue of their bizarreness, but that was all. He was inadvertently alienating with his "praecoxgefuhl," but he was not invested in distancing others as was Betty. On occasion he was overtly negativistic; that is, restless and assaultive—but most of the time his negativism was passive; that is, staying in bed, not eating, and remaining mute with his eyes closed.

Ben's schizophrenia contained episodic negativistic eruptions that were extreme, e.g., assaultiveness, but that compelled the milieu to engage him by controlling him. He behaved "like an infant" in his first hospitalization, but since he was a grown man, this often led to the need for restraints. While this behavior was undoubtedly alienating in one sense, it was engaging in another. He forced people to hold him by holding him down. One could not ignore his distress. As such, Mark's schizophrenia was highly interactive. Remarkably, this aspect of his illness was relatively *new* behavior. Previously isolated, he became object-hungry. He started to complain about loneliness, and isolation was now more painful than soothing. A fitful, convulsive change seemed to be taking place. Long denied needs for contact were bubbling forth through the symptomatology of his illness.

Joanne's schizophrenia was both private and interactive. She was hungry for relatedness but fearful of it. In her illness she resolved this conflict by elaborating a transitional fantasy space absolutely loaded with people. Via her seven Irian worlds, she never ceased to be actively related even when she was withdrawn from "real" people. Her behavior could be alienating, although it seemed cultivated and clearly defensive: nose-picking, obesity, unkempt hair, bitten-off fingernails, and unbrushed teeth. Despite this, her underlying warmth and vulnerability showed through and she was clearly a very attractive patient. She had a capacity to accept care with gratitude and she displayed a well developed social empathy or awareness of the needs and realities of others. She could see beyond herself and was unique among our four patients in this way.

Joanne was negativistic, but her negativism was largely internalized as conflict. For example, she was a harsh critic of her peers ("Do I have to split infinitives to get along with them?") and her teachers. In fact, she had a strong endowment of jealously and envy. Her psychological tests were loaded with aggression: death, murder, attacks, accidents, sexual assault, operations, mutilations. At the same time, if she expressed any of this aggression, she would suffer paralyzing guilt or paranoia. When her meanness "just came out" she would in turn be mean to herself and hurl scathing criticisms at her reflection in the mirror. Aggressiveness, even in the form of normal exhibitionist wishes to display her giftedness in school (reciting poetry, showing paintings) led to shameful ideas of reference that others were laughing at her. Her negativism boomeranged back upon herself, often actively as self-punitive behavior. She cut her wrists, burned and pulled off her skin, and thought about slashing her body. All four of our patients had well developed consciences, but only Joanne's carried a big stick. It gave her nightmares, but it also gave her an advantage. Because she was slugging it out with herself, her intense negativism and aggression was not driving other people away.

Illness Parameters: Recapitulation

Close inspection of the schizophrenic disorder reveals its likeness to the mythological Hydra. As one cuts into its phenomenology, more and more heads appear. The monster changes with every slice. Dissection along the parameter of onset, for example, separates Ben's schizophrenia, with its sudden appearance, from that of others whose schizophrenia emerged gradually. Dissection along the parameter of early course, however, identifies Mark's illness as intermittent in contrast to the continuous and progressive quality of Joanne's and Betty's syndromes. The probe of affects teases forth yet another cleavage plane in the specimen: Joanne's feelings remain largely intact and Ben's feelings gush forth with frightening intensity, but Betty's and Mark's feelings seem, most of the time, to have been replaced by embalming fluid. The scalpel of relatedness carves out still different anatomical structures. Mark's schizophrenia captures most of his attention, leaving him tenuously connected to others. Betty's schizophrenia growls like an angry dog, warning approachers to remain at a respectful distance. Ben's schizophrenia is just the opposite, commanding attention and demanding contact. Joanne's schizophrenia also involves the observer, but as a sympathetic audience watching her struggle to create a coherent plot on stage. The remaining parameter, severity, counts the number of heads, or lines up the illnesses by size and virulence. Mark's appears to be the worst, followed closely by Betty's. Ben's schizophrenia is heavy, but relatively new, whereas Joanne's schizophrenia, while chronic, is relatively mild compared to that of the other three patients.

Have we exhausted all of the relevant ways to look at the illness? Hardly. What we would most like to know about—etiology—has yet to be articulated. In the meantime we must continue to develop our descriptive skills. Schizophrenia is not one-faced or even Janus-faced. It is multifaced or faceted, and this must be taken into account in every clinical evaluation. Schizophrenia may be common, but it is an *individual* disease. It is also a disease which affects individuals, and thus far we have not even considered them; that is, the people who become afflicted with schizophrenia. If we focus our attention on these persons we will find, no longer to our surprise, yet another range of dimensions awaiting our measurement.

HOST FACTORS: THE PERSON WITH THE ILLNESS OF PERSONHOOD

When does a person with schizophrenia become a schizophrenic? Medical parlance in other specialties seldom blurs host and disease. People with carcinoma, for example, may be referred to as "cases" of carcinoma, but never "carcinomics." Having schizophrenia, similarly, need not make one "schizophrenic." But the term does exist. Everyday linguistic usage suggests that it is often difficult to separate this illness from the person. The reason for this unclarity is that schizophrenia affects the very development and expression of personhood. For example, an observer would be hard-put to decide whether Mark was a person with a weird malady or simply a weird person. For Betty, illness appears to *be* the personality. In terms of invasiveness, her schizophrenia seems to have taken over. It might even be said that she never had a distinct personality, or that from the beginning her personality was warped into schizophrenia. Either path leads in the same direction; Betty seems more "schizophrenic" than like a person with schizophrenia. Ben also seems to be totally gripped by schizophrenia, and one can see from his case study why demonic possession was a popular etiologic hypothesis in the Middle Ages. He was a very different person when ill than he was before illness. Ben, the diffident, preoccupied loner, exited stage left while Ben, the horny, exhibitionistic jock, entered stage right. Joanne, more than the others, conveys the impression of being a *person* with schizophrenia, or something akin to schizophrenia. Amidst the profusion and confusion of her Irian worlds another presence can always be felt, a normal person looking for someone to help her come out of hiding.

The first task in describing the person with schizophrenia, then, is to estimate the degree to which the individual and the illness are separable. How much personal meaning is embodied in the illness, or how much of a person is present to register the impact of the illness? We call this the *thematic story line* of illness. Our analysis of the person with schizophrenia inevitably carries us back into his or her history, in search of the individual that was "premorbid" or preexistent to the schizophrenia. Sometimes "premorbid" cannot be distinguished from "early morbid," but that in itself is important to know. Crucial "host factors" can be defined only after careful reconstruction of the historical premorbid person and his or her development within the family matrix. This archaeologic endeavor unearths at least two broad domains of relevant parameters, the heterogeneous *developmental vulnerabilities* to schizophrenia, and the various *premorbid dimensions* which are useful in predicting the likely long-term course and outcome of particular cases of schizophrenia.

Thematic Story Line of Illness

The chimerical interface between person and illness can sometimes be palpated through the clinical use of that equally abstract instrument, the psychodynamic formulation. To apply the psychodynamic formulation in this sense means to consider, in each case, whether there is a clear human story line. Is there a recognizable plot in the story of the patient's struggle with illness, or a narrative about a person becoming sick that has a beginning, middle, and denouement? Does the illness reflect, or even amplify, the patient's otherwise expectable life preoccupations? Can *meanings* be discerned in the symptoms? Do recognizable wishes, defenses, and conflicts about a limited number of themes emerge through the psychopathology in ways that are easy to formulate without unjustified embellishment?

Joanne's illness pulsated with a story line about conflict. She presented herself as a person with many wishes for contact, for expression, for competition, and for success. She seemed endowed with an overabundance of aggression and envy, manifested early in her life in overtly murderous wishes toward her baby sister, Betsy, or in her perception of the nursing situation as Betsy devouring mother's breast. Arrayed against these drives were many inhibitions that reflected her family's style; for example, father's condemnation of her enuresis ("pants-wetting stinker") and her fears of rape going back to father's rages at the breakfast table about Hitler and the Czechs. She elected not to tell her parents about anti-Semitism at summer camp, figuring they would castigate her for it. These conflicts between drive and defense were readily discernible in her symptoms and personal history. For example, her clinging, fearful dependence upon mother during latency could be interpreted as a reaction formation against competitive feelings so strong that, in recognition of them, father suggested Joanne's mother actually give up painting. Even in Joanne's symptoms, early conflicts were identifiable. For instance, a conflict over basic trust was revealed in the symptom of hallucinating the smell of ether, which came on in the presence of perceived deception. Empathic observers could regard her symptoms not just as manifestations of illness but also as signals readily translatable into a story about human passions and strivings.

Meaning is harder to track in Ben's schizophrenia. The illness itself seemed to appear precipitously, confusingly out of the blue. The wide variation in recorded accounts of his first 24 hours of breakdown attests to the fact that no one knew exactly what happened. His symptoms, however, eventually began to cluster around a few identifiable themes: concretely naked displays of sexuality, nightmare elaborations of castration (the Nazi dream), and concerns about masculine identity and potency (homosexual panics). One can, with some imagination, formulate a story about Ben's breakdown. Premonitory hints of strain appeared as inhibitions and negativism during high school. When, in college, this girl-shy young man quite uncharacteristically became involved with two women, it seemed he was trying to change somehow. The pressures proved too much, however, and his world fractured. His schizophrenia left Ben's personality in pieces, as if there had been a breakthrough, with the intensity of an earthquake, of grid-locked developmental pressures. It was as if Ben tried to negotiate adolescence all at once, to become a masculine, outgoing adult overnight. Instead, the fault lines of his personality precipitously shifted.

The stories for Betty and Mark are primarily about the relentless *anschluss* of illness and its subjugation of their characters. There is no sense of a resistant populace of persons struggling against these forces. The only theme apparent in Betty's dynamic was that of massive retreat from all developmental tasks. She could not tolerate separation. She returned from college to her bedroom, but there was no drama, no longer any mention of the kind of felt separation anxiety that could be inferred when she called on her first day of college and asked to come home. After that it was totally denied, right up to her abrupt return. She also could not tolerate sexuality, even so much sexuality as is normally experienced in the oedipal constellation. She demanded her father remove his presence, thus actualizing her regression to preoedipal infantile relatedness with mother.

Mark's story is simply that of an eccentric kid becoming progressively more bizarre. While the story has a clear narrative line, there is little to no meaningful interaction between his illness and dynamic life issues. Movement is unidirectional, a progressive disengagement that had its own momentum. Mark's withdrawal did increase substantially when his brother returned from the army and took a position in the family business. The link between this and Mark's behavior, however, is speculative at best, because there was nothing in his symptoms or behavior to signal that he was struggling with sibling rivalry or with conflicts about competition. Mark's written note about becoming the greatest man in the universe does contain vague references to people in his life (father and siblings), but linking them to his grandiosity is definitely "stretching it." Virtually all that is apparent in this note is the grandiloquent, fantastic fabric of burgeoning delusion, not a story of human struggle and conflict.

Our purpose in trying to tease forth psychodynamic themes from the fabric of illness is purely a descriptive one. We do *not* maintain that the hypothesized dynamics *explain* the vicissitudes of the illness. They may have such value in certain cases, but that is another matter. What we are interested in here is how readily apparent such dynamics are. We suggest that the easier it is to formulate such hypotheses, the more intact is that person with schizophrenia. The explanatory validity of psychodynamic formulations may be questionable, but their descriptive validity is not. At the psychological level, the mind does function, in part, by the dynamics of drive, defense, and conflict, and the less deranged the mind, the more these dynamics will be intact and discernible.

Developmental Vulnerabilities

We now know that many people who develop schizophrenia are preprogrammed with a propensity for the disorder. They are "vulnerable" or carry one or more of a variety of "risk factors." We know neither how many potential patients carry these vulnerabilities nor the nature of all the risk factors. A fair degree of scientific progress has been made in this area, however. Genetic predisposition, for example, is now recognized as a clear source of vulnerability. The individual with the greatest risk for developing schizophrenia is the monozygotic (identical) twin of a person who already has schizophrenia, even if he or she was raised from birth in a different environment from the twin sibling. First degree relatives (parents, children, siblings) of patients with schizophrenia carry a significantly higher risk for the disease than do people in the general population. Birth complications, especially those that disrupt cerebral integrity, constitute another clear source of vulnerability to schizophrenia.

Many more developmental risk factors have been postulated but have not been well tested for validity yet. Among the biological candidates are gestational infections (especially viral), subtle neurologic compromise, and medical illnesses in childhood and adolescence. Among the psychological candidates are deviance in parental communication and general level of psychopathology in the rearing family milieu. Chronic stress of varying sorts may also be considered risk factors, such as low socioeconomic status, attenuated social networks, or critical family environments.

The temptation to wander off into the literature is strong here, for this is an area of intense research activity at the present time. The temptation will be resisted, however, for two reasons. First, knowledge about the host risk factors for schizophrenia, except for genetics and perinatal complications, remains tentative. Second, the developmental histories for Ben, Betty, Joanne, and Mark were gathered at a time preceding knowledge about these risk factors. Their medical records, therefore, are devoid of the information which today would be considered important to know. Their histories were influenced by the prevailing developmental theory at the time that regarded schizophrenia as psychologically generated by persistent family psychopathology, the so-called "schizophrenogenic" theory. Accordingly, the records of our four patients contain rich descriptive data about deviant interactions among family members, but virtually no useful information about risk factors currently believed to be important, such as family history of mental illness from a rigorous diagnostic perspective.

Despite these omissions, it is possible to see that Mark's history was basically "clean" vis-à-vis most postulated risk factors. This is all the more surprising because his illness was quite severe and long-standing. There were no perinatal complications, medical illnesses, or neurological abnormalities. His growth and developmental milestones were traversed without noticeable deviance. He experienced no major losses. His family was intact, well-to-do, and geographically stable. His parents provided Mark with a reasonable milieu for growing up. They had their quirks; father worked excessively and perhaps found mother too distracted by their large number of children. But it would be reading too much into the data to label this as deviant. Given the paucity of childhood and adolescent risk factors, we might be particularly suspicious of genetic vulnerability in Mark's case. His records, unfortunately, are suggestive but unclear. Mark had a maternal uncle treated for mental illness at a Veterans Administration hospital, a paternal grandfather with a history of alcoholism, and a 20-year-old brother still attending high school. All of these descriptions are diagnostically enigmatic, too vague, and incomplete to be useful. They suggest Mark *may* have carried some kind of genetic vulnerability, but that is all. We have no clue regarding any such risk or its direction; that is, toward schizophrenia or toward some other form of mental illness.

The records strongly suggest that Betty's mother suffered from depression or something similar for the 10-year period when Betty was between the ages of 6 and 16. The other potential risk factor of note includes the nuchal cord at birth. Other stresses were the loss of the family business in the Great Depression, father's unemployment for one year, and the family's subsequent and uncomfortable move to the maternal grandparents' home. Relationships within the family were odd to the point of deviance, especially the parents' tolerance of Betty's irrational behavior; for example, acquiescence to her demand that father remove himself from the household because of his alleged sexual interest in her. In all, we cannot prove, but we might suspect, the existence of both genetically and environmentally linked vulnerabilities to schizophrenia in Betty's case.

Ben's record contains no information about family history of serious mental illness. His mother saw a psychiatrist, but this was apparently for adjustment problems after her husband's death. Ben's father was portrayed as a tyrannical man, curiously overdependent on his wife, but he never sought treatment for this behavior. Ben's birth was difficult, painful, and complicated by a posterior presentation, but we have no further details about this or about possible sequellae. His growth and developmental milestones were remarkable only in that he resisted nursery school with temper tantrums at age three and was described as overly compliant during latency, perhaps in response to his father's harsh disciplinary temperament.

Separation and loss were prominent stress factors: Father went into the army for one year when Ben was 10 months old; his beloved caretaker, Anna, was fired when he was 9 years old; and father died several months after Anna's dismissal. It is difficult to conclude anything from this incomplete potpourri except that Ben may have had more than a normally troubled relationship with his father. Whether this engendered an actual vulnerability to developing schizophrenia is, of course, unknown.

Joanne's mother was said to have been depressed several times. We have no further details about this or about other mental illness that may have existed in her family. Birth was uncomplicated as were Joanne's developmental milestones. Medical illness, however, played an important role in her childhood. She had difficulty with bladder control, necessitating painful and intrusive operative procedures. The problem involved an extra urethral opening to the vagina for which she underwent cystoscopy and two operations. This condition was problematic in its own right, but it also served as a focus for much family deception that Joanne found troubling. Joanne's history is replete with many examples of parental distortion or empathic failure such as father's frightening temper or mother's overprotectiveness. It is hard to conclude, however, whether this means that Joanne's parents were irrational, or that Joanne was supersensitive to normal variations, or that the history-takers in Joanne's case were looking (exclusively) for irrationality to confirm their theory of schizophrenogenic parental influence. The data collected, unfortunately, are not very objective and leave us with the impression that genetic vulnerability may have been present and that chronic stress from strained family relationships was probably present.

Unfortunately, the quality of our archival data severely limits the assessment and identification of vulnerabilities to schizophrenia in our four patients. Even if we had the data it would be hard to apply them to the identification or vulnerabilities in a clinically meaningful way, since the relative impact of most of these purported vulnerabilities upon the course of illness is still a matter of speculation. Overall, the data available on Ben, Betty, Joanne, and Mark render them more similar than different on dimensions of vulnerability. All three of the patients about whom we have data concerning family history of mental illness could have had a genetic predisposition. Two out of four had birth complications and possible vulnerabilities therefrom. All four patients grew up in families that were described as psychologically abnormal in the records. Rescoring their charts while mindful of the etiologic theories in vogue at the time they were recorded, however, casts a different light on vulnerability.

We find little to label as deviant in any of the cases except, perhaps, for Betty's. Even there, however, it is hard to know if Betty's schizophrenia represented the warp of her parent's distortions or whether their irrationalities represented the woof of Betty's schizophrenia.

Premorbid Dimensions and Prognosis

Maps of the vulnerabilities to schizophrenia are largely a promise of the future. In the meantime, are there any currently available host factors useful for clinical purposes? The answer is decidedly affirmative. What the patient-to-be is like as a person before the onset of illness can strongly determine his or her response to schizophrenia. To everyone's information, but to no one's surprise, research over the years has demonstrated that stronger people deal with schizophrenia better than weaker people. By strong and weak we mean the degree of health as reflected in the person's native talents and demonstrated capacities to work (or go to school), to socialize (especially with peers), and to love. On the average, the more the person has developed these capacities or "premorbid dimensions," the better their overall short and long-term prognosis.

Betty and Mark cut similar profiles of poor premorbid adjustment. Both were socially isolated with few or no friends. Neither ever dated and both appeared uninterested in or negative about the opposite sex. Both shared similar cognitive deficits: a lack of insight, no capacity for self-observation, and a certain concreteness to their thinking. Both were intelligent enough to reach college. However, only Mark proved industrious enough to complete his studies and to work, at least for a time, in his father's business.

Ben cut a healthier premorbid profile than Mark and Betty. He, too, was a loner, especially in elementary school, but he struggled against it. His isolation came from a painful self-consciousness and a vulnerable self-image. He seemed to want desperately to change and, for example, cried in front of a mirror when he was unable to part his hair. Ben eschewed the opposite sex for a time, but eventually charged past his heterosexual inhibitions shortly before his illness began. While Ben probably was not as intelligent as Betty or Mark, he possessed a capacity for insight, self-observation, and psychological abstraction far superior to theirs. He also had an ability to work that carried him up to and partly through college.

Since Ben's illness was acute, his behavior prior to its onset can legitimately be labelled *pre*morbid. For Betty and Mark, however, the illness was insidious, and slowly progressive, starting in their childhoods. Their premorbid periods, therefore, may be more accurately designated as *early* morbid periods. Joanne's picture, in contrast, fits neither categorization. Her illness began early and progressed steadily, but a normal personality also developed concomitantly. In fact, this normal personality could be viewed as super normal. Instrumentally, she was well endowed and gifted in many ways. She had a strong vocabulary as a child and psychological testing at age 14 revealed that she had a superior I.Q. She was remarkably able to function in school despite being actively symptomatic. While she created a private language, she also had a marvelous command of regular discourse, including a special gift for metaphor. She alone, among our four patients, could reflect and view herself objectively and, for example, look at herself in the mirror and see two people, "she and her." Socially she was relatively isolated, but this came in part from being choosy. She preferred the company of adults and was rather contemptuous of pressures to relate with peers. While too young for sexual relationships, she had developed a sexual interest that, in fact, caused her a fair amount of turmoil.

Host Factors: Recapitulation

Overall then, our four patients were very different in their "premorbid" endowments and, accordingly, in their prognostic potentials. Premorbid social, sexual, and instrumental functioning are among the most frequently validated key predictors of outcome in patients with schizophrenia. Given this, we would probably score Joanne highest and Mark and Betty lowest on any of the classic prognostic scales, regardless of the nature of their illnesses. The same hierarchy would hold for the first host factor under consideration; that is, the psychodynamic or story line dimension. The vulnerability dimension proved to be less discriminating, largely because our understanding about the constituents of this host factor has just begun.

We have concluded our cursory inquiry into schizophrenia and its victims, and find bewildering heterogeneity in both. Let us now follow them, if we can, into the human therapeutic encounter, mindful that we risk still more confusion, but hopeful that it will expand our perspective and deepen our understanding.

Introduction to Treatment Process

Schizophrenia can be treated biologically and interpersonally. The biology of schizophrenia, however, is not our focus here, important as it is. Our interest lies with the interpersonal aspect of treatment, for three reasons. First, interpersonal strategies constitute at least a part of the treatment of *every* patient with schizophrenia. Even a treatment that is primarily biological in nature must be administered to the patient somehow by someone. This negotiation is an interpersonal encounter, the nature and quality of which may be crucial to the success of the overall treatment. Second, we need to look for new perspectives on the interpersonal encounter because, while we have a sense that it is very important, the utility of psychotherapy as a treatment for schizophrenia has been seriously challenged by a quarter of a century of empirical research. Finally, long-term individual psychotherapy has been the principle treatment of schizophrenia at Chestnut Lodge for over 50 years. We therefore have more data about the interpersonal treatment of schizophrenia than about anything else!

Schizophrenia, after all, can be treated both successfully and not so successfully. However, the efficacy of any particular treatment is also not our focus here. Our interest lies in how a particular schizophrenic patient with a known outcome behaves in the interpersonal treatment matrix. We hope this will tell us more about schizophrenia and give us clues, in retrospect, about the process of interpersonal treatment in successful and unsuccessful cases. While we cannot link process and outcome causally, we can try to describe a typology of process that might be correlated with success or failure, against which we can evaluate our ongoing efforts more objectively.

This typology of interpersonal treatment process consists of process levels and parameters. Levels refer to the complexity and richness of interaction achieved between patient and therapist(s). Parameters are dimensions that characterize the process in more global terms. Sometimes they serve to refine levels; sometimes they arch across levels. Chapter 9 will be devoted to the conceptual elaboration of these levels and parameters, along with an outline of our method of case study. In Chapters 10 and 11, we will illustrate how our four patients negotiated their interpersonal treatments, focusing on key aspects of process. In Chapter 12, we will discuss the implications of this perspective for treatment and research, and will conclude with speculations about an integrated psychotherapy for schizophrenia.

Psychotherapy Process Descriptors

THE PROCESS CONCEPT

All psychotherapies have one thing in common: they are treatments based on human interaction, and, like most human endeavors, their variety is endless. Literally hundreds of forms of psychotherapy exist today and far more have come and gone over the years. In this plethora lies the unique strength of the human interaction as treatment; there can always be a potential match between mode of therapy and type of human disorder or misery. However, such a variation also generates many headaches. To the therapist–practitioner, wedded to a particular form of psychotherapy, such variety is often irritating. To the patient–consumer, preoccupied with his or her distress, such variety is often baffling and intimidating. To the treatment researcher looking for specific forces that move the psychotherapeutic process, such variety is often paralyzing.

Much as we may wish, we cannot escape the reality that psychotherapy and complexity appear to be synonymous. Psychotherapy can be short or long, casual or deeply probing, intermittent or frequent, and involve two or more people, to list just some of the variations. However, prolonged observation of this form of human interaction identifies recurring themes and patterns. Each of the more commonly used psychotherapies possesses a certain structure, includes a set number of participants who meet regularly, assumes that a certain time is required for the desired changes to occur, involves a reasonably coherent theoretical rationale, and abides by specific rules of conduct. For example, psychotherapy as usually practiced at Chestnut Lodge, and in which our four patients participated, is quite specific in its form. It is individual, involving doctor and patient who meet four to five times per week either on the patient's ward or in the doctor's office close by. It is long-term, lasting at times for years, and aims to bring the patient back to a reasonably stable, extrainstitutional adaptation. It is psychoanalytic in its theoretical orientation, the rationale being that personal control follows upon an expanded understanding of one's symptoms and behaviors. And this understanding is achieved through verbal communication; that is, talking about one's feelings rather than acting upon them.

Whether long-term, intensive, psychoanalytically oriented, individual psychotherapy constitutes the *ideal* form of psychotherapy for these patients, although an important question, lies outside our current investigation. The global question of whether psychotherapy works, in fact, is somewhat akin to asking whether parenting works. As noted earlier, research shows that psychotherapy is efficacious generally, but the question must be asked more specifically. What patient with what disease can undergo what changes with what form of psychotherapy? To this expanded question we would like to add: With what form of psychotherapy *in which the patient achieves what process levels and parameters*?

While in Chapter 6 we dealt with the complexities of disease and host, here we deal with the complexities of the treatment interaction. Doctor and patient generate an ongoing experience together that we term the treatment process. The psychotherapeutic treatment process is not uniform, just as parenting is not uniform, although both are designated by only one word. A paranoid patient may enter psychotherapy willingly but become convinced that the therapist is an FBI agent and leave the hospital without permission. Another paranoid patient may come to psychotherapy under protest, sit snapping chewing gum, and stare out the window. Still another paranoid patient may enter psychotherapy suspiciously, but slowly develop trust, and use the therapist to test new, more adaptive behaviors. Each patient creates a different psychotherapy process with the therapist. The first achieves tenuous contact leading to flight. The second establishes static resistance leading to stalemate. The third develops an alliance leading to positive change.

The variations are legion. For example, the situation could involve three different patients with three different therapists, or three different patients with the same therapist, or the same patient with three different therapists, or the same patient with the same therapist who uses three different approaches at different times. And so on. The actors may vary, but the process configurations they create are meaningful, and, we hope, specifiable. We further assume that the levels achieved are linked to expectable outcomes. As Greenspan and Sharfstein (1981) wrote:

> The challenge to each psychotherapeutic approach is to delineate its process steps, relate these steps to different outcomes, and develop reliable procedures at either clinical, judgmental, or quantitative levels for determining these process levels. The capacity to predict with some reasonable certainty the relationship between process and outcome at each stage in a therapeutic procedure is the relevant clinical test of "efficacy." (p. 1218)

Methods and Assumptions Guiding Our Study of Process

To recapitulate briefly what we outlined in Chapter 1, our method for delineating psychotherapy process levels and parameters involved several steps. First, we chose patients who met the *Diagnostic and Statistical Manual of Mental Disorders, Third Edition (DSM-III)* (American Psychiatric Association 1980) criteria for schizophrenia upon retrospective chart review. From this sample we selected patients about whom we had reliable knowledge of long-term outcome from the Chestnut Lodge Follow-Up Study (McGlashan 1984a, 1984b). This cohort was further narrowed to include those for whom there was rich archival documentation of their psychotherapeutic treatment. Ben, Betty, Joanne, and Mark comprised the final group, but the study in total involved 10 patients, 6 males and 4 females, divided roughly in half between good and poor long-term outcomes. This sample included 11 individual psychotherapists and (in Betty's case) 3 group therapists, and covered a total of 36 years of psychotherapy.

Three narratives were written for each patient from literally thousands of pages of case records, case conference transcripts, and follow-up notes: a description of the patient's manifest illness (a typical anamnesis); a description of the patient's course at Chestnut Lodge, particularly the course in psychotherapy; and a description of the patient's long-term course after hospitalization. The first allowed us to characterize the patient diagnostically and beyond, as detailed in Chapter 7. The second allowed us to characterize the patient's process in psychotherapy, as will be detailed in the coming chapters. The third allowed us to put the first two narratives in a lifetime perspective. The four cases already presented illustrate the composite narratives which were constructed from these records.

To study the process of psychotherapy, the treatment narratives were scrutinized with studied naivete and with the compulsive application of the query, "What was happening here?" While we tried to do this as objectively as possible, our efforts were influenced by some explicit assumptions and some implicit ones.

Explicit Biases.   The most important explicit bias was that we studied the treatment process with full knowledge about the patient's long-term outcome, hoping, in fact, that this perspective would inform our judgments about process. We were not interested in the degree to which a given psychotherapeutic process adhered to a particular theoretical scheme, but we were interested in constructing a matrix of process levels and parameters that might correlate empirically with outcome.

Since our data consisted primarily of archival descriptions of the patient's course in psychotherapy and in the hospital over a number of years, we were observing behavior at a "macro" level; that is, across broad sweeps of time and circumstance rather than at the "micro" level of who-said-what-and-when in a particular therapy session. The latter perspective guides the data collection for most psychotherapy research. Our perspective, of necessity, departs radically from this tradition. Much important information of this nature was simply not available. Nevertheless, we hoped our "macro" bias would offer the advantages of observing *average* behaviors and *phasic* changes that were relatively free of short-term artifactual or "random" fluctuations. Not finding ourselves among the trees but above them, so to speak, we hoped that our perspective might outline the forest.

Finally, we focused upon the psychotherapeutic dyad and assumed that this relationship was prototypic of the patient's interactions within the milieu and institution at large.

Implicit Biases.   While we tried to be as atheoretical as possible in our review of the process narratives, our training and experience undoubtedly influenced what we considered important. Our descriptive vocabulary, for example, reveals our medical backgrounds, our years as clinical psychiatrists, and our subspecialization in psychoanalysis. Other implicit biases undoubtedly derive from our research and clinical work with schizophrenic patients prior to and during this project.

Studies of the process of recovery from acute breakdown in remitting schizophrenic patients at the National Institutes of Health, for example, led to the formulation that this process could be divided descriptively between patients who integrated their psychotic experience and those who sealed it over (Levy et al. 1975; McGlashan et al. 1975, 1976, 1977). Integrators were curious about their symptoms, regarded them as part of their life's pattern, and gained information from them, resulting in their having a more flexible attitude toward illness than patients who sealed over. The latter had rather fixed, usually negative, views of their illness, tended not to strive to understand their psychotic symptoms, nor to place their psychotic experiences in perspective with their lives before and after breakdown. Our subsequent clinical experience with schizophrenic patients at Chestnut Lodge generally upheld this distinction. Both integration and sealing-over could lead to stable recovery, although long-term follow-up investigation demonstrated superior outcomes among the integrators (McGlashan 1987).

Just prior to beginning the follow-up study, two reviews of the literature were conducted regarding the psychotherapy of schizophrenia (McGlashan 1982a, 1983). Reviewed were 50 years of accumulated knowledge—what experts maintained should be done in psychotherapy with schizophrenic patients. The survey revealed a great dichotomy in technical strategies over this half-century of observation. On the one side were supportive techniques, largely following the medical model of a doctor doing to or for a patient. On the other side were investigative techniques, largely following the psychoanalytic model of a therapist helping a patient broaden his or her understanding. These strategies, in a sense, seemed to match with the recovery styles described in the prior work with remitting schizophrenic patients; that is, supportive techniques matching with sealing over recovery styles, and investigative techniques matching with integrative recovery styles. This recurring distinction between technique, recovery behavior, and outcome, implied at least two process levels and, indeed, informed our formulation of the distinction between the levels of Fortification and Integration (to be described).

The review of investigative, individual psychotherapy strategies (McGlashan 1983), furthermore, collated a series of technical interventions that, viewed longitudinally, outlined a sequence of treatment process phases or levels. These were: 1) establishing a relationship; 2) elucidating the patient's experiences in the here and now; 3) tolerating the mobilized feelings, especially those arising between doctor and patient; 4) integrating the patient's experiences into an expanded perspective of the self; and 5) working through sequences 2–4 over and over, to consolidate understanding and the associated behavioral changes. These recurring themes, collected from the observations of experts, closely influenced our formulations of process levels and parameters.

We also carried into this project certain convictions concerning the nature of *long-term* psychotherapy derived from our clinical experience. Specifically, we regarded it not only as a technical process but also as a developmental one. A patient enters the dyadic interaction at certain levels of emotional maturity and, hopefully, advances to more complex and adult levels of organization. We did *not* regard the process as a recapitulation of normal human development, but felt aspects of developmental sequencing could be applied to psychotherapy, at least conceptually and metaphorically (Sroufe 1982). This perspective, for example, broadened our view of the therapist. To the image of him or her as a technician translating transference we added the image of a parental figure facilitating the epigenesis of relational capacity and complexity (Wynne 1984). The developmental perspective also focused our attention on the *dyad* as the basic unit of study. While some of the process levels and parameters we defined refer more to the patient-in-the-dyad and others refer more to the therapist-in-the-dyad, no dimension described one or the other participant independent of the dyad. Finally, we speculated that the process of long-term treatment, like emotional development, might involve phases or levels arranged in a somewhat predictable, hierarchical sequence.

A consideration of two sequences will illustrate our developmental thinking: the engagement process of the doctor and patient in psychotherapy, and the smiling response of the normal human infant at three months of age. Might both processes be described in epigenetic terms? Take the smiling response. The neurological capacity for the smile is determined phylogenetically, but its ultimate expression arises within an interpersonal matrix. Its appearance, so to speak, is *mutual*. Who knows who starts what, parent or infant? There is no "A causes B" sequence, but rather maturation, evolution, organization, interaction, and integration. The infant engages the parents with a smile but the parents reinforce that engagement by smiling back. So, too, perhaps the patient has to engage the therapist initially in some fashion, but the therapist must reinforce that engagement. In both processes (developmental and psychotherapeutic), there may exist preexisting *anlage* or *potentials* in both participants that are realized when they interact. The relevant question is not who triggers what, but whether the participants become engaged in this *anlage* or not, and, if not, how not? Perhaps, as in normal development, there are average expectable "a priori" levels of psychotherapeutic process that preexist and are usually inconspicuous when the process is working, but observable when it is not. We usually are not aware that "engagement" between doctor and patient is an important event unless it fails to occur, just as we are not aware of the infant's smile as a developmental step unless it is delayed.

In viewing psychotherapy as a largely technical maneuver, one that, for example, can be presented as a manual, or text, we may be too caught up in the medical model that sees the doctor applying "X" to the patient and causing "Y." The medical model may, by itself, be too narrow. Psychotherapy is not just a technical maneuver, it is also a special kind of personal encounter. We felt the medical model needed to be supplemented by the developmental model in order to describe the process of psychotherapy more fully. While one cannot write a manual for parenting, one can describe good and poor parenting. In like fashion, through our project we hoped to describe good and poor long-term psychotherapies with schizophrenic patients, the good versus poor judgment deriving from long-term outcomes, rather than from the degree to which the psychotherapy adhered to any particular theoretical schema.

Schematic Outline of Process Levels

At this point we leap forward and present the *results* of our investigation. Detailed below are the psychotherapy process levels that emerged from our scrutiny of the treatment narratives of all 10 patients in the study, including Ben, Betty, Joanne, and Mark. For heuristic purposes, we felt it best to proceed in reverse and present the resultant levels before illustrating how we arrived at these levels with our four cases.

Figure 1 presents a schematic hierarchy of proposed process levels and some hypothesized correlations for our population of inpatients with schizophrenia. As one moves down the figure, the process levels become more complex, developmentally advanced, and associated with better long-term outcomes. Preliminary definitions for each process level are advanced below.

No Engagement. At this lowest level, dyadic participants are out of contact. Interactions are incomprehensible, random, and unpredictable. The patient is autistic in the descriptive sense, lost in psychopathology. The therapist feels that he or she does not exist for the patient, at least as a *human* object. Or the therapist may feel consumed by the patient's psychotic distortions, transformed into bizarre objects of the patient's psychopathology. Here an *apparent*

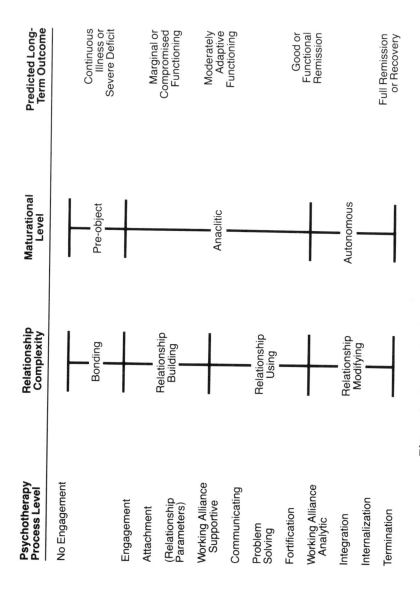

Figure 1 Process levels and hypothesized correlations

relatedness exists, but closer scrutiny reveals it to be transference psychosis and therefore *pre*object in nature by virtue of the absence of self and object differentiation. If this proves to be the only process level the patient is capable of achieving, no matter who the dyadic partner, then the patient's long-term outcome is likely to be bleak, indeed, riddled with psychopathological defenses that are life-threateningly maladaptive.

Engagement. Here the patient and therapist engage with each other in some form of relationship. That is, the behavior of one participant clearly makes a difference in the behavior of the other participant, at least part of the time. This relatedness may be very primitive. It may, for example, be characterized by paralyzing ambivalence in which the patient oscillates endlessly between approach and avoidance, driven by the so-called need/fear dilemma (Burnham et al. 1969). Or a patient with a negative or deficit syndrome may mold compliantly to the therapist in a structurally intact but affectively empty form of contact. This has been described elsewhere as "aphanisis" (McGlashan 1982b), a state of relatedness involving rudimentary, stable defensive structures that provides a minimally adequate, if not rigid, stimulus barrier. The patient can at least control conflict behind psychological silence or blankness and relate by creating a false self concordant with the profile demanded by the dyadic partner. Still other patients are "object hungry" and relatedness has not become blunted or burned out. For such patients, interactiveness and intensity of relatedness are valued. They seek objects, reach out for contact, and readily lock in to available people. Engagement here is likely to be more robust.

Attachment. Attachment represents a step above engagement. Here the therapist becomes a *unique* object of engagement; that is, differentiated and special among the larger world of objects. Therapist and patient become *individuals* to each other. This may be signalled in the therapist by dreams and fantasies about the patient. This may be signalled in the patient by imitative behaviors, weekend separation reactions, or defensive behaviors that are dyad-specific, such as transferences, psychotic transferences, or wishes to avoid and flee from the therapist. The therapist becomes an anchor of sorts; when present the patient may be less anxious, but when absent the patient may become more symptomatic and regressed. Without the therapist the patient may display less tolerance for novelty, more poverty of exploration, diminished comfort-seeking, and a compromised capacity to be soothed.

The attachment may be insecure and troubled, but present. For example, the patient's ambivalence about the therapist may be un-integrated and split off. The patient may relate positively with the therapist in a conscious form of *folie-a-deux* anaclitic dependence while the negative is unconsciously split off and projected onto persecutory objects. Or, the patient may relate with the therapist in a hostile dependent fashion where negativity is conscious, but object need is denied and projected onto idealized nurturing and rescuing objects. In either case, attachment implies that the patient's engagement with the therapist has become important and unique enough that ambivalence becomes a source of danger (anxiety) requiring some form of defensive resolution.

Attachment presupposes or demonstrates differentiation of relatedness. The patient can relate to different people differently. Not everyone is treated the same. The therapeutic dyad in particular has a boundary within the hospital milieu and enjoys relative immunity from intrusion by the surround. The patient's relationship with the therapist is different from his or her relationship with other people in the hospital community. A similar interface exists between the patient's relationship with the therapist and the patient's relationship with family members.

We feel that patients capable of attachment, no matter how primitive, no matter how troubled, are assured of at least a marginally functional long-term outcome. They are capable of bonding and mobilizing defenses that, however maladaptive, at least preserve the bond over time.

Relationship.   Relationship level refers broadly to the existence of an ongoing meaningful interaction between dyadic partners. Broadly conceived, it encompasses *all* process levels from Attachment to Termination. Relationship is characterized by multiple dimensions, the so-called "process parameters," some of which relate to process levels, some of which are orthogonal to the hierarchy. Accordingly, these parameters will be elaborated in the next section, and we have signalled the nonspecificity of the Relationship level here by placing it in parentheses in Figure 1.

Working Alliance—Supportive.   At the level of Alliance, the relationship becomes more complex than at Attachment, in that each participant relates, at times, according to particular roles. Specifically, participants accept and adopt their respective roles as *doctor* and *patient* or *therapist* and *client*. The relationship shifts from being built to being used. A treatment aim is present, as is some form of therapeutic rationale or myth, however tacit. The dyad is sufficiently beyond issues of survival and cohesion so that focusing and planning are possible, and so that "technique" has a meaning. The dyad as a working pair can isolate and compartmentalize issues and elaborate specific technical strategies for dealing with them. In the *supportive* alliance the doctor–patient roles follow the medical model wherein the doctor "does" more or less actively and the patient "receives" or complies more or less passively. Patients who reach this level in their psychotherapeutic process, we postulate, are likely to realize at least a moderately adaptive long-term outcome. Being able to "work with" another person opens up countless avenues of potential help and support with which even the severest of illnesses might be controlled.

Communicating. At the process level of communicating, the relationship is used to build a common language or matrix of meaning. The dyad is stable and quiet enough to foster learning, to broaden experience, to look at and contemplate thoughts, feelings, and behaviors. Communicating includes the following dimensions or activities:

1. *Elucidating.* Thoughts and feelings are elucidated in the here and now. The process involves listening, questioning, narrowing focus, demanding facts, elaborating concrete details, asking the "stupid" question, treating psychotic content as signal, asking "what," "where," "when," "how," "how much," and "how often." Noncritical acceptance is offered in the service of achieving a shared focus of attention upon the patient's experience.
2. *Naming.* Feelings are identified and named, such as joy, anger, sadness, and so on. Primitive or nonverbal experiences are translated into verbally identifiable and describable states.
3. *Differentiating. Who* is feeling *what*? Experiences are clarified and differentiated; that is, thoughts from feelings, certain feelings from other feelings, and whether the feelings arise from self or other.
4. *Consensual validating.* Participants in the dyad compare perceptions to establish common symbols, meanings, and syntax. They try to attain "interrater reliability" in their use of language.

Problem Solving. At the process level of problem solving, the dyad participants use their shared vocabulary to explore and solve problems. The spotlight is on the patient's assets and strong points. Carefully timed pressure is applied persistently toward incremental

advances in functioning. Participation in current social or instrumental pursuits, whether in the hospital or in the community, is
encouraged. The patient is expected to be doing something and such
behavior is not regarded as acting out or as a defensive flight into
health. Strategies are developed for pragmatic adaptations to continued defects. The patient trains in the conduct of daily living and
the therapist facilitates this with advice, teaching, and modeling.
Solving problems often means facing the unfamiliar. At this level,
the dyad shows a willingness to address new levels of anxieties and
concerns, to emerge from defensive havens, to contemplate alternate
ideas, to explore novel behaviors or coping styles, and to chance trial
and error. The essence of this level is that the therapist and patient
can use their relationship to focus together on something; that is,
a "problem," outside the relationship.

Fortification.   Fortification is the highest or most stable process level that can be reached within the anaclitic or dependent mode
of relatedness and within the supportive mode of the working alliance. The patient uses the relationship with the therapist, sometimes indefinitely, to fortify himself or herself against the disease
and its functional consequences, to "seal over" the psychosis in much
the same way as the body walls off chronic infection. The therapist
actively facilitates this process. For example, positive transference
is welcomed and fostered. Negative transference is skirted and not
forced into treatment. If it comes up, however, the therapist avoids
reacting critically, angrily, or defensively. The therapist serves as a
stimulus barrier of sorts. He or she defines reality and presents it
in tolerable enough amounts to foster acceptance and to avoid collapse of coping capacities and self-esteem. The therapist also as-
sesses the patient's long-term deficits and helps him or her find or
create an altered environment that conflicts less with his or her
psychopathology. The dyad is manipulated to support existing defensive strategies at times of stress and to fortify them with additional strategies during quiescent periods. Patients are frequently
taught to ignore symptomatic demands on their attention and to
hide their "craziness" from others with conscious suppression. Patients who achieve a process level of Fortification are likely, in our
view, to have a good functional long-term outcome. They can, with
ongoing help, control their illness to a degree that it interferes minimally with everyday life.

Working Alliance—Analytic.   At the process level of the analytic working alliance, the therapist and patient share a conflict-free,

task-oriented collaboration to deal with the patient's problems together, *including the patient's problems with the therapist.* That
is, the relationship that supports the work no longer remains tacit,
but itself becomes a focus of the work. It is recognized and accepted
that many of the patient's patterns of relating are problematic and
that their solution involves modifying the patterns, usually first within
the doctor–patient relationship. The analytic alliance presupposes
that the patient possesses the capacity for participant observation;
that is, the capacity to step back from participating to objectify the
self and to observe the self in interaction. In psychoanalysis this is
known as analyzability, and candidates for psychoanalysis must be
capable of this process level at the *beginning* of treatment.

Integration. At this level of process, therapist and patient engage in very complex and shifting modes of relatedness, sometimes
experiencing together and sometimes analyzing that experience,
sometimes discussing the here and now and sometimes recalling
the past, sometimes focusing upon their dyadic relationship and
sometimes reflecting upon relationships beyond the consulting room.
The aim of all this activity, however, is to expand the patient's understanding and to integrate this new information into an altered
and more mature perspective of the self. Integration involves at least
two processes, developing a metaperspective and accepting dystonic
aspects of oneself as real. Each will be briefly elaborated.

Metaperspective. The patient develops perspective and dynamic
insight, can use interpretation, and understands his or her illness
in reconstruction. The patient in the dyad demonstrates an ability
for self-analysis and a capacity for taking the "meta" position. Symptoms become meaningful in a larger life context. Behavior is viewed
from multiple perspectives and contradictory data become interesting counterpoints rather than craziness. The patient develops respect for, and curiosity about, the complexities of the mind. The
patient understands emotional relativity and therefore can use interpretation, which asserts that what appears to be real may in fact be
a distorted creation of fantasy, memory, and desire. This requires
the ability to differentiate self from others and, in particular, to see
the therapist as real and to discriminate the transference as a distortion that makes sense vis-a-vis past wishes. Finally, the patient
in the dyad can detail his or her history of illness and symptom
formation both phenomenologically (what, when, where) and inter-
actionally (why, what relevant stresses, etc.). Specific vulnerabilities
and patterns to break down are identified. The patient can see his
or her illness as such and elaborate some reasonable nonmoralistic

theories regarding its etiology. The precursors to illness are extended back historically to establish continuity between the sick self and the well self. The patient can "own" his or her illness with less shame about prior irrational behaviors. The contributions of past objects, such as parents, are clearer, more balanced, and better understood, if not forgiven. The paths to recovery, including relevant treatment contributions, are also reconstructed.

Accepting dystonic aspects of the self as real. Negative feelings can be experienced consciously against the positively regarded therapist without undue anxiety about survival of the relationship. Negative realities about the self are also realized and accepted. The patient accepts responsibility for wishes, especially aggressive wishes and acts against others. This generates depressive anxieties, genuine guilt, and attempts to repair and undo. Related attitudes are fairness, tenderness, consideration, forgiveness, concern, and mutuality. Such feelings and attitudes lead to new patterns of relating, to resolving negative interactions and disjunctive rhythms. They also foster greater tolerance of noncomplementarity (differences) in relationships and often make natural divergences exciting and pleasurable rather than threatening.

Internalization.   At this level of process the patient "takes in" or internalizes the therapist of Engagement, Attachment, Alliance, etc. This process may involve introjection or identification or mixtures of both. With introjection, the patient internalizes an ongoing relatedness and dialogue with his or her therapist imago. In this dialogue, the patient remains the patient and the therapist remains the therapist. With identification the patient "metabolizes" the therapist imago by identifying—that is, actually changing and becoming like—the therapist. The internal dyad or dialogue disappears as the patient "becomes" the therapist, capable of taking care of himself or herself. The operational result, with either introjection or identification, is a capacity to function self-therapeutically or self-analytically without needing the presence of the therapist. This level also involves two related processes: progression via disillusionment and mourning, and individuating.

Disillusionment and mourning. Confrontation with reality results in acceptance and not antipathy. In fact, the broader perspective of multiple realities is enriching. Tolerance develops for error, ambiguity, uncertainty, and unanswered and unanswerable questions. Illusions of omnipotence and magical cure are relinquished, leading to wisdom and affirmation rather than despair. There exists a more realistic view of one's assets and limitations. Sadness and grief can be experienced nondefensively. The patient accepts the reality of separation, aloneness, and the fact that loss is essential to relating and growth. Healthy resignation is achieved with acceptance that life's earlier losses and failures cannot be undone. Infantile wishes and entitlements are let go and put to rest with sadness, but without painful bitterness or paralysis. Emotional health is accepted and preferred. The patient wishes not to be a patient, relinquishes secondary gain, and develops anxiety about regression. The patient feels no longer alien among other people, but also no longer unique. The self is accepted as an adult among other adults.

Individuating. The patient in the dyad demonstrates initiative to master areas of weakness and deficit and wants to progress to more competent, adult levels of functioning. At some point in the process, without being asked or told, the patient initiates conscious and willful efforts to change "therapeutically," the most frequent targets of change being maladaptive aspects of character. Important here is the distinction between change that is intended and change that "just seems to happen." Spontaneity and striving supersede passivity and perseveration. Self-starting balances reacting. Personal will is strengthened by the exercise of working through. The patient repeats the cyclical work of integration over and over again, each time with greater autonomy, will, and self-control and with less need for the cycle to be catalyzed by the therapist. The patient takes more and more initiative for starting the work and generating change as he or she becomes able to articulate personal wishes and devise reasonably effective strategies for their satisfaction.

Termination.   In this final and most advanced process level, the patient is able to leave the dyad because the work of therapy is done. The patient, having accrued strength and internalized the process, is capable of independent functioning. This stage is signalled by a diminution in transference. The therapist is seen more clearly and objectively as someone real, different, and imperfect in empathy. Interests and investments shift toward extradyadic relationships. The patient feels confident he or she can survive the loss of the actual therapeutic dyad because the functional dyad is now a working part of the self. Patients who achieve this level—that is, completion of the process—are patients for whom the terms "recovery" or "full remission" can be applied.

Schematic List of Process Parameters

The psychotherapeutic narratives yielded more than the process levels elaborated above. They also contained many other forms of interaction that we postulated might be important signifiers of the utility of the psychotherapy. Once again, we say "might be" and emphasize that these "parameters" of psychotherapeutic process are not proven entities but educated guesses; that is, hypotheses that require future empirical study for validation. All of the parameters to be outlined below and illustrated by the cases in Chapter 10 describe various aspects of the psychotherapeutic dyad. These descriptors were named "parameters" rather than "levels" because they conceivably could apply to many different levels; that is, they appeared orthogonal to the hierarchical frame of levels. They are as follows:

Commitment. The commitment level of the dyadic participants to each other and to the work appeared to be an important descriptor of the process. We conceived of commitment level in very simple, concrete terms. Did the participants meet regularly? Did they set aside regular time for sessions, the integrity of which they protected against other interests or demands? How easily did external pressures from family, hospital milieu, or their own preoccupations impinge on these meetings? We noted especially the actual time and energy invested in the psychotherapy: number of sessions per week, length of treatment, continuity of therapist, quality of psychotherapeutic record keeping by the therapist, and so on.

Dyadic Match.   We tried to estimate whether the patient and the therapist made a good personal match. Did they bond? Did they fit well together? Did they hit it off initially and lock into a groove comfortably and casually? Was the dyadic coupling natural or forced? A good fit was often silent; that is, hard to spot when present, but easy to identify when absent. Patient and therapist could also be alike as people; that is, be concordant, but still match poorly (that is, be noncomplementary). An example would be a pair of stubborn people who became mutually competitive, controlling, and retaliatory.

Structure of Relatedness.   We found that the dyadic relationship could be described from the perspectives of time, ritual, range, heterogeneity, and flexibility.

Time. Was there a sense of time to the relationship? Did it have a past, present, and future or was it endless, timeless, drifting without beginning or end?

Ritual. Dyads that were not totally random or fragmented developed interactions that were stable by being repetitive, even if their sequences were stereotyped and perseverative. The dyad evolved "routines" or "rituals"; that is, consistent and predictable background behaviors that provided a rhythmic underpinning to the dialectic. Through the creation of ritual the participants were able to remain "in phase" with each other most of the time.

Range. This referred to dyadic interactions that extended beyond ritual. Here the relating was repetitive and stable but not stereotyped. Instead the participants groped for change amidst the continuity and sameness. Their interactions gradually evolved, branched, and differentiated into multiple forms, often integrating antecedent patterns. There was a sense of development, accrual, and deepening of the relationship with time.

Heterogeneity. This was similar to range of relatedness and referred to the different roles that the patient in the dyad was capable of assuming, in fantasy or in actuality. For example, could this patient relate from the position of caretaker, peer, lover, collaborator, or child with the same people at different times or with different people at the same time?

Flexibility. This referred to the ease with which the patient in the dyad could shift roles or move within his or her range of relatedness. Was the patient rigidly stuck with one exclusive role (e.g., victim) and one mode of relating (e.g., hostile dependent) or could he or she relate flexibly depending upon the situation?

Hedonic Tone.   Hedonic tone related to the pleasurable, motivating, energizing character of the dyadic relationship. What was the overall feeling tone to the relationship? Was it alive or dead? Did the dyad radiate tension and drive, or was it flat, empty, and burned out? If the interaction was alive, could it be described as pleasurable, warm, and satisfying, or was it painful, dysphoric, or repulsive? Did the patient and therapist like each other or did an observer sense the presence of alienating mutual malevolence, disdain, contempt, or lack of caring? Also, what in their relatedness did the dyadic participants find compelling and pleasurable; that is, did they get their "kicks" out of healthy relatedness such as humor, or out of unhealthy relatedness such as sadomasochistic power struggles? Finally, did the dyad contain admiration? If so, the patient was special to and liked by the therapist. The therapist was hopeful, confident, and optimistic (although realistic) about treatment. He or she imagined the patient as having a good prognosis within reason; that is, as capable of getting better and developing a viable future. The patient, in turn, responded positively to this attitude by feeling energized, confident, and grateful. The antithesis was a dyad with interactions that were critical, devaluing, scolding, belittling, or contemptuous.

Empathy.   Empathy related to the therapist in the dyad and the degree to which he or she was able to imagine, share, and understand the patient's experience. Our process narratives contained examples of three types of empathy: descriptive, dynamic, and existential. *Descriptive empathy* meant the degree to which the therapist conveyed (in the record) an objective description of the patient's manifest illness, clinical presentation, and behavior in the therapy. *Dynamic empathy* meant the degree to which the therapist conveyed a clear and sensible description of the patient's psychodynamics, especially as they were manifest in the dyad. This involved four elements: 1) identifying, often through countertransference, with the patient's experience, including disavowed and inarticulate aspects; 2) formulating the correct developmental level of the patient's psychopathology; 3) articulating a cogent and operational core conflict; and 4) continuously testing these intuitions against subsequent experiences. That is, the therapist did not simply "smear" the patient with his or her own unconscious or force the patient into established theoretical constructs.

A therapist with *existential empathy* regarded the patient with basic human respect as an esteemed person who struggled with problems not entirely foreign to those of the therapist. The therapist did not insist on the validity of his or her reality sense and realized that psychosis and sanity were not so different. The patient was regarded as capable of teaching the therapist a great deal. The therapist approached and regarded the patient without biased perceptions and procrustean preconceptions. The therapist was committed to the patient as a person, and not as a theoretical construct. The therapist was open to discovery and saw (with celebration) the unique and spontaneous in the patient, like a mother who lets a baby influence her vision rather than vice versa. This meant individualizing care, learning what *this* patient needed. At the most basic level, the therapist recognized that while the patient's experience may have been highly pathological, it was nevertheless *real* to the patient. The therapist acknowledged what was valid in the patient's perceptions, the kernel of truth in the patient's distortions. The therapist declined to challenge the reality of hallucinations and delusions, but did not accept their validity either; he or she disagreed without arguing or focused on timing rather than content. At a more sophisticated level, the therapist knew when an interpretation was premature and impinging; the therapist also was sensitive as to when to allow the patient room simply to be, without regarding everything the patient presented as derivative or determined; that is, sometimes a cigar *was* just a cigar. The patient's reality was not denied, and the impingements of the therapist's cherished notions were minimal. The patient was not force-fed therapy (for example, told to "get out his anger" when he was not feeling angry), or forced into the therapist's conceptions of cure (for example, "real change" versus "social recovery"), or coerced into change without reason or reward.

Containment. The concept of containment comes from D. W. Winnicott (1965) and means the degree to which the relationship between patient and doctor, or the dyad, can "contain" a variety of conflicts and dysphorias without serious derailment of the relationship. The dyad could experience crisis but "go on being." Containment, like many of our parameters, was also multidimensional. Our review of the process narratives suggested six elements: limits, therapeutic regression, tolerance of dysphoria, capacity for soothing, therapeutic restraint, and being-with.

Effective *limits* created a setting of mutual safety. The therapist sat in "the most comfortable chair," meaning that he or she felt reasonably safe and in control of the situation. At the most primitive level this involved instituting graded but appropriate precautions against assaultiveness. It also involved appropriate control against overwhelming affects such as anxiety or panic that might otherwise "break out" in the form of acting out behavior or "break in" in the form of symptomatic regression. Furthermore, these limits were instituted through soothing and pacifying interactions (including medication) as opposed to coercive and intimidating commands or "rules." The most effective limits achieved a well modulated interaction without lability of mental state in the patient, or rapid vacillations between intense involvement and indifferent withdrawal between participants.

Regressions in treatment were antitherapeutic if they threatened the patient's existence, failed to change, proved wearing on staff, dehumanized the patient, or led to *greater* distance between patient and therapist or between patient and the milieu because of quantum leaps in paranoia, autism, etc. At the very least, regression should have remained within the dyad or milieu without disorganizing or escaping it. Regression may have been therapeutic if it forced individuation of care and informed the surround about the patient's unique needs, assets, and liabilities; that is, if it helped the patient become special. Regression may also have been positive if through such a state the patient allowed greater contact and care and developed more tolerance for being nurtured consonant with the patient role. It may have been useful if the regressive ideas and affects were elaborated *thematically* in psychological space and not behaviorally and symptomatically.

A dyad that *tolerated dysphoria* could experience but contain and bear disturbing aspects such as frustration, anger, depression, pessimism, anxiety, agitation, negative transference or counter-transference, and continue work without rancor, distancing, or major disruption.

A dyad with a *capacity for soothing* could provide stimulus modulation on an everyday basis and emotional support at times of distress. In stimulus modulation the therapist actively manipulated stimulus load in order to render the dyad sufficiently free from urgency that attention could be focused or that the course could be held without derailment via inhibition or regression. The dyad created a conflict-free sphere or a low anxiety, low guilt, work place for relating and learning. At times of distress, crisis, or urgency, the therapist provided active relief through direct reassurance, structuring, and pacification. The therapist helped the patient maintain engagement and organize coordinated behavior in the face of high levels of arousal and tension. This may also have involved helping the patient organize differential affective abreactions; for example, transforming vague distress to laughter or inchoate agitation to sadness.

Therapeutic restraint involved the therapist achieving a careful balance between closeness and distance in the dyad, often by creating the paradox of therapeutic "neutrality" and by tempering therapeutic zeal.

Optimal distance was set in response to the patient's ambivalent anxiety. Consistent friendliness, kindness, understanding, and acceptance were in order, but not to the point of nonprofessional closeness. On the other hand, attitudes of utter caution or lack of spontaneity were also out of place. The therapist also tempered his or her curiosity and eagerness to "find out" about the patient, thus respecting and honoring the latter's need for privacy, for room, and for defensiveness. Within reason, the patient was allowed to determine the distance and create privacy. The patient's boundaries were respected and not invaded. Efforts of either party to dominate or to submit were successfully restrained.

The therapeutic paradox meant the therapist's capacity to hold the "real" relationship and the therapeutic relationship simultaneously. The therapist offered a real relationship of sorts, yet went about the business of being a therapist, of being concomitantly active and reflective, participating and observing, involved and detached, passionate and rational, close and distant, in a harmonious dialectic. There was a natural neutrality deriving from role specificity (doctor and patient) or from an understanding that the therapist was both real and transferential; that is, not real but a reenactment. The therapist effectively presented himself as both a person and an instrument. In a poorly modulated paradox, the therapist became a technical automaton, or the real relationship eclipsed everything, and doctor and patient related to each other without therapeutic intent.

Tempered therapeutic zeal meant the therapist was not too ambitious or demanding of "cure" which depersonalized the process and imparted a message that the patient was unacceptable. The therapist did not need therapeutic success and conveyed that his own well-being did not depend upon the patient's progress. The urge to "help" was not as productive as a willingness to "be of use." The latter attitude was active but not domineering.

Finally, containment in relatedness allowed for the therapist to *be with* the patient. That is, the therapist frequently accepted the patient as he or she was without regard for where the therapist wished the patient to be. The therapist "sat with" the patient rather than always "doing business" (doing to or for the patient). It involved being a real object in the patient's life with one's own identity as a person rather than relating exclusively through a role. Patient and therapist developed a common "here and now" without becoming frightened or rejecting.

Process Descriptors: Recapitulation

The above constitute the process levels and parameters we were able to specify from our psychotherapeutic narratives. Let us now return to Ben, Betty, Joanne, and Mark to see how they profile on this complex matrix. Review of their cases will also illustrate how we generated this matrix to begin with; that is, how we worked from case to concept.

Case Illustrations of Psychotherapeutic Process Parameters

We shall now *repeat* the last part of Chapter 9, outlining the psychotherapeutic process parameters. This time, however, the grid will be peopled with our four patients.

COMMITMENT

Joanne and Mark present the best and the worst levels, respectively, of commitment to the treatment dyad and process. Both Joanne and Dr. Fromm-Reichmann were highly invested in the psychotherapeutic work, which lasted 4½ years. Joanne, in fact, attended a local university in order to remain in treatment. Mark, on the other hand, was marginally committed. He would be around and *apparently* committed but then suddenly disappear or become involved in activities (such as flying lessons) that caught his caretakers by surprise. The record did not suggest that Mark was actively secretive, but rather that his caretakers lost track of him easily, perhaps betraying a casual commitment on their part as well.

Commitment to treatment was less clear for Ben and Betty. While Ben's therapist, Dr. Schwarz, was clearly committed to the work, Ben's enthusiasm was compromised by conflict and defensiveness. He accepted treatment but did not work hard at it. Betty was actively negativistic about treatment, denying its necessity, but passively receptive to its imposition. Her caretakers, on the other hand, presented an interesting split on this dimension. There was a strong commitment to Betty at the institutional level, but a weak commitment to her at the individual level. Institutionally, the hospital reduced her fee twice and made special efforts to move her to less expensive day patiency so that she could remain in treatment. Individually, no particular person on the staff sustained a substantial commitment to her. Individual therapists came and went mysteriously. Dr. Norris' termination was not documented or justified. Likewise, the record was mute concerning Dr. Thorpe's reasons for stopping. He cited "administrative duties" and later said treatment was not progressing. Perhaps this was so, but treatment doesn't progress in one year for many patients at Chestnut Lodge, and he wrote that Betty's capacity to relate to him had actually improved. It is doubtful that Dr. Thorpe gave up all of his patients, so why was Betty selected to be among those to be dropped? Whatever the reason, the fact that she was transferred to another treating person suggests a lack of commitment to her at the individual level.

Dyadic Match

Ben and Joanne matched well with their therapists. Ben and Dr. Schwarz were explorers into the territory of psychosis that was relatively uncharted for both of them. That is, psychosis was new to Ben, and treating psychosis with intensive psychotherapy was new to Dr. Schwarz. Both were curious and flexible in their approaches. They were also alike in being men capable of containing intense feelings. In his first session, for example, Ben fell asleep when he became too affectively aroused. Dr. Schwarz, on the other hand, could entertain fantasies of assaulting Ben but siphon these into proper interventions.

Joanne and Dr. Fromm-Reichmann were definitely well matched. They were capable of balanced give and take. Joanne, for example, could be angry and petulant when Dr. Fromm-Reichmann did not talk to her colleague prior to going on vacation. Dr. Fromm-Reichmann heard this criticism and apologized. Joanne, in turn, was quick to forgive and stated in wonderment that she never knew someone like Dr. Fromm-Reichmann to admit error. Dr. Fromm-Reichmann, in turn, pointed out to Joanne that she rather passive-aggressively took an inordinate amount of time in conveying her displeasure and the reason for it. Joanne heard this and was able to use it. In short, they could both give and take observations and criticisms in a complementary fashion. Another example revolved around the uncanny fashion in which the issue of specialness arose in both therapist and patient. In one of the case conferences, Dr. Fromm-Reichmann expressed her concern that she might be making Joanne special. The very next day, in their session, Joanne wondered how they could take care of her problem of making herself special so that she could give it up. This could also be seen as an example of dynamic empathy, insofar as there was a concordance between the preconscious thoughts of both doctor and patient.

At first, Mark's match with Dr. Norton was excellent, especially in their bonding together as strangers in a new land, Dr. Norton to America, and Mark to Maryland. Later, however, they uncoupled when Dr. Norton tried to become more analytic with Mark. At first, Mark stayed in the relationship, but as a compliant shadow rather than as a partner; then, he drifted away.

Betty did not match individually with anyone. Curiously, however, she did match well with the institution. Chestnut Lodge seemed to provide Betty with what she needed in a way that complemented her hostile-dependent style. Specifically, the institution presented itself as an institution rather than as an individual. She had several caretakers, not just one. Thus her need for distance was respected and her negative transference was spread around sufficiently so that no one grew impatient to the point of finding reasons to discharge her or to transfer her elsewhere. This match did not happen at once. In fact, in her strange sojourn with Dr. Norris there was a reversal of roles. Dr. Norris accepted Betty's projections as real because they meshed with her own self-critical leanings. Too great a degree of closeness was a danger for that dyad. An awareness of this situation may have prompted the institutional decision to place Betty in group therapy rather than individual therapy for the next few years.

Structure of Relatedness

Time Structure.   Time is present in Joanne's process but absent in Betty's. The relationship between Joanne and Dr. Fromm-Reichmann begins, flowers in distinct sequences, and then wanes, becomes internalized, and is left behind. Their story has a beginning, a middle, and an end. In Betty's case, however, there was no past or future but only an endless present. Her relationships had the same character from beginning to end.

Mark's story had a sense of time at first in the development of his relationship to Dr. Norton. But then their relatedness plateaued into an endless latency through which Mark and Dr. Norton drifted timelessly, until Dr. Norton and his supervisors became aware of time and grew impatient, whereupon Mark's relatedness to Dr. Norton disappeared like Cinderella at the stroke of midnight.

The sense of time was present but vague in Ben's case. His relationship with Dr. Schwarz evolved and therefore had a history, but somehow the temporal sequences were not clearly marked. By the end of his third month with Dr. Schwarz, for example, Ben became more self-observing. He recalled being disoriented and having the delusion he was in hell at the time of admission. The fact that he *recalled* something suggests the emergence of a time perspective. However, he next maintained his current problem was that his penis was too big. Although Ben was capable of distinguishing past from present, this was in some ways a distinction without a difference, since his state of mind in both periods was delusional.

Ritual. Ben's process with Dr. Schwarz most strikingly illustrates the development of a repetitive, ritualized interaction between dyadic partners. In this case, it was the behavioral sequence of their opening hour that evolved into a "ritual." Ben would do something forward or forthright, fall asleep, and then wake up and shake Dr. Schwarz's hand at the end of the hour. This sequence was intact and stable over time. It also expressed a recurrent conflict between aggressive impulses and wishes to repair. In a sense, Dr. Schwarz and Ben built their relationship upon this ritual.

Ritual was also central to Mark's relationship with Dr. Norton. Their ritual involved playing with things, gadgets such as cameras, around which they could interact with a shared focus and purpose. In fact, during times of stress, Mark would use this ritual of sharing objects or projects in order to master and emerge from his symptomatic confusion. Doing something familiar, or "ritualized," with Dr. Norton was soothing and focusing. Thus, Mark was able to use ritual defensively as Ben had done. Unlike Ben, however, Mark did not build further upon the earlier sequences that he developed with Dr. Norton.

Betty's behavior was repetitious but not ritualized because ritual involves a give and take. Ritual is a form of relatedness and Betty eschewed all forms of relatedness.

Ritual served as a means of introducing Joanne and Dr. Fromm-Reichmann to each other. Joanne spent her first month of psychotherapy, for example, coming to her hours, "lounging" there, and smoking a pipe. This helped her become familiar with a strange and new situation and to relax. Dr. Fromm-Reichmann and Joanne began quickly to build upon this trust, however, and developed a relationship far beyond the stereotypes of ritual.

Range. The relationship between Dr. Fromm-Reichmann and

Joanne became deeper and more complex. After the month of "loung-ing," for example, Joanne became tense from the development of transference suspicions about Dr. Fromm-Reichmann's power to control her life. That is, she brought something new to the relation-ship and tested the relationship by pushing it to more broadly reach-ing levels.

Ben also increased the scope and variation in ritualized themes, although he was more conservative than Joanne had been. After several sessions of the assertion–withdrawal–reparation ritual, Ben came in and said, "How the fuck are you?," then went to sleep, woke up, and passed wind, thus bringing Dr. Schwarz a new, somewhat more engaging aspect of himself. In doing so he was groping for change, although the differences were small, certainly smaller than those introduced by Joanne into her dyad. She took quantum leaps forward, as when she introduced transference issues after only one month in treatment.

Betty and Mark displayed no range in their relatedness. Betty showed relentless hostile dependency, all of the time, to everyone. Mark developed a ritual but it never evolved. When Dr. Norton fo-cused on their relationship in an effort to analyze it more closely, Mark drifted away and formed his stereotypic superficial chumships with other players.

Heterogeneity. Over her course in treatment, Joanne dis-played a rich heterogeneity of relatedness ranging from preoedipal (wanting care, nurture, safety) to Oedipal (interest in men). She wanted to be passive, or to receive care, but also to give as a peer, as a lover, and as a caretaker. With many people she was superficial; with some, especially Dr. Fromm-Reichmann, she was close.

Ben displayed varied fragments of relatedness all jumbled to-gether: sexy, paternalistic, childish, chummy, and competitive. His first session with Dr. Schwarz, for example, was filled with a rich collection of part-behaviors and part-wishes. He was curious, loving, aggressive, but obedient to limits; object-seeking but fearful of re-lating and responsive to soothing—truly a humpty-dumpty of per-sonality parts. Ben's heterogeneity lacked integration compared with Joanne's. Variety gave her character richness; it only increased the level of confusion in Ben's character.

Betty demonstrated no heterogeneity of relatedness. She was not active with one person, passive with another, sisterly with one peer, seductive with another. She treated everyone in the same way, as if they were a rock and she were a window. Mark also had no repertoire of relatedness beyond forming chumships. Everyone and anyone could be a chum, men or women, doctors or patients, family or friends. Outside of this mode, however, Mark seemed to vanish.

Flexibility.   Lack of heterogeneity also means absence of flexibility. Betty, however, was rather interesting in this regard. Her character was rigid and inflexible, but strangely robust. She was maladaptive, but not fragile. When moved "prematurely" to day patiency, for example, she did not collapse, to everyone's surprise. Father described her as a forceful personality, able to make others bend to her will. Indeed, her father moved out of their house for two years, even though Betty's demand was psychotic; and Chestnut Lodge as an institution, by treating her with group therapy alone, deviated for some time from its policy that every patient be in individual psychotherapy.

Ben, if anything, was too flexible during most of his course with Dr. Schwarz. *Fluid* is perhaps a better term to describe his rapid shifts from one fragmentary type of relatedness to another; for example, from knocking over the pipes, to falling asleep, to holding Dr. Schwarz' hands in their first session. In fact, marked personal fluidity and instability was a prominent aspect of his acute and florid psychopathology. Later, however, it resolved into flexibility and became a strength.

Joanne's flexibility was optimal among our four patients. In fact, greater flexibility of personal style was one of her goals later in therapy. She would not allow her poems to be published, for example, because she wanted an opportunity to have a "normal" teenager's experience. She was aware of this deficiency in her repertoire and wished to rectify it so as to expand her range of choices and improve the flexibility of her character.

Hedonic Tone.   Our four patients were very distinctive on this parameter.

Mark could be described as "sort of" alive. He was around a lot and busy, although he didn't seem to generate sparks of enthusiasm. In fact, the tone of his interactions was mostly flat or anhedonic. He was often active with people, but not pleasurably or painfully so. His interests were largely focused on the inanimate, in gadgets and with depersonalized projects. Admiration was not palpably present. Mark and Dr. Norton liked and respected one another, but specialness somehow eluded them. Few people imagined that Mark had a good prognosis and almost everyone was surprised with the progress he made.

Betty was unattractive, at times repulsive, but alive and fighting,

unquestionably *there*. The overwhelming affective tone of her relationships was dysphoria. It was so exaggerated as to be humorous
at times. Unfortunately, however, Betty seldom laughed along. Even
when successfully cajoled into smiling, she would turn her face to
the wall and wipe off all expression. She thrived on the hostile part
of hostile-dependency, saying right off to Dr. Norris, "You are of use
to me if I can fight you," (that is, "you are of use to me only as a
hated persecutory object.").

Betty was clearly invested in sadomasochistic power struggles.
She relished Dr. Beasely's characterization of her as a powerful,
controlling person. Rather than take what he said in the spirit in
which he presented it—as a confrontation—she took it as a com-
pliment! Betty was happy to know that her power was finally recognized. The pleasure she derived from sadomasochistic power
struggles could be inferred by the regularity with which she seduced
people into them; for example, sparring with Dr. Norris over coming
to her office, accusing the student nurse of molestation, provoking
Dr. Thorpe into blocking her exit from the group, or demanding that
an apartment be obtained for her by the social worker without her
taking part in the effort.

Admiration was absent. The institution held Betty like a dutiful
but unenthusiastic mother who was weary, puzzled, and confused
with her patient-child. Dr. Thorpe said, "I can't find the answer with
her. No approach works. She is always here, though." Dr. Xeno said
he was never sure where he stood with her. Her therapists had no
optimism about her case and Betty, in turn, had no gratitude, but
only a corrosive scorn for her therapists.

Ben's course was intensely alive, but with libidinal juiciness
rather than with hateful acidity. He walked around nude and with
erections, sexually propositioning all who passed by. Despite the
inappropriateness of this behavior, Ben was warmly received and
well liked in the milieu. Even his grabbing a female occupational
therapist across the chest elicited "Hold it!" rather than "Get away!"
Ben related to Chestnut Lodge much as he related to his mother
during one of her visits, pounding her on the back as if she were
an old buddy. His treatment was fun at times, amusing at others.

Most striking, however, was the positive "mirroring" or admiration Ben received from his caretakers. Dr. Schwarz tolerated Ben's
overblown image of himself as a baseball slugger. Instead of con-
fronting Ben's grandiosity, Dr. Schwarz said it must be difficult for
him to expect such perfection of himself all the time, thus giving
Ben a good reason for giving up his inflated expectations without
challenging his self-image. To use Kohut's term (1971), Dr. Schwarz

had a "gleam in his eye" for Ben. He saw Ben's illness as reactive, a response to loss. He noted Ben's lack of chronicity, his ability to contain and limit symptoms, and his good functioning socially and instrumentally in college. In short, he saw many good prognostic signs. At follow-up, Ben said of Dr. Schwarz, "He seemed to care about me, not because of his career or something." Staff, as well, mirrored pleasure with Ben's exhibitionism. When he would rush on the unit exclaiming "Guess what I just did!," they caught his enthusiasm and stopped what they were doing to attend.

Joanne's dyad with Dr. Fromm-Reichmann was deeply alive and generally positive in its hedonic tone. They were important to each other and liked each other. They joked and laughed together frequently. Furthermore, Joanne frequently experienced relief as a result of her interactions with Dr. Fromm-Reichmann. She worried, for example, that Dr. Fromm-Reichmann would take away her defenses, but was relieved and reassured by Dr. Fromm-Reichmann's reply that they would not be taken away until Joanne was ready to give them up. The dyadic ambiance overall was warm, pleasurable, and satisfying. Their focus of pleasure was not with the illness, but with the work and with health.

Mutual admiration was unquestionably present. Dr. Fromm-Reichmann was almost always pleased with the work and proud of Joanne's progress. Although she guarded against unduly treating Joanne in a special way, Joanne was always a special patient, not only to Dr. Fromm-Reichmann but also to the entire institution.

Empathy. Empathy for Mark's experience varied widely during his course at Chestnut Lodge. For the most part, the record clearly and fully depicted the way he presented himself, except for the account of his periods of withdrawal and confusion, which was rendered in a truncated, incomplete fashion. This incompleteness itself may be an accurate reflection of the phenomenology. Dynamic empathy, however, was generally lacking. Mark presented a blank screen upon which everyone projected their dynamic hypotheses without noticing that there might be something meaningful about the blankness itself; that is, that it might signify deficits rather than defenses.

Mark did receive good existential empathy early in his course. For example, Dr. Ricardo, the admitting physician, acceded to Mark's request to visit his sister, recognizing the reality of the patient's anxiety and fright, and reacting with tolerance rather than with controlling behavior. Dr. Norton began his contacts with Mark by showing an interest in whatever Mark brought up, rather than requiring him to talk about "problems." Since Dr. Norton's early efforts to link the here and now with Mark's past drew only compliant agreement without further associative material, the therapist abandoned any "orthodox" effort to interpret transference. Instead he drove Mark around the countryside, with apparent good results; Mark was then described as getting better.

Later in Mark's course, however, existential empathy was lost. Dr. Norton became restive, ceased driving with Mark, and instead insisted on meeting in his office. Dr. Norton also shifted to a more strictly analytic model in his dealing with Mark. He had been influenced by his Greek chorus of analytic supervisors to believe that the negative transference was missing from the work, and that it would be wrong to continue without addressing it. Accordingly, Dr. Norton began to identify negative transference in the patient's behaviors; for example, interpreting mockery in one of Mark's comments. Mark laughed for five minutes, clearly anxious. At this point their dyad began to fall apart. Dr. Norton continued interpreting much of what Mark presented, linking past and present, analyzing the meaning of the patient's confusion as resistance to change. In so doing, Dr. Norton lost touch with Mark. Mark's reaction was to buy a piece of land, which, insofar as it depleted his funds, jeopardized his day patiency and initiated his deterioration. At this point the mis-empathy escalated. Mark's ineffectiveness was *again* interpreted as negative transference. His increasing regression and dishevelment after a home visit was labelled by Dr. Norton as defiance, as Mark's open rebellion against therapy. Dr. Norton saw it as the long lost negative transference they had all been waiting for rather than as despair, which it probably was. Patient and therapist were so far apart at this point that the patient never came back.

Empathy was variable in Betty's case as well. The record was vividly descriptive, perhaps because her self-presentation was so invariant. The record contained no discussions about her psychodynamics, however, despite the fact that most who dealt with Betty had a fair idea of how she worked, except Dr. Norris, who temporarily lost perspective and took Betty's projections to be reality. Perhaps there was no communication of any dynamic understanding, especially to the patient, because of a sense that she would not recognize, accept, or appreciate it. Existential empathy, too, was incomplete. Betty was left alone, but without empathy for her need of isolation, or for her right to it. Her aloofness was accepted but never celebrated. Her imperviousness to influence, her ability to swat away therapists like mosquitoes was never admired, but rather interpreted entirely as a defense by the Director of Psychotherapy.

Ben was shown consistent empathy. Descriptions of him in the record are alive and compelling. Dynamically, the Chestnut Lodge psychologist constructed a fairly coherent picture of Ben's core conflicts from the psychological tests. Dr. Schwarz was able to apply this understanding to their dyadic rituals, to identify Ben's anxieties about aggression and his fear of its destructive consequences. Existentially, Dr. Schwarz proved sensitive to Ben's experience and let him simply "be" at crucial times. He honored Ben's boundaries and, for example, did not intrude on his sleeping or reading during the hours. He dealt humorously with Ben's passing of wind for what it was, a fart, rather than interpreting it as a malodorous communication filled with transferential meaning. When Ben screamed in cold wet sheet pack, Dr. Schwarz held his ears, but said, "Go ahead and scream if you want to," recognizing the patient's need to scream. And all of this seemed to register with Ben at some level, because, at follow-up, Ben said of Dr. Schwarz, "He really took an interest in me as a person."

Joanne was also the recipient of fine tuned empathy. The description of her in the record was exceptionally clear. Dr. Fromm-Reichmann was consistently in touch with Joanne's psychodynamics, often through analysis of her own feelings. An example was her concern about regarding Joanne as special, thereby enacting maternal countertransference. The next day Joanne brought up the same issue, validating Dr. Fromm-Reichmann's hunch.

The account of therapy abounded with Dr. Fromm-Reichmann's existential empathy. Early in their work, when Dr. Fromm-Reichmann asked Joanne to write down her history, Joanne became subdued, did not do the task, and later complained that it sounded like school. Dr. Fromm-Reichmann did not interpret this as resistance, but said, "Gee, why didn't you say so!" acknowledging the kernel of truth in Joanne's distress. Later Dr. Fromm-Reichmann went on vacation and returned to find Joanne a defiant adolescent complaining bitterly about her interim therapist. After three sessions, Joanne acknowledged being upset that Dr. Fromm-Reichmann did not talk to the interim therapist before leaving as she had promised. Instead of interpreting Joanne's petulance as resistance, which it was in part, Dr. Fromm-Reichmann apologized and admitted her error. Joanne did not believe this and responded with idealization, following which Dr. Fromm-Reichmann wondered how come it took Joanne so long to express her displeasure. This transaction involved the therapist's acknowledging the part-truth in Joanne's conflict or distortion, thus preventing her feeling odd and defensive.

Dr. Fromm-Reichmann was exquisitely sensitive to Joanne's boundaries, to her need for privacy and space, especially as she moved closer to Dr. Fromm-Reichmann in the dyad. As such, Dr. Fromm-Reichmann asked Antilobia, Joanne's chief Irian god, whether he would reveal the secret of Joanne's confusion. When he replied negatively, because "Nobody can share anybody else's experiences," Dr. Fromm-Reichmann agreed, but still requested permission to try. Dr. Fromm-Reichmann was also mindful of Joanne's need for symptomatic defenses, such as her excess weight. She was reluctant to challenge this state of affairs, recognizing that Joanne "needs to look the way she does" until she really wanted to change. Later in their work, Joanne regressed after giving up her Irian gods. Dr. Fromm-Reichmann remained empathic, respecting the gods' importance to Joanne and understanding her difficulty getting along without them. Overall, Dr. Fromm-Reichmann approached her work with Joanne with humility and presented herself as fallible and willing to be corrected. She was empathically in touch with a similar, all too human person within Joanne hiding behind grandiose defenses. By accepting her own existential reality, Dr. Fromm-Reichmann gave tacit permission for Joanne to do the same with hers.

Containment

Limits. The issue of limits was most conspicuous in Ben's case because his behavior was often highly disorganized and on the edge of control. At times restraints were necessary—for example, when he became too enthusiastic libidinally with the women in the milieu. Most of the time, however, he could be "talked down" into more appropriate behavior. His first session with Dr. Schwarz is illustrative of this. Although Ben behaved in such a way as to produce some anxious moments, there was no disruption of the overall flow. Dr. Schwarz remained in control, albeit quietly, via his self-assurance and calm tolerance of Ben's presence. He articulated limits when necessary, as when he told Ben not to knock the pipes off his desk. For the most part, however, he set limits by example. He tried to understand rather than react. This was not threatening to Ben and may in fact have been actively soothing, because Ben spent a good part of that hour fast asleep. Ben, in turn, was easily calmed and responsive to soothing. For him, it was enough simply to be in the presence of someone in control. He could borrow, in a sense, another's equanimity. He could use the other for "containment."

In contrast to Ben, Mark's and Betty's behaviors were more controlled but less contained. Physical safety was not an issue with Betty or Mark. Their dyads were civil. Neither Betty nor Mark, however, were really *in* their dyads. After initial engagement with Dr. Norton,

Mark escaped containment via activities that went unnoticed; for example, buying an engagement ring for a student nurse, or taking flying lessons. Was Mark being secretive or were his caretakers losing interest? Whatever the reason, effective limits to distractions were not in place. Betty perceived treatment almost entirely as a limit being enforced coercively, and while she was controlled behaviorally in her treatment, she made sure her therapists were not really in control of the situation. To her, therapy meant control of her will and, in Betty's world, freedom and containment were mutually exclusive. For Betty and Mark, it may be said that treatment failed to provide limits to their *lack* of involvement.

Limits of this type were unnecessary in Joanne's dyad. She could engage in well modulated interactions with Dr. Fromm-Reichmann without lability of mental state or rapid vacillations from intense involvement to indifferent withdrawal. Like Ben, she was also fully *in* the relationship with her therapist. Yet there were times when she wanted limits and craved to be "held." Recall her retrospective account of what it was like to be in cold wet sheet pack. She felt held by many hands, but impersonally, without cost. "It was like being held in arms without the price of commitment." This might be the prototypic definition of effective limits: circumstances that allow holding *in* relationship while protecting autonomy of will. These circumstances have to be produced by *each* member of the dyad.

Therapeutic Regression.   Regression can mean several things: exacerbation of symptoms, deepening of psychosis, infantalization of behavior, or all of these. Whether this turn of events has therapeutic potential or not probably depends on whether the regression can be contained within the treatment relationship.

Ben's breakdown was a massive regression, a catastrophe to be sure, but one with hidden potential. He "broke" while trying to change, while attempting to become more related. His psychosis, paradoxically, fostered this process because in his regression he became more connected with people. After the initial phase of outrageous behavior which elicited being held rather concretely, Ben entered a phase of little boy behavior that elicited being held warmly. Ben's unpredictable and at times frightening boisterousness became amusing bluster. Staff liked him, listened, and took time to care. He became special to them, and this, more than anything else, may identify his regression as "therapeutic."

Mark did not regress *in* his relationship with Dr. Norris, he regressed *outside* of it. While engaged in the therapeutic dyad, in fact, Mark became less confused and withdrawn. When disengaging from the dyad, Ben became more disheveled, quietly negativistic and isolative. Dr. Norton interpreted the latter as a therapeutic regression—that is, as a breakthrough of negative transference; but it was probably only regression—that is, exacerbation of psychosis, precipitated by a loss of empathic relatedness. Mark's regression was not contained within his treatment relationship, nor did it foster relatedness.

Betty never regressed, at least beyond her usual stable psychotic baseline. In her first one-to-one dyad with Dr. Norris, there was a regression, but it was the therapist who regressed! Furthermore, this regression proved to be antitherapeutic. Dr. Norris' inability to contain Betty's projections resulted ultimately in disorganization and dissolution of the dyad. After that, no one ever pushed Betty again to be close. Closeness was probably avoided out of a sense that it would lead to a marked, and therefore antitherapeutic, increase in her paranoia and retaliatory distancing. This may have been wise, but it also foreclosed on the (admittedly remote) chance that a deeper regression might have allowed Betty to become more comfortable with human contact and to begin accepting care.

Joanne regressed—that is, became more symptomatic in her psychotherapy with Dr. Remington—before coming to Chestnut Lodge. This was a negative development because it rendered her less capable of handling the demands of everyday life. She was admitted to Chestnut Lodge, therefore, to remove these demands, and to allow her to focus more fully on the task of treatment. She was hospitalized, in effect, to allow her regression to become therapeutic. In the hospital, Joanne wouldn't have to hide and to hold on for dear life; she could "fray forth" and open up a bit. Hospitalization to maximize the therapeutic potential of regression was a gamble, a gamble seldom taken these days, but it worked. Joanne translated symptomatic regression into a meaningful dialogue with Dr. Fromm-Reichmann. She tested the relationship and relaxed, allowed more contact and care, and developed more comfort with dependency, consonant with her role as a patient. Her regressions became part and parcel of her relationship with Dr. Fromm-Reichmann, rather than unrelated psychopathological creations. Once in the relationship with Dr. Fromm-Reichmann, her regressions had clear dynamic meaning. For example, after approximately 2½ years of work, Joanne began burning herself again and had to be restrained. Dr. Fromm-Reichmann interpreted this regression as Joanne's resistance to some transference feelings. This reversed the regression, and later Joanne stated that she fought the idea about Dr. Fromm-Reichmann's being so important that she would burn herself over feelings about her.

Joanne's regression, then, was clearly transference related. Furthermore, it was reversed with transference interpretation. This sequence may be prototypic of a regression that deserves the adjective "therapeutic."

Tolerance of Dysphoria.   Mark had virtually no tolerance for dysphoria. Most of the time he felt nothing, especially unpleasurable sensations. When he did feel something he became confused, or withdrew. Mark could not conjure up, much less tolerate, negative transference. He must have been baffled, indeed, by Dr. Norton's repeated references to this transference, to something he couldn't and didn't experience.

Betty could withstand dysphoric affects, especially negative transference, but they were poorly tolerated or contained in her therapeutic dyads. In fact, her overt negativism repeatedly disrupted containment. Dr. Norris felt devastated, Dr. Thorpe gave up, and Dr. Xeno retreated to silence and to reading. Because of this, the institution held Betty, but at arm's length. They spread her around, so to speak, so that no one person had to deal with all of her projections. Tolerance could be achieved, but only with distance.

Ben could handle dysphoric affects, including negative transference, and they were well contained or tolerated most of the time. Dr. Schwarz could let Ben scream in pack. He could entertain countertransference assaultive fantasies but recognize their empathic value. He could also detoxify some of Ben's aggression in ways that enhanced their relationship, as when he gave Mark a reasonably good (but not grandiose) grade for his fart.

Joanne could not only experience dysphoria, but she also sexualized it as masochism. She brought both into her dyad with Dr. Fromm-Reichmann, for example, as a fear and a wish that she would be deceived (the wish part being implied by the fact that she *repeated* her fearful expectation in the transference). Dr. Fromm-Reichmann was able to contain Joanne's dysphorias, to identify their distorted roots from the past, but also to endorse them as facts of life that must be tolerated ("I never promised you a rose garden"). In this context Joanne was able, through identification with Dr. Fromm-Reichmann, to relinquish many of her demands for affection and unblemished love, and to become wiser and more tolerant of her and others' foibles. She could accept disappointment and continue on rather than retreat. When her English professor did not match up to the crush she had on him, she could give up the fantasy and enjoy his real company as her English professor.

Capacity for Soothing.   Betty's therapeutic dyads might have been soothing had she ever allowed them to be. For her, quiescence or stimulus modulation was achieved in her dyads only when there was virtually no interaction. She seemed comfortable with Dr. Xeno, for example, only after he stopped talking, stopped looking at her, stopped reading to her, and started reading to himself! She never received support or help at times of distress, because she never shared her distress. Only once in several years did she go to her administrative psychiatrist and make a request when upset. Every other time she folded her arms, clenched her jaw, and slammed her doors. If she found anything soothing, it was isolation.

Dr. Norton's interactions with Mark were soothing, or at least not disruptive, early in their work when he decided to shelve "orthodoxy" and to be with Mark concretely. Once he pushed his analytic model, however, their interaction became overly stimulating, and Mark, for example, laughed for five minutes (clearly anxious) and then withdrew.

As mentioned, Ben was easily soothed or calmed by interactions, even at moments of deep psychosis. Dr. Schwarz intuitively monitored and modulated Ben's stimulus tolerance. In their sessions, for example, he gave Ben access to withdrawal, especially sleep. Dr. Schwarz' style was casual. He did not challenge or confront. He gave Ben enough space to hold his shaky male ego intact and thereby avoided urgent eruptions of homosexual panic.

Joanne did not really require a dyad to achieve stimulus modulation and emotional equanimity. She brought with her an adequately developed capacity for pacification. From the beginning, the dyad with Dr. Fromm-Reichmann was more or less free from urgency, high arousal, or tension. Their attention could be focused on the work and held there without derailment. Joanne alone among our four patients was able, right away, to create with her therapist a work place for relating and learning, free enough from anxiety, guilt, and conflict.

Therapeutic Restraint. Dr. Schwarz achieved a good balance between closeness and distance with Ben. He was not overly friendly and respected Ben's boundaries and autonomy. He was also both a real and a transference object for Ben, a person and a doctor. He took Ben to a basketball game, but also relayed understanding of dynamic issues to him as well. Their dyad was not always "therapeutic" but it was also never without "therapeutic" intent. We had no information from the records upon which to elaborate a judgment about Dr. Schwarz' therapeutic zeal. Our overall sense was that he was invested in, but not overly ambitious about, a therapeutic result.

Betty never achieved any modulation between closeness and distance. If close to objects, she disregarded boundaries and invaded them with massive projections. In fact, she enslaved Dr. Norris with her projective assaults. She seemed comfortable only at great distance from objects. She demanded almost total privacy, even when among people. On the unit she sat and read, so withdrawn that people were surprised if she said hello. At the activity center she even climbed into a cupboard to avoid being seen. This demand was very consistent across dyads and across time. Perhaps the distance she achieved at Chestnut Lodge was optimal; that is, was the only distance of which she was capable. It may have been optimal in reducing her anxiety, but it did not stand her in good stead. No therapist was ever able to get close enough to Betty to make therapeutic restraint an issue.

Dr. Norton and Mark varied widely over time on this parameter. They seemed to strike a good balance at first. Dr. Norton was friendly and kind but respected Mark's privacy and need for a comfortable distance. Later, however, the therapist and treatment team somehow stopped hovering, and allowed Mark to wander too far away (e.g., the flying lessons). Then, toward the end, Dr. Norton suddenly moved close and attempted to pry open Mark's head with interpretations. This vacillation may have reflected Dr. Norton's puzzlement with Mark, for Mark certainly did not understand therapeutic paradox. To Mark there was no such thing. He could relate to Dr. Norton so long as Dr. Norton was real—that is, so long as he drove Mark around the countryside. But when Dr. Norton became "therapeutic" and pushed the analytic side of their relationship, Mark dropped out and left for home, there being nothing for him to hang around the hospital for. With Mark, *any* therapeutic aim was too zealous.

Dr. Fromm-Reichmann's work with Joanne was a study in therapeutic restraint. She was open and available, but respectful of Joanne's need for privacy. As already noted, she reassured Joanne that she wouldn't take away any of Joanne's symptoms until she was ready to give them up. Dr. Fromm-Reichmann maintained a therapeutic paradox as if it were second nature. She was real with Joanne, but used her own reality to show Joanne that not all people were the way she expected them to be. That is, she used her reality to exemplify; that is, to interpret. Finally, while keenly interested in Joanne's progress, she was willing to allow change to proceed at its own pace.

Being-With. Betty was striking in that she would not allow even this form of relatedness. She could tolerate someone in her proximity only so long as they did not expect her to relate.

Mark and Dr. Norton, on the other hand, cut an excellent example of being-with, at least at the beginning of their relationship. Dr. Norton allowed Mark to be his mentor, to advise him about American customs, to build a bridge between them. He treated Mark with matter-of-fact gratitude and gave him the status of a useful person. What he was not able to see was the slipperiness of Mark's cathexes and the depth of his deficits. Engagement by being-with required constant effort on the therapist's part. Once Dr. Norton and the administrative psychiatrist engaged Mark, they assumed, as one does with people who are not mentally ill, that the relationship would carry itself, with Mark locked in and cathected. Not so. When Dr. Norton and the administrator relaxed a bit, Mark drifted. At this point they lost their being-with status and tried a therapeutic transformation, which only drove more nails into the coffin of relatedness.

Ben and Dr. Schwarz spent much time together being-with, active times at a basketball game, or quiet, nonurgent, nondemanding times with Ben resting in bed or on the couch sleeping or reading. This was a comfortable part of their dyad and not experienced as an autistic or defensive retreat.

Dr. Fromm-Reichmann actually defined set times to be with Joanne. She called it their "practical relationship." She invited Joanne to play the piano, or present poetry, or otherwise participate in a "real" relationship. Dr. Fromm-Reichmann would state, "Well now we know what your poetry is like," and Joanne would be relieved and happy about being heard. Perhaps it was this ability to be with another person that Joanne was referring to at follow-up when she described the people she had liked at Chestnut Lodge. They shared one thing in common, "It was a kind of matter-of-factness, and ordinariness; they looked across at me, not up or down at me, but across at me."

— 11 —

Case Illustrations of Psychotherapeutic Process Levels

We now illustrate the process levels defined in Chapter 9 with data from our four cases. Our format will differ from that of the preceding chapter because not all of the patients reached the same levels outlined in Figure 1. Whereas the process parameters, by and large, apply to all cases, the process levels do not. As will be detailed, we judged that Joanne reached the level of *Termination*, Ben reached at least the level of *Fortification*, and both Betty and Mark hovered between *Engagement* and *Attachment*. Accordingly, we shall proceed by patient rather than by variable, starting at the lower end of the hierarchy and moving up.

BETTY

Betty presented us with the least ambiguous case. She wanted to have nothing to do with anyone, and she succeeded. At her core she remained actively psychotic with grandiose and persecutory delusions. To the world, she related with a split ambivalence seen as paranoid, hostile-dependency. She "owned" neither side of her ambivalence. The hostility was projected onto persecutors, and the dependency denied. She saw herself as the embattled victim and felt justifiably oppositional.

We felt that Betty was able to *Engage*, but not to *Attach*. She engaged consistently with the institution as an impersonal shelter.

She also engaged, briefly, with various individuals in a lively and negative way that proved to be short-lived. She might begin to attach, begin to develop a special relationship with a therapist, but this closeness was too threatening and would trigger a vehement reflex negativism that severed the relationship. She decided to stop with Dr. Xeno, for example, because she began to think of him outside her sessions. Thus she retreated from attachment to individuals, but could engage with a more impersonal group and with an institution.

Betty was curiously *in* the milieu, but not *interactive* with it. She was clearly dependent on the hospital, but did not acknowledge any such need psychologically. She did acknowledge dependency behaviorally by staying so long. She complained that it was too difficult for her to move out, or even to move to another room on the unit, and she never said no to efforts aimed at prolonging her stay.

Her course at Chestnut Lodge involved no movement from this process level. There was no change except for an important flip in the valence of her split ambivalence about her parents. She moved from being negative about her parents to being negative about the hospital, allowing her ultimately to live an institutional existence at home, where we found her at follow-up. This change was foreshadowed by her negative transference with Dr. Xeno and her parallel improvement in the milieu: asserting herself, playing bridge, learning how to dance. Later, when her negativity led her to terminate with Dr. Xeno, her positive feelings about her parents blossomed and she ultimately went to live with them in a sick, but viable, relationship. She transferred her dependence back to her parents. At follow-up it was clear that Betty had succeeded in keeping the split negative side of her ambivalence with Chestnut Lodge; for example, her hostile letter to the Medical Director and her father's anxiety lest we infuriate her by contacting her.

MARK

The strength and stability of Mark's defenses made it look as if he were suffering from a stable defect state. Most of the time he was able to raise global barrier defenses of denial, isolation, and obsessional ordering that were effective but rigid. This structure seemed to provide an adequate stimulus barrier and internal quiescence or blankness. He was able to focus on external projects and things, but seemed to need psychological defenses against awareness of himself as a person with feelings. For example, he could participate but not observe. Or, when threatened with dysphoric feelings, he "fragmented"; this state could be seen in his intermittent confusion. He was unable to differentiate or articulate affects in a way that they could be projected. That is, he could not organize affects with positive and negative polarities in order to create ambivalence, much less split and project them.

All this rendered his relatedness compliant but empty. In our judgment he was able to *Engage* at this level of compliance, but was unable to *Attach*. He did imitate Dr. Norton's posture, mannerisms, and speech, but there was always a sense that Dr. Norton could be replaced by someone else, especially someone else who would enter into Mark's latency-like rituals. That is, he engaged to a function, but not to a person. He was object related but not object seeking; his relatedness was slippery and nonspecific. There was no interface between the therapeutic dyad and the community. Objects were important but equally substitutive: Don Brett for Dr. Norton, one student nurse for another, a nurse for his sister, or the hospital for his family. He could engage the therapist on a concrete level—that is, as a companion or shelter object—but not as a therapist. He never regarded Dr. Norton as possessing an instrumentality that he needed or could use. Therefore, when Dr. Norton shifted to this mode of relatedness, Mark disappeared and reengaged with his family.

Mark's course at Chestnut Lodge was marked by initial improvement and stabilization at a defect level because Chestnut Lodge and Dr. Norton offered him asylum, protection, and play. He later deteriorated because this was taken away and he was challenged to do more than he was capable of doing. In a sense, he required and sought an alternate living environment, an indefinite asylum. This was ultimately not forthcoming at Chestnut Lodge, and so Mark returned home. There his family created an altered environment that worked; that is, a job in the family company that was not really a job, and permanent care-taking, primarily from mother.

BEN

Ben's record contains many gaps, especially around his later course in the hospital and with Dr. Schwarz in psychotherapy. Accordingly, our reconstruction of his case is more speculative than we would have liked.

Ben experienced a typical acute schizophrenic nervous breakdown. He was obviously and floridly ill, his personality "busted" wide open and in pieces, floating around in a fluid, jumbled confusion. He presented Chestnut Lodge with a polymorphous collection of "relatedness fragments," often loosely organized and contradictory: active–passive, adult–child–peer, male–female, oedipal–preoedipal, aggressive–libidinal, exploratory–withdrawn, and so on. He was, like all the King's men, trying to put his pieces back together. His course at Chestnut Lodge was the story of this process, at least its beginning phase.

There was little question in our minds that Ben *Engaged*, not only with Dr. Schwarz, but with many others in the milieu. He seemed, in fact, to be voracious for relatedness, standing inches away from people, pinching women, propositioning everyone. Ben and Dr. Schwarz made a good match and Ben seemed committed to him and to the work.

Ben also seemed to *Attach* to Dr. Schwarz, although the archival documentation of this is thin. Ben did develop a special relationship with Dr. Schwarz that was different from his relationships with others in the milieu. Early on, for example, Ben seemed to be more silent with Dr. Schwarz than he was with others. Their dyad evolved its own unique character, specific to the therapy hour.

Their psychotherapeutic dyad had a time structure and rituals that were both repetitive and evolving. Its hedonic tone was lively, positive, and hopeful. Dr. Schwarz provided all forms of empathy and spent time simply being with Ben. Their interaction contained effective limits, stimulus modulation, tolerance of dysphoria, and a capacity for soothing. Ben's regression was well contained by their relationship and proved, therefore, to be therapeutic.

Did Ben form an *Alliance*? We judge that he did, at least a supportive one. He accepted that he was a patient with something wrong and that he needed a doctor. But we sense that he didn't like it, was eager to get it over with, to get out of treatment, and to get on with his life. And who could blame him? Sometimes the only important part of having a nightmare is in the waking up.

We also felt that Ben probably reached the process levels of *Communicating* and *Problem Solving*. While we have very little information about their later sessions, Ben and Dr. Schwarz did develop a dialogue with similar language (e.g., sports and "jock" metaphors). They reviewed Ben's life and past, and worked together exploring specific problems such as his sexual relationship with Mrs. Jones. We judge that the highest process level Ben achieved, at least by the time he left Chestnut Lodge, was *Fortification*. While at Chestnut Lodge he experienced a steady reappearance of sanity, mostly in the form of bolstered defenses and effective sealing off of psychosis. Social recovery and control over psychosis was the overall treatment plan for him while he was in Chestnut Lodge, as it is in just about every inpatient setting. His irrationality was both tolerated and controlled, at first with external restraints, and later with efforts to build internal restraints, such as getting him to hide his craziness (literally to cover his nudity), to check and delay peremptory behavior, or to distract himself with projects. A good part of Ben's reintegration was probably spontaneous. This momentum was not challenged. In fact, it was facilitated by Dr. Schwarz and the staff who tried to help Ben return gently from grandiosity to reality and to rebuild more mature defenses such as displacement, suppression, or sublimation. Once Ben achieved adaptive recovery, he wanted out. Like a typical "sealing-over" patient, he was anxious to put the experience behind him, leave the hospital, make up for lost time, and rediscover what health had to offer.

When Ben left Chestnut Lodge, however, he was still in flux. He had reached *Fortification*, but had not clearly plateaued at this level. In fact, while he was at Chestnut Lodge, there were times when he demonstrated behaviors that might be regarded as antecedent to higher levels. At times, for example, he demonstrated an ability for (although not much interest in) perspective and dynamic insight, as when he was able to work with dreams, or to recognize aspects of family characteristics in himself (for example, his grandmother's stubbornness, his mother's ability to care). He could also, at times, be very responsible, as in relating to his roommate with concern or taking an interest in other patients needing assistance. As noted, the milieu liked him and found him warm and gentle, despite his bluster. We did not feel, however, that this behavior was dominant or consistent enough to say he had reached an *Integrative* process level.

The picture when he left Chestnut Lodge was largely *Fortification* or sealing over. He then joined the currents of restless American youth and drifted among his late adolescent peers. He always seemed to be searching, however, trying out different jobs, different lifestyles. He continued to be fluid, but at the level of character style and identity rather than at the level of relational fragments. Later, however, Ben felt the need for a major consolidation. He wanted to grow up, to find a partner, to consider parenting, and to integrate aspects of himself that were already there nascently such as perspective, insight, responsibility, concern, and caring.

He signaled this by returning to Rockville (but not to Chestnut Lodge) and reentering psychotherapy (but not with Dr. Schwarz). We know very little about this treatment experience, but suspect this time he entered into an analytic alliance, because the result was a developmental progression. With this treatment experience, he may have reached the process level of *Integration* and *Internalization*. About this, however, we simply do not know.

Ben did effect a kind of termination while he was at Chestnut Lodge, but not the kind we refer to here as a process level. There was, instead, a natural disengagement. After a time Ben became capable of functioning independently. Much of the work seemed done. His interest in treatment waned as the outside world beckoned. So he left. But this was a termination from a supportive alliance. Ben originally came to treatment because an illness peremptorily forced him. It was as if he had been in an accident, found himself in a hospital, and had to deal with it. But neither the accident nor the hospital nor the treatment was chosen. And so when the worst of his injuries seemed healed, he wanted to leave. Later on, however, he seems to have *chosen* treatment for the purposes of modifying his relationships and negotiating developmental progression. But at the time he left Chestnut Lodge, his termination was not like the termination level reached by Joanne with Dr. Fromm-Reichmann, which was termination from an analytic alliance.

JOANNE

Joanne was severely compromised when she came to Chestnut Lodge. While her schizophrenia was mild in comparison to that of Mark and Betty, her schizotypal personality disorder was quite pervasive and crippling. She also brought with her, however, many talents and personal strengths. While her illness distorted her perceptions, she could prevent it from invading her capacity to test reality. Thus her image of, and reactions to, Dr. Fromm-Reichmann were often twisted by transference, but this transference was never psychotic in intensity. Interpretation or a simple "Hey, that's not right!" from Dr. Fromm-Reichmann was enough to set Joanne back on track. Joanne was capable of organizing affect and generating ambivalent feelings about herself and others. Ambivalence, in fact, was a major source of conflict and anxiety for her, against which she erected defensive (symptomatic) barriers. At times she disavowed her hate, at times her love. But they were always there, embedded in her symptoms and behaviors when not in her consciousness. Thus she could hate Dr. Fromm-Reichmann for leaving her on a vacation but, finding that threatening to her loving bond with Dr. Fromm-Reichmann, she could deceive herself by displacing the hate to the interim therapist, Dr. Ward.

Joanne's plethora of defenses, paradoxically, was a source of great strength. Defense as mental "structure" can foster adaptation as well as the formation of symptoms. Joanne displayed many "higher order" defenses; that is, healthy rather than pathological ways of dealing with psychological conflict. She had an obsessional ability to structure her daily life. She could organize, plan, and be active in a number of pursuits simultaneously. Most importantly, she could repress conflict. For example, she was totally unaware for three days that her hostility toward Dr. Ward had anything to do with Dr. Fromm-Reichmann. And Joanne could use defenses creatively; that is, sublimate many of her conflicts through school, art, poetry, humor, and so on. In fact, the ready availability of these strategies and their precocious use led to a problematic skew in her personal repertoire; that is, an overabundance of talent covering an underdeveloped "normal" character. Joanne was aware of this toward the end of treatment when she eschewed publication of her poems lest it eclipse her pursuit of "normal teenage" experiences.

Joanne's capacity for relating was largely intact. As noted, she possessed robust object hunger and adequate heterogeneity and range in her relatedness. Her problems here, too, were more in the realm of emphasis. She was fearful of many encounters and this led to a constricted and stereotyped range, especially with men. She was always watchful and tentative, treating everyone as a potential critic or rapist.

We felt that she *Engaged* immediately, and quickly formed an excellent match with Dr. Fromm-Reichmann, to whom she was optimally committed.

Within one month she developed transference tension with Dr. Fromm-Reichmann, a signal par excellence of *Attachment*. Joanne became resistant and convinced that Dr. Fromm-Reichmann would be perfectionistic, hostile, and retaliatory like many of her important objects. Thus invested with Joanne's personal past, Dr. Fromm-Reichmann became unique and different from the rest of the people in the milieu. Evidence for this included vacation separation reactions (symptomatic regressions, retreat, and diminished capacity to be soothed) and Joanne's strong resistance to the idea that Dr. Fromm-Reichmann was important to her. Dr. Fromm-Reichmann dealt with this insightfully. She rapidly challenged the reality of Joanne's early distortions in order to move them aside so transference would not be the only basis of Joanne's attachment. She also wanted Joanne to see her as real. For example, Joanne quickly came to view Dr. Fromm-Reichmann as a powerful, all-knowing, and potentially devastating critic. Dr. Fromm-Reichmann essentially said "Nonsense," insisting she was neither God-like nor incapable of being wrong.

She encouraged Joanne to correct her when appropriate. Against Joanne's protest that it was not possible, Dr. Fromm-Reichmann tried to show her that people could be different; that is, spontaneous without having temper tantrums like Joanne's father, or friendly without being saccharine like Joanne's mother.

The dyadic connection between Joanne and Dr. Fromm-Reichmann was relatively distinct and very stable. Joanne had active relationships with other staff and patients in the milieu, and, in fact, often assumed leadership in a patronizing and condescending fashion. She also typically established split relationships. One nurse was always a staunch ally whereas another nurse was always an abandoning, betraying enemy. She played out some of the same split ambivalent themes with Dr. Fromm-Reichmann, but not to such an extent. With her Joanne displayed more overall respect and humility. Her relationship with Dr. Fromm-Reichmann was always more whole and integrated than her relationships with others.

During the course of treatment, an interface developed between the dyad and Joanne's family in important ways. At first, Dr. Fromm-Reichmann actively fostered a boundary and said, in effect, "I am different from your mother and father." She essentially "coaxed" Joanne away from her primary objects. Later, Dr. Fromm-Reichmann reacquainted Joanne with the positive aspects of her parents, but not until such time as Joanne was capable of appreciating a wider perspective.

As noted, their dyadic structure was well defined, their relatedness contained, and their interactions characterized by an overall positive tone with a full range of empathy.

Joanne entered into a *Treatment Alliance* with Dr. Fromm-Reichmann almost immediately. They adopted and accepted their respective roles as doctor and patient, and the ultimate aim of this relating was treatment. From the beginning, their alliance was largely *analytic* rather than supportive in nature. One of the most striking things about Joanne was her love of truth. When she was originally told by Dr. Remington that she was sick, her response was relief and gratitude, rather than denial and resistance. As such she was ready and willing to enter into an alliance with Dr. Fromm-Reichmann, who quite correctly invited Joanne to engage collaboratively with her against Joanne's illness. Their alliance had many supportive elements, but their commitments to exploration, learning, and understanding carried it beyond support into the analytic realm. Joanne's wish to broaden her experience was strong enough to overcome many of her resistances to leaving the supportive nest. She leaned on Dr. Fromm-Reichmann to be sure, but she also wanted to stand by herself. Accordingly, she used Dr. Fromm-Reichmann as a consultant as well as a mother.

Joanne and Dr. Fromm-Reichmann reached the *Communicating* process level without too much difficulty. Joanne brought many of the requisite components of this level with her to the dyad—an ability to know and name her feelings, to identify who was feeling what, and to express herself understandably. Dr. Fromm-Reichmann, in turn, learned what Joanne meant with her language and gods, and quickly achieved linguistic consensual validation. Dr. Fromm-Reichmann also used other techniques to develop communication. She did not force, she *elucidated* Joanne's narrative, usually by simply being interested. Sometimes she was creative, as when she asked Joanne's chief Irian god for permission to understand a symptom or as in playfully acting the part of Joanne's father, hunting around the house looking for his children, a technique identified by Leston Havens (1986) as empathic projective statements. She used another strategy discussed by Havens, the counter-projective statement, when Joanne mercilessly castigated herself for behaving destructively in the torn pillow and feather melee on the unit. Dr. Fromm-Reichmann projected or assigned responsibility for Joanne's behavior to an "It," thus sufficiently freeing Joanne from guilt to look at this "It" and understand how her behavior, now objectified, related to other anxieties.

Joanne and Dr. Fromm-Reichmann also reached the process level of *Problem Solving*. Joanne was world oriented and eager to learn strategies for negotiating her way further into it. Dr. Fromm-Reichmann actively supported Joanne's pursuit of a variety of activities, educational, socially rehabilitative, and recreational. She did not regard them as competitive with treatment or as a resistance to it. In fact, she joined Joanne in considering solutions to some of the problems that Joanne encountered. For example, when Joanne complained that her mother had typed up her poems rather poorly, Dr. Fromm-Reichmann advised her to send them back and insisted, over Joanne's objections, that she had to let people know when she was displeased. Dr. Fromm-Reichmann helped Joanne in an actively supportive way and admonished her to experiment, to try new ways of responding and doing things.

Joanne achieved the *Fortification* process level, but did not plateau here. Treatment fortified her assets and defensive repertoires, but she went beyond this. Ultimately, Joanne found strength in *knowing*, not in disavowing more successfully. For this reason Dr. Fromm-Reichmann did not avoid negative transference but let it enter the dialectic according to Joanne's capacity to handle it. For example, she waited three days for Joanne to realize that her negative feelings for Dr. Ward really belonged with Dr. Fromm-Reichmann. Once Joanne knew that she was angry with Dr. Fromm-Reichmann, and realized that Dr. Fromm-Reichmann also knew it without batting an eyelash, Joanne felt accepted or validated in a wider sense. Dr. Fromm-Reichmann did not bolster or challenge Joanne's defenses in this example, but let Joanne's use of displacement stand until Joanne did not need it anymore. Dr. Fromm-Reichmann was supportive and at times fortifying, but she did not pursue it as a primary strategy or process goal. She expected that Joanne would need an altered environment only for awhile. She always assumed that Joanne's need for treatment would not be interminable.

Using her analytic alliance, Joanne achieved an *Integration* process level with Dr. Fromm-Reichmann. She was able to use interpretation, construct a dynamic narrative interweaving her illness and her life, and develop an ever widening perspective on her internal complexity and depth. She could take a symptom—for example, the olfactory hallucination of ether—associate it to an event of the past—for example, the anesthesiologist with the ether gun—recognize this as a symbol of parental deception, and come back to the present via transference to her conviction that Dr. Fromm-Reichmann was dissembling when she promised to visit Joanne on Christmas day. When Dr. Fromm-Reichmann's behavior failed to conform to expectation, Joanne was able to interpret her conviction as transference; that is, as self-generated distortion. Joanne's perspective expanded and often integrated split ambivalences. For example, she regarded her mother with a more forgiving humor when mother sent Joanne and Dr. Fromm-Reichmann some exquisite cookies at Christmas. Dr. Fromm-Reichmann expressed her appreciation and Joanne, with a certain pleasant irony, noted they were typical of her mother. She said, "She knows that I can't eat them, yet I am delighted that she made them."

As a result of integrating, Joanne developed a greater sense of responsibility and concern. She could accept mental acts as *her* productions. The complex interchange between Joanne and Dr. Fromm-Reichmann concerning Joanne's self-loathing about her excess weight is illustrative. Dr. Fromm-Reichmann pointed out to Joanne how she used her gods to be responsible for what she herself felt and said. As the analysis of this symptom proceeded, it became increasingly clear that Joanne's excess weight stood for a feeling of humiliation and was also generated by that feeling. In essence, Dr. Fromm-Reichmann held Joanne responsible for producing and elaborating at least some of her symptoms. Furthermore, when Joanne accepted this responsibility, she began to do something about it; that is, to lose weight.

Joanne did not disavow illness. In fact, she tried to establish continuity between it and the rest of her life. This effort was seen most clearly in her residual symptom of skin pulling which symbolized her illness and gave her a "sense of continuity" between the college undergraduate and the once-crazy girl on the fourth floor. Joanne not only reconstructed the place of illness in her life, but she also reconstructed the narrative of her treatment. Toward the end of their work, Joanne reviewed many of the important interactions that she had with Dr. Fromm-Reichmann, such as the time she was resistant to the idea that Dr. Fromm-Reichmann was important to her, or the time Dr. Fromm-Reichmann expressed her genuine concern about Joanne's self-mutilation, or Dr. Fromm-Reichmann's collaborative attitude, or her rose garden statement, and so on.

Joanne achieved the *Internalization* process level, too. She mourned necessary losses, let go of cherished but unprofitable symptoms, and steered perpetually toward reality and health as she orchestrated the work of therapy increasingly on her own. She gave up Gloria, her Irian persona, accepted herself as real, and set about addressing some very real problems such as her grooming and appearance. She felt badly within a few months of beginning school, until Dr. Fromm-Reichmann clarified this as her loss of specialness as a sick person. Upon realizing this, Joanne let go of much secondary gain, a substantial change, considering that early in her course she competed to be the sickest patient on the ward. Ultimately, she came to prefer the rewards of being an adult and, for example, grew restive with her father's infantilizing paternalism and longed to have a "real mutual adult relationship with him." She was able to hear and accept Dr. Fromm-Reichmann's caveat that the real world was not a rose garden, but still to choose that world with excitement and anticipation. Joanne *wanted* to develop, to progress. She wanted to relate to men, sought Dr. Fromm-Reichmann's advice on the matter, and responded to her suggestion that Joanne look in the mirror.

As the therapeutic dyad developed its own history and began to "work through" increasingly repetitive themes, Joanne's illness waned and her regressions could be reversed quickly with the use of interpretations. An example was the session in which Joanne revealed having a fantasy about a Japanese-American caught between both ethnic groups accusing him of being a spy and giving him enemas. From this she associated to receiving enemas from her father and to her subsequent masochistic reaction formations to Oedipal wishes. In the aftermath of this, she had a clinical setback signalled by poorer concentration at school and wishes to mutilate herself. Dr. Fromm-Reichmann linked the setback to the Japanese-American fantasy, whereupon Joanne recovered quickly. The fact that she turned around so quickly indicated the degree to which she had internalized the process. It was now a familiar vehicle. She knew how to use it, what it could do, and what it couldn't do.

Joanne also began to drive the "process vehicle" more and more on her own. For example, shortly before giving up Iria for good, she burned herself. In the next session, *she* initiated a series of exploratory associations that went from burning to anxiety to her frustrated passion for men. The Dr. Fromm-Reichmann on the outside only needed to listen, while the internalized Dr. Fromm-Reichmann initiated and carried the work. The process of internalization was so natural and automatic that it was largely silent, noticeable in one place as a slight increment in strength or in another as a subtle accrual of instrumental capacity. One day a confused and frightened girl entered a hospital. Years later, she had a boyfriend who marveled at her degree of insight. Some of the steps in between involved internalization of the therapeutic dyad, although most of these steps escaped notice. Joanne struggled mightily against recognizing her strong attachment to Dr. Fromm-Reichmann. Through the therapeutic work, however, she was able to acknowledge and accept her need for a relationship with Dr. Fromm-Reichmann and, in so doing, actually became less dependent in a pathological way but more interdependent in a healthy way.

Finally, Joanne achieved a capacity to do the therapeutic work on her own, thereby reaching the process level of *Termination*. With time, her extra dyadic investments multiplied and she made many changes in her life. She started school, but instead of concentrating exclusively on academics, she also attempted to develop social skills through singing in church choirs or entertaining and cooking for friends. As Dr. Fromm-Reichmann said, "Your activities in life will begin to be more important than our meetings. Soon you're just not going to want to fit them in." So it came about. Joanne no longer needed to fit in the dyad because it was already installed in her mind. Dr. Fromm-Reichmann accepted her well earned place as one of Joanne's cherished maternal "introjects."

Over her 4½ year course, Joanne made steady and measurable progress. The record documents that she experienced regular symptom relief, although it does not detail the timing. However, by one year in treatment we know Joanne had stopped mutilating herself.

She discontinued eating extra food and the nonedible substances. There was a diminution of her gut pains, trances, and confusions. She no longer continuously listened to the radio to drown out hallucinated voices. By 1½ years in treatment her relations with others had moderated to the extent that she was not as precocious and angry as she had been in the beginning. By the second year in the hospital she had few symptomatic complaints, continued to get along better with others, and her insolence frequently vacillated with states of self-depreciation. In the third year she started school and involved herself in numerous community activities. By the fourth year she was basically asymptomatic and functioning effectively as a student and young adult.

Repeated psychological testing in Joanne's second year recorded some progress but found her more constricted overall. The final set of tests in her fourth year documented marked improvement with a reversal of the constriction. Perhaps she went through a phase of fortification/sealing over before shifting over to an integrative mode. The pattern and pace of test changes were interpreted as being compatible with steady psychological growth.

Chapter
— 12 —

Research and Treatment Implications

What can we make of all this, these patients with this illness, and their stories of treatment? Except for outcome, which we assessed concurrently, our study was entirely retrospective. We rediagnosed, estimated prognosis, and created process dimensions based upon data that were collected for medical, not for research, purposes. We were lucky that the records proved fairly complete, but much information was still missing. Prospective studies could assure a more complete set of data. Nevertheless, our study has implications. They differ depending upon whether we are taking a research or a clinical perspective.

RESEARCH IMPLICATIONS

We postulate that interactive or process *levels* and *parameters* apply not just to psychotherapeutic treatments, but to many forms of treatment of schizophrenia, and perhaps to the treatment of many forms of mental illness. No treatment that we know of bypasses or completely eliminates the human encounter. Accordingly, a closer and more systematic study of this encounter may hold promise. We suggest that three classes of investigation are relevant: articulation studies, psychometric studies, and treatment efficacy studies.

ARTICULATION STUDIES

The first step in the study of process dimensions involves their further articulation and definition. The design of such a study is illustrated schematically in Figure 2. Each horizontal line represents the course of a single patient. Each box represents an assessment event or period. Four assessments are vital: *diagnosis* and *prognosis* at the beginning of treatment (whatever that may be), *process dimensions* (levels and parameters) after a period of treatment, and *outcome*, whether assessed at the end of treatment or many years later. Once outcome is known, the patients' diagnoses and prognoses can be characterized according to some common standard, and then the process of treatment can be scrutinized retrospectively for dimensions that seem "meaningful" vis-a-vis outcome.

This was essentially the model we followed. We restricted our study to patients with *DSM-III* schizophrenia, but investigating a single diagnostic class of patients is by no means mandatory. The study schematically presented in Figure 2, in fact, contains three broad diagnostic categories: neurotic, borderline, and psychotic. Mixed diagnostic and prognostic cohorts could produce a detailed and expanded matrix of process levels and parameters. Schizophrenic patients, for example, especially those who are chronic, would tend to cluster around the lower end of the process spectrum, with patients varying mostly between the No Engagement and the Supportive Alliance process levels. Neurotic patients, on the other hand, would tend to cluster at the upper end and help us define and refine the variations between the Analytic Alliance and the Termination process levels. A study of patients completing psychoanalysis from the Columbia Psychoanalytic Institute demonstrated, for example, that patients with a good outcome almost uniformly reached what they termed "an analytic process" during the course of their treatment (Weber et al. 1985).

It may be that certain diagnostic groups or prognostic subsets of these groups would be associated with specific process dimension profiles. In such an event, process measures could be used, in turn, to refine diagnosis and/or prognosis. It is well known in psychotherapy research, for example, that establishing a working alliance has strong positive prognostic value (Luborsky and Auerbach 1985). From this perspective, the psychotherapeutic process crucible becomes a living, interactive "psychological test" with powerful diagnostic and prognostic implications.

The treatment variable in Figure 2 is just that: variable. Treatments other than psychotherapy, such as behavior modification, cognitive psychotherapy, or social skills training, could be substituted into the design and investigated. It is interesting to speculate whether the levels and parameters generated would be specific to treatments or more universal in their character and hierarchy. A

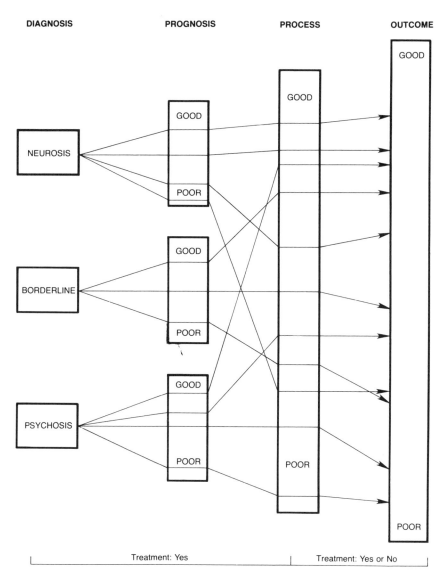

Figure 2   Articulation studies of process dimensions

study of short-term (20-session) cognitive psychotherapy with depressed patients is an example (Shaw 1986). Certain process developments within the first two or three sessions predicted outcome with regularity. Patients ultimately failing treatment were either too cognitively disorganized to collaborate, or unable to formulate their depressive assumptions and stereotypes, or unwilling to do their homework assignments, believing that "treatment" took place only in the sessions. While such process dimensions may sound different from those elaborated for our long-term patients with schizophrenia, closer inspection may identify common elements.

It may also be useful to elaborate process levels and parameters in treatments that are primarily biological. For example, we would hypothesize that phenothiazine drug compliance would be significantly better in schizophrenic patients capable of a Problem Solving process level than in schizophrenic patients reaching no higher than an Attachment process level. Drug studies using comparison groups could achieve greater control by matching the groups on process levels and parameters.

PSYCHOMETRIC STUDIES

Articulating the process levels and parameters is only the first step. Next, the variables so defined must be tested and refined psychometrically. This involves first establishing interrater reliability and, second, testing the reliable variables for predictive validity by correlating process levels and parameters with independently (that is, blindly) assessed outcome.

Concurrent validity may also use factor analysis. That is, many process parameters undoubtedly intercorrelate highly. We have, in fact, grouped many together that we guessed were different weaves of the same cloth; for example, the component variables under Structure of Relatedness (time, ritual, range, heterogeneity, and flexibility). Whether these variables actually do intercorrelate and group together, however, can be tested empirically by measuring their correlations with each other or by seeing whether they emerge as discrete factors in a factor analysis.

We could use similar empirical analytic techniques to study the relationship(s) between process levels and process parameters. In this book we have made a distinction between them, perhaps erroneously. It seems reasonable to consider that some, if not many, process parameters could be process levels, and vice versa. We are not sure, in fact, what distinguishes a level from a parameter. Perhaps this, too, is an empirical matter, with levels being those parameters that prove to be tightly correlated to outcome but not tightly overlapping with each other. A level could be the parameter with the highest correlation with a particular outcome, or it could be a multivariate "equation" of parameters generated from a discriminant function analysis; that is, a set of parameters with the highest predictive power for a specified outcome.

If process levels and parameters can be shown to be valid predictors of outcome (a relationship that we assumed, but did not prove in our effort), then a related question, not strictly psychometric, becomes important. What is the time course of development of various process levels and parameters and, more importantly, when can one count on them to be predictive? Joanne, for example, reached our highest process level (Termination), but it took her 4½ years to get there. Could her levels and parameters at an earlier time, say at one month or three months in treatment, have predicted her long-term outcome as well? Such a question could be addressed by including two or more process dimension assessment periods in the design in Figure 2. Some of these assessments would be made early and some late in the patient's course.

TREATMENT EFFICACY STUDIES

Process levels and parameters can be incorporated into controlled comparison, prospective outcome studies. They may be especially helpful for investigating long-term treatments. A sample design is presented schematically in Figure 3.

The boxes again represent assessment periods, but in this case the lines stand for comparison treatments. X, for example, may be long-term, intensive, analytic psychotherapy and Y may be long-term, intermittent, supportive psychotherapy. Process levels and parameters may serve as either independent or dependent variables in this design.

If treated as independent variables, process levels and parameters could be used to match the two treatment groups beyond diagnosis and prognosis. Note in this design that both comparison groups come from the same diagnostic pool, and that the patients in this pool have been selected for good prognostic characteristics and randomly assigned to the two starting treatment comparison groups. Each group then begins its respective treatment for a specified period of time (Treatment Period 1). At the end of this period, patients in each group will be segregated according to whether they achieved "good" or "poor" process levels and parameters. They then continue their treatments through Treatment Period 2 to outcome.

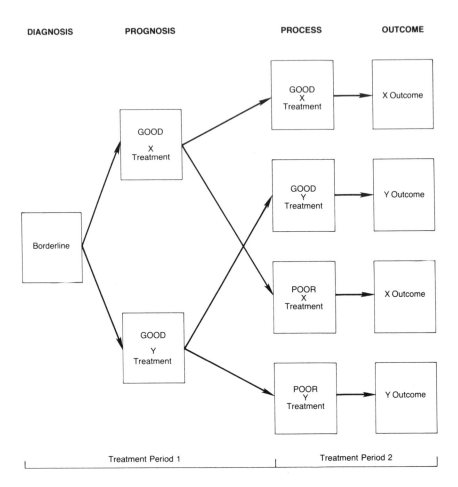

Figure 3   Treatment efficacy studies using process dimensions

Treatment Period 2 may be long, but Treatment Period 1 can be limited to the amount of time necessary to ascertain process levels and parameters that, from prior work, have been shown to possess predictive value vis-a-vis outcome. Segregation of the comparison groups into pairs with good process levels and parameters versus pairs with poor process levels and parameters can be done retrospectively, for purposes of analysis, at the end of the study; during the study they remain intact as comparison groups. Such a study matches the comparison groups more closely than can be accomplished by diagnostic and prognostic stratification alone. This design provides a better test of the long-term differences between treatments X and Y because it controls more for natural history effects. This design, theoretically, could also allow an investigator to start with comparison groups that are more heterogeneous diagnostically and prognostically because later segregation along process levels and parameters would tend to "homogenize" these differences.

Process levels and parameters could also be used in this design as dependent variables; that is, as outcome measures. If prior investigation has demonstrated a high correlation between shorter-term process levels and parameters and longer-term outcome, then assessment of the short-term process levels and parameters might substitute for the outcome assessment. Studies of long-term treatment or of outcome even beyond Treatment Period 2 could then be done in a shorter period of time.

The permutations on this design are multiple, but will not be elaborated further. It is important to note that process levels and parameters could not be used effectively for this type of study until their utility as predictors of outcome had been established by the type of investigation detailed above and illustrated in Figure 2.

TREATMENT IMPLICATIONS

In assessing the treatment implications that our four cases suggest, we must be very cautious. Ben, Betty, Joanne, and Mark were treated between 20 and 35 years ago when many current strategies, especially pharmacotherapy and rehabilitation, were not in vogue or not regarded favorably by the institution (a state of affairs which no longer holds). We must first, therefore, try to estimate what their courses might have been like with today's treatment regimens. Next, given the heterogeneity of schizophrenia and host factors, we must estimate the contribution of natural history to the patients' courses. Only then can we speculate about treatment effects and implications or, indeed, try to define what is meant by "treatment."

Ben, Betty, Joanne, and Mark in Contemporary Treatment Climates

What would be the likely long-term courses of our four patients today, especially if they were given medication and did not enjoy socioeconomic advantage? The question is particularly cogent for Betty and Mark, whose outcomes were poor by our follow-up standards. Would that we could say their experience was like a bad dream from which we wake up with relief and exclaim, "I'm glad we're in the present!" Unfortunately, however, the treatment of schizophrenia is not like the treatment of bacterial infection before and after penicillin. We wake up to a new day, to be sure, but on the way to work we see a bag lady cursing at unseen presences or we encounter a homeless drifter glancing furtively at us, and we wonder where they came from. The treatment revolution in psychiatry is real enough, but it has not resulted in a panacea, especially for those with chronic disorders.

Drugs might have made a striking difference with Betty, especially in the intensity of her delusional apprehension. But it is also likely that she would still have become chronic, either nonresponsive to drugs or repetitively noncompliant with their use: a typical "revolving door" patient. Her negativism and fanatical preoccupation with encroachment on her space would apply to drugs and to rehabilitation as well. Today, whatever hospitalizations were necessary to protect Betty's safety would be brief. Without family support, and unable to work, she would become a ward of the state. The state, which used to care for patients like Betty in public hospitals, would today be laissez-faire about its responsibility. In fact, the state would let Betty drift, having found it more expedient and less expensive to protect her "rights" than to protect her health. It is not absurd to speculate that in our contemporary treatment climate Betty might be that bag lady we avoid on the way to work.

Mark may also have benefited from drugs, even though he presented with a marked deficit syndrome. Mark's confusions, especially, may have responded. It is not likely, however, that his long-term course of inadequate functioning would have been altered by medication. He did, in fact, receive drugs during his hospitalizations in the follow-up period. They probably shortened his periods of inpatiency. However, they did little to advance his social or instrumental capacities.

Mark, as opposed to Betty, may have been able to use a structured program of rehabilitation. In fact, while at Chestnut Lodge he was attracted to "projects," but never stuck with any of them, possibly because their therapeutic potential and legitimacy was not recognized by the institution. Today his projects would be part of a structured program designed to rehabilitate his instrumental skills. With such a resource, Mark may have reclaimed enough functioning to be capable of more than makeshift work in his family's company.

Without his family's financial backing and overall umbrella of caring, however, Mark would probably become a participant in his state's system of community mental health. Because of his compliance, the system would have more to offer Mark than it would have to offer someone like Betty. He would most likely be on injectable drugs, live in a semistructured community facility (e.g., board and care home) and attend a sheltered workshop, if one were available that provided compensation clearly superior to social security disability. In the absence of such facilities, an absence which is still all too common, Mark would probably also be on the street, the homeless man who avoids us on our way to work.

Joanne is difficult to transpose into today's treatment climate. She did not present herself as unambiguously schizophrenic or as unambiguously in need of hospitalization. Her regression in psychotherapy with Dr. Remington would probably be viewed as a negative development, which it was, but the response today would be to discontinue the psychotherapy rather than to provide her with the structure of a hospital while she continued psychotherapy. Instead of psychotherapy, she would probably now receive medication, perhaps a brief hospitalization, and a program of treatment designed to keep her in school and with her family; for example, special scholastic tutorials and family therapy. It is likely that Joanne would respond positively to such a program since she had a good prognosis to start with. Whether she would have accomplished all she did with Dr. Fromm-Reichmann in a shorter period of time and at less expense is difficult to say. She might have made a social adjustment, but might never have moved beyond adjustment to realization of her individual potential.

We seriously doubt that Ben's course would have been any different with drugs. Ben is a good example of how unpredictable schizophrenia can be. He, among our four patients, displayed the form of disorder which usually responds rapidly to neuroleptic medication; that is, acute, floridly symptomatic, highly "positive" schizophrenia. Yet prior to admission at Chestnut Lodge, Ben was impervious to months of neuroleptics at high doses, whereas he achieved remission in 1½ years at Chestnut Lodge on no medication. Nevertheless, in today's treatment climate Ben would have remained on medication. Other neuroleptics would be tried, or thymoleptics (lithium or antidepressants) would be added because of the affective component of his illness. It is impossible to say that the "quality" of the remission he achieved would be different with or without drugs; that is, deeper, more resilient, or more integrative as compared to fortified.

It is possible Ben would respond to a rehabilitative focus, given his amenability to participant activity, but here too it is impossible to know. He had a mind of his own and was eager to leave the structure of institutional establishment in order to sample a variety of lifestyles and instrumental options. He might have found modern rehabilitative programs confining to his restless spirit and inadequate to his grandiose plans.

Could his hospitalization have been shorter without ill effect? Quite possibly, especially if a drug were found that accelerated his momentum toward remission, and if organized options to inpatiency were available such as day patiency or a structured living and treatment setting in the community. His own strengths probably would have carried him through the potentially rocky transitions from one program to another, especially if he had the backup of continuity of care.

Overall, it is difficult to speculate with confidence about what differences current day treatments and less advantaged economic circumstances might have made in the courses of our four patients. In each case, "outcome" may have occurred more quickly, and may even have been better, than the outcome described. Or it may be that modern, cost effective, expedient measures would have involved a sacrifice of quality in outcome. We simply do not know. Until modern psychiatric treatment can be shown to have made an unequivocal quantum leap ahead, we are left to fight the hydra of schizophrenia with sticks, stones, and whatever wit we can muster.

The treatments that Ben, Betty, Joanne, and Mark received were ambitious and not unreasonable for the times. Whether they would be reasonable for all times we cannot know, since we still see the beast before us through a glass darkly. Nevertheless, their treatments were reasonable enough that we might learn something of value by retrospective scrutiny.

OUTCOME AND NATURAL HISTORY EFFECT

In trying to determine the effect of any treatment in schizophrenia, we must first contend with the overwhelming influence of natural history of the disorder. This means the lifetime course and outcome of the disease without treatment. Schizophrenia is heterogeneous. The disorder varies in its manifestations and severity; the people afflicted with the disorder vary in their vulnerabilities and strengths. Much of this variety itself determines outcome, no matter what treatments are applied.

A fair amount is known about natural history effect. We are not lost in a sea of confusion but have ways of measuring these variables and predicting their short- and long-term effects on course and outcome. We have discussed some of these prognostic variables in Chapter 7 and will not repeat that discussion here. Their relationship to long-term outcome is depicted in Figure 4, a schematic and somewhat oversimplified form. Long-term outcome is on the ordinate. Prognosis makes up the abscissa, combining the influences of illness virulence and host resiliency. Quite simply, but also quite without exception, recovery varies directly with host strength and inversely with severity of illness.

We have also depicted our estimate of where our four patients were situated on this prognostic continuum. Joanne was clearly the best, followed fairly closely by Ben. Betty and Mark were down at the lower end. Between them, we felt Betty had the worst prognosis because she had not managed college and her illness continuously

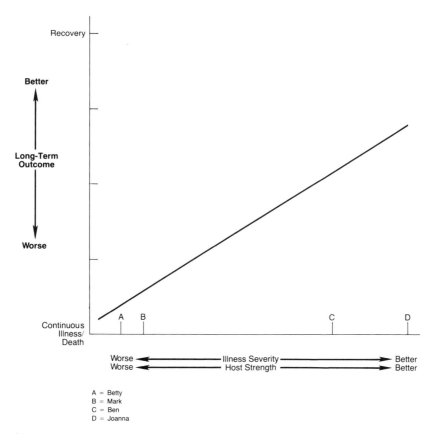

Figure 4 The natural history of schizophrenia: prognostic factors and outcome

interfered with relatedness. Mark, in contrast, had completed college, and while his illness resulted in significant deficits in his capacity to relate, it did not interfere with all levels of that capacity as did Betty's illness. The hierarchy in Figure 4 makes it obvious that much of the outcome we encountered at the time of our follow-up was determined even before our patients entered treatment at our hospital.

What are the implications of this powerful but frequently ignored natural history effect? Foremost is the need to intensify our efforts at finding out what schizophrenia is. Basic research into the nature of schizophrenia is the first priority of treatment; better understanding of etiology and pathogenesis will suggest treatments with greater specificity. Next in importance is refining prognosis. The more accurately the natural history of a particular case of schizophrenia can be predicted, the better treatment planning can match that individual's needs.

Finally, it is obvious that for many cases the natural history of schizophrenia is chronic and life-long. For such people, we must redefine what we mean by treatment. For them, treatment is not a discrete endeavor. It is something that must last for their whole life. We guess that brief hospitalization and drugs are necessary and sufficient treatments for about 10 percent of schizophrenic patients. For the other 90 percent such approaches may be necessary but by no means sufficient. For many of this 90 percent, time limited interventions do not even scratch the surface. Despite all the treatments we have to offer, a significant number of our patients remain maladaptive, and their existence requires that we alter the environment around them to fit their disabilities. We have no other choice, unless we follow the example of our primate ancestors and abandon our deviates to the wilds of the jungle (or to the detritus of the inner city). For such patients treatment means asylum. Treatment is asylum.

Ironically, Betty and Mark ultimately received the treatment they needed. Their families managed to create viable asylums for them, living situations which did not demand more than they could handle, living situations where they were cared for indefinitely. This was possible, in part, because their families were financially well off. But what they received every patient with chronic schizophrenia should receive, and could receive if society ever stops denying the illness. Quadriplegia is paralysis of the arms and legs. Chronic schizophrenia is a similarly disabling process that may affect the "final common" pathways that support higher psychological functions such as self-sense, will, and judgment. What seems to be freely chosen behavior may be paralysis of the capacity to self-determine, a paralysis of will. Taking this perspective seriously may lead us to think twice about allowing our bag lady her "freedom" to freeze to death on the stairs of the train station.

OUTCOME AND TREATMENT EFFECT

When addressing the effect of treatment on outcome, we must distinguish between the contribution of "treatment" and the contribution of natural history. Our estimate of the treatment contribution and its relationship to prognosis and natural history is schematically represented as the shaded area in Figure 5. This being a graph about treatments, we have also added process levels and parameters. We line up process levels on the ordinate in keeping with our hypothesis that they correlate tightly with outcome. We suggest process param-

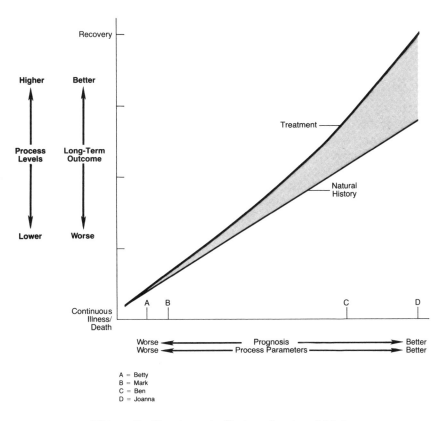

Figure 5 Treatment effect and natural history

eters have much in common with prognostic variables and, therefore, belong on the abscissa.

As depicted in Figure 5, we hypothesize that current treatment
efforts of all kinds, biological and psychological, have less impact
the more severe the illness; that is, the more severe the illness, the
poorer the prognosis. With schizophrenia as with so much else in
life, the rich get richer and the poor get poorer.

Joanne and Ben were well enough to use psychotherapy positively, Joanne quite specifically and Ben somewhat nonspecifically
(he may have used psychotherapy more specifically in the follow-up
period). Betty and Mark were too sick to use psychotherapy profitably
as their primary treatments. Betty's illness poisoned her ability to
relate so that "relationship therapy" couldn't get off ground. Mark's
illness snuffed object investment and therefore precluded meaningful relating. Schizophrenia did not drive him away from contact,
however, as it did for Betty. Mark's schizophrenia was "negative"
and Betty's was "positive" by current subtype nosology. While much
is made of this distinction phenomenologically, Betty and Mark demonstrate that whether schizophrenia is "negative" or "positive," the
illness can be equally catastrophic.

Chestnut Lodge did not need to change its approach for Joanne
and Ben, who were able to use psychotherapy. In Betty's case, the
institution adapted itself appropriately to her state. Chestnut Lodge
offered protection and as much interaction as she could stand. The
hospital, in effect, created a viable asylum in which she could function more or less comfortably. It also provided a model of care that
she could accept later on with her parents. In Mark's case the institution failed to accommodate to his psychopathology and made
the mistake of trying to force a mode of therapeutic relatedness he
couldn't handle. This had no major lasting negative effect, however,
because Mark found what he needed eventually; that is, a "home
grown" asylum.

In other economic circumstances and at other times, Betty and
Mark might have become semipermanent state hospital residents.
Today they might well be among the homeless and it is for this reason
that we regard asylum as treatment, and, accordingly, make one
final adjustment to the treatment graph. Figure 6 depicts a hypothesized relationship between asylum and outcome. In contrast to "active" treatment, asylum has greater impact the more severe the illness.
Here the poor do get richer. Betty and Mark were able to sustain
marginally functional lives under the umbrella of their extrainstitutional "institutions." While their outcomes were not great, they
were certainly (in our estimation) superior to what could have been

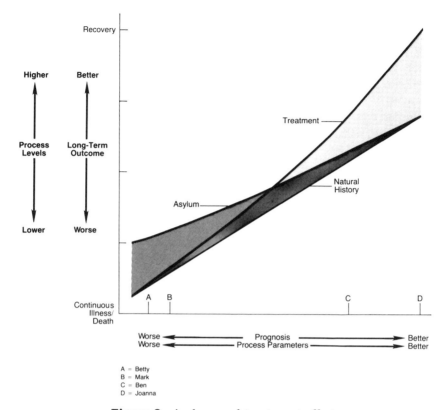

Figure 6 Asylum and treatment effect

expected in the absence of such protection. Without the family co-coon, they would have been lost and quite possibly at mortal risk. It is knowledge of this reality, in fact, that keeps countless families imprisoned at home with their schizophrenic offspring today.

Betty and Mark also illustrate that asylum need not be synonymous with indefinite inpatiency. Unfortunately, however, few programs offer asylum other than the state hospital or the home. Day patient and outpatient asylums sufficient for the need cannot become realities without more solid commitment of social resources and less paranoid regard of social paternalism. Furthermore, patients will probably not accept these alternatives unless there is continuity of care from one setting to another. The difficulty in human relations experienced by chronic patients creates resistance to entering new programs with new caretakers.

Was psychotherapy antitherapeutic for any of our four patients?

We would judge no for Joanne and Ben. We would also judge no for Betty; psychotherapy did not touch her positively or negatively. Supportive psychotherapy was therapeutic for Mark, but analytic psychotherapy was antitherapeutic. Dr. Norton's supportive approach engaged and organized Mark but the shift to investigation disorganized him. We found no examples of mistakes in the other direction; that is, being supportive when being analytic was called for. Perhaps this is not a mistake, or at least not an uncorrectable one.

What are the treatment implications for schizophrenia which our four patients suggest? While Joanne and Ben had a good treatment effect, Betty had a good asylum effect and Mark did, too, at least initially. These two pairs of patients had very different treatment needs. This was suggested initially by their differences in prognosis, and later more forcefully by their different behaviors in the psychotherapy process. Their process parameters paralleled their prognostic profiles and their process levels portended their outcomes. All these signs pointed to the need for active therapy for Joanne and Ben and to the need for active asylum for Betty and Mark.

Joanne and Mark actually received what was indicated and they profited from it. Betty did not find most of what she needed but did find most of what she could use. In fact, she could probably have done just as well without so much psychotherapeutic attention. Mark was given more than he could use and therefore did not receive what he needed. What he needed was more of what he had been offered initially by Dr. Norton.

Proper treatment assignments follow from careful evaluation of the patient, both initially and during the early stages of the patient's interaction with the doctor. Evaluating this interaction according to process levels and parameters may offer a greater "fix" on natural history and the treatment consequences. Many questions remain, of course, such as how long it should reasonably take for a patient to reach his or her "natural" process level or how one knows that the patient has attained level X or Y or Z? All this, however, is work for the future.

A PROPOSED INTEGRATED PSYCHOTHERAPY FOR SCHIZOPHRENIA

Embedded in the contours of Figure 6 is the assertion that we have something to offer the schizophrenic patient, whatever his or her expected natural history. We have treatments that can help, treatments as active therapy, treatments as asylum, or both. There are many good forms of active therapy from biological to psychosocial. There are also many good forms of asylum, from institution-based to family-based. But we wish to focus on psychotherapy, as we have done throughout this book, not because it is better or worse than any of the other treatments, but because, in our conception, it is a part of every treatment of schizophrenia.

We propose a psychotherapy which integrates the "therapy" and "asylum" aspects of treatment. In fact, we maintain that psychotherapy contains both, and that it always has. In the history of psychotherapy, however, the therapy aspect has been progressively separated from the asylum aspect, the so-called "T–A split" of therapy and administration or the split between investigative (analytic) psychotherapy and supportive psychotherapy. We propose reuniting these divergent dimensions into a broadly conceived psychotherapy that contains both asylum and therapy in combinations that are tailored to the individual patient.

We offer Chapters 8 through 10 and our process dimensions as a preliminary outline of this broader psychotherapeutic endeavor. That is, our process levels and parameters may be regarded as goals and/or techniques to be considered in any ongoing psychotherapeutic work with schizophrenic patients. We will not try to amalgamate this outline into a specific body of psychotherapeutic techniques because much of this corpus needs to be developed. Also, preliminary attempts at such an amalgamation can be found elsewhere (McGlashan, in press; Dingman and McGlashan, in press). We are interested here in placing the notion of an integrated psychotherapy in a broader perspective.

At its most complex and sophisticated level, our integrated psychotherapy of schizophrenia is an alloy of three traditions: psychoanalysis, Sullivanian interpersonal therapy based on Sullivan's theories, and existential Gestalt therapy. Dr. Fromm-Reichmann's treatment with Joanne was a prototypic example of this alloy at work. All three traditions were there. Dr. Fromm-Reichmann spent time being with Joanne, she participated and observed, and she interpreted. She was supportive and analytic, offering her presence for asylum and her mind for work. Her approach was informed by several "schools" but dominated by none. She tailored technique to fit Joanne's case and person and made the psychotherapy absolutely unique. Her work with Joanne may, in fact, be an example par excellence of the more general form of psychotherapy, not limited to schizophrenia, proposed recently by Havens (1986). It contained the elements that are universal to all psychotherapies as outlined by Jerome Frank (1971): a mutually accepted therapeutic rationale or myth; an emotionally charged, confiding relationship that facilitates the arousal of emotions and the strengthening of hope; the provision of new information and new perspective transmitted by idea, example, or self discovery; the provision of success experiences.

At its most primitive level, our integrated psychotherapy is a struggle toward engagement; that is, an exercise in holding, managing, and supporting another's life. It is also an exercise in waiting; that is, being-with while waiting for the patient to signal he or she is ready to progress to the next process level, or being-with while waiting for more help from research about the disease. Dr. Norton's early treatment of Mark is a prototypic example of this level of the work. It is possible that if Dr. Norton continued being with Mark, Mark might have advanced in process levels. Considering the severity of Mark's illness, we do not consider this very probable. Dr. Norton's premature move to an analytic strategy, however, foreclosed on such a chance.

At the least complex level, the therapist offers a relationship that is an asylum. This, in our view, is as important an aspect of psychotherapy as, say, interpretation. Simply because the patient cannot use all we have to give, or even a fraction of it, does not provide us with license to relinquish the effort. The asylum is a place the patient can be, where he or she may find some sort of comfort, some regard and dignity. This may seem an obvious, and rather pedestrian, conclusion. Unfortunately, it is obvious only to those who deal with schizophrenia every day; that is, the patients, their families, and their treaters.

At its most existential level, the therapist offers a relationship that creates both the therapist and the patient. For 50 minutes, the world changes; each is the center of the other's universe. The magnitude of this effect is greater for the individual with schizophrenia because of the impoverished relations he or she has with others outside the hour: To paraphrase Karl Jaspers, the doctor is the patient's fate. But the therapist who has worked for years with the same patient knows that the patient is his or her fate, as well. Therapist and patient define each other; each, alone, is one self too few.

References

American Psychiatric Association: Diagnostic and Statistical Manual of Mental Disorders, Third Edition (DSM-III). Washington, DC, American Psychiatric Association, 1980

Bleuler E: Dementia Praecox as the Group of Schizophrenias (1911). Translated by Zinken J. New York, International Universities Press, 1950

Burnham DL, Gladstone AI, Gibson RW: Schizophrenia and the Need-Fear Dilemma. New York, International Universities Press, 1969

Dingman CW, McGlashan TH: Psychotherapy of schizophrenia, in A Clinical Guide for the Treatment of Schizophrenia. Edited by Bellack AS. New York, Plenum Press (in press)

Eysenck HJ: The effects of psychotherapy: an evaluation. Journal of Consulting Psychology 1952; 16:319-324

Frank J: Therapeutic factors in psychotherapy. Am J Psychother 1971; 25:350-361

Gomes-Schwartz B: Individual psychotherapy of schizophrenia, in Schizophrenia. Edited by Bellack AS. Orlando, Grune & Stratton, 1984, pp 307-335

Greenspan SI, Sharfstein SS: Efficacy of psychotherapy: asking the right questions. Arch Gen Psychiatry 1981; 38:1213-1219

Havens L: Making Contact. Cambridge, MA, Harvard University Press, 1986

Hogarty GE, Anderson CM, Reiss DJ, et al: Family psychoeducation, social skills training, and maintenance chemotherapy in the after care treatment of schizophrenia, I: one-year effects of a controlled study on relapse and expressed emotion. Arch Gen Psychiatry 1986; 43:633-642

Horwitz WA, Polatin P, Kolb LC, et al: A study of cases of schizophrenia treated by direct analysis. Am J Psychiatry 1958; 114:780-783

Irl G: Das "Praecoxgefuhl" inder Diagnostic der Schizophrenie. Archiv fur Psychiatrie 1952; 203:385-406

Kohut H: The Analysis of the Self. New York, International Universities Press, 1971

Kraepelin E: Dementia Praecox and Paraphrenia. Translated by Barklay RM. Huntington, New York, R.E. Krieger Publishing, 1971

Levy ST, McGlashan TH, Carpenter WT: Integration and sealing over as recovery styles from acute psychosis: metapsychological and dynamic concepts. J Nerv Ment Dis 1975; 161:307-312

Luborsky L, Auerbach AH: The therapeutic relationship in psychodynamic psychotherapy: the research evidence and its meaning for practice, in Psychiatry Update: American Psychiatric Association Annual Review, Volume 4. Edited by Hales RE, Frances AJ. Washington, DC, American Psychiatric Press, Inc., 1985

McGlashan TH: DSM-III schizophrenia and individual psychotherapy. J Nerv Ment Dis 1982a; 170:752-757

McGlashan TH: Aphanisis: the syndrome of pseudo depression in chronic schizophrenia. Schizophrenia Bull 1982b; 8:118-134

McGlashan TH: Intensive individual psychotherapy of schizophrenia: a review of techniques. Arch Gen Psychiatry 1983; 40:909-920

McGlashan TH: The Chestnut Lodge follow-up study, I: follow-up methodology and study sample. Arch Gen Psychiatry 1984a; 41:573-585

McGlashan TH: The Chestnut Lodge follow-up study, II: long-term outcome of schizophrenia and the affective disorders. Arch Gen Psychiatry 1984b; 41:586-601

McGlashan TH: Schizophrenia: psychosocial treatments and the role of psychosocial factors in its etiology and pathogenesis, in Psychiatry Update: American Psychiatric Association Annual Review, Vol. 5. Edited by Frances AJ, Hales RE. Washington, DC, American Psychiatric Press, Inc., 1986

McGlashan TH: Recovery style from mental illness and long-term outcome. J Nerv Ment Dis 1987; 175:681-685

McGlashan TH, Levy ST, Carpenter WT: Integration and sealing over: clinically distinct recovery styles from schizophrenia. Arch Gen Psychiatry 1975; 32:1269-1272

McGlashan TH, Docherty JP, Siris S: Integrative and sealing-over recoveries from schizophrenia: distinguishing case studies. Psychiatry 1976; 39:325-338

McGlashan TH, Wadeson HS, Levy ST, et al: Art and recovery style from psychosis. J Nerv Ment Dis 1977; 164:182-190

Shaw BF: Cognitive therapy of depression. Panel discussion, in Psychiatric Update: A Clinical Continuum in Psychiatry, vol. 6, no. 3. Edited by Usdin G. The American College of Psychiatrists, 1986

Smith ML, Glass GV, Miller TI: The Benefits of Psychotherapy. Baltimore, The Johns Hopkins University Press, 1980

Sroufe LA: The organization of emotional development. Psychoanalytic Inquiry 1982; 4:575-599

Stone MH: Exploratory psychotherapy in schizophrenia-spectrum patients: a reevaluation in the light of long-term follow-up of schizophrenic and borderline patients. Bull Menninger Clin 1986; 50:287-306

Weber JJ, Bachrach HM, Solomon M: Factors associated with the outcome of psychoanalysis: report of the Columbia Psychoanalytic Center Research Project (II). International Review of Psycho-Analysis 1985; 12:127-141

Winnicott DW: The Maturational Process and the Facilitating Environment. New York, International Universities Press, 1965

Wynne LC: The epigenesis of relational systems: a model for understanding family development. Fam Process 1984; 23:297-318

Index

A

Active phase of schizophrenia, 94
Adaptive failures, 98
  See also Social behavior and
    relationships
Adolescence, treatment
    implications, 57
Affective disorders, 94
  relationship of schizophrenia
    to, 101
Affective psychopathology, 103
Affect states
  difficulty of identification, 101
  flat, 95
  inappropriate affects, 96, 102
  rage, 83
  and schizophrenia diagnosis,
    103, 109
  See also Feelings
Analyzability, patient capacity for,
    133
Anxiety
  patient defenses, 47
  patient relief techniques, 45
Articulation studies, 175–178
  schematic design, 177
Asylums
  integration with therapy, 191
  as only viable treatment,
    186–187, 188–189
  relationship with outcome, 189

Attachment process level
  case illustrations, 164, 167
  description, 129–130
  and outcome, 130

B

"Ben" case study
  affective presentation, 102–103
  attained process level, 163–166
  "being-with" relatedness, 159
  commitment level to therapy,
    143
  containment of dysphoric
    affects, 156
  course of illness, 99, 100
  developmental vulnerabilities,
    116
  diagnosis, 94
  empathy during treatment
    process, 151–152
  flexibility during therapy, 148
  hedonic tone of dyadic
    relationship, 149–150
  illness severity, 105–106
  imposition of limits during
    therapy, 153
  instances of therapeutic
    restraint, 157
  narrative description, 13–21

"Ben" case study (*cont.*)
  onset, 97
  potential outcome with
    contemporary treatment,
    183–184
  premorbid adjustment
    assessment, 117
  prognosis, 16
  range and heterogeneity of
    relatedness, 147
  record of outcome, 21–26
  relationship with therapist, 144
  ritualized interactions, 146
  therapeutic regression,
    154–155
  time structure, 146
Bender Visual Motor Gestalt Test,
  47
"Betty" case study
  affective presentation, 102
  antitherapeutic effects of
    therapist's regression, 155
  attained process level, 161–162
  avoidance of interaction, 108
  commitment level to therapy,
    143–144
  course of illness, 99, 100
  developmental vulnerabilities,
    115, 117
  diagnosis, 95
  empathy during treatment
    process, 151
  flexibility during therapy, 148
  hedonic tone of dyadic
    relationship, 148–149
  illness severity, 105
  lack of containment of
    dysphoric affects, 156
  lack of limits during therapy,
    153–154
  narrative record, 27–38
  onset, 97–98
  potential outcome with
    contemporary treatment,
    181–182
  premorbid adjustment
    assessment, 117
  prognosis, 185–186
  record of outcome, 38–39
  relationship with therapists,
    145
  time structure, 145

Biological risk factors, 114
Birth traumas
  case examples, 14, 27, 114
  as source of schizophrenic
    vulnerability, 114
Bleuler, Eugen, 98
  interpretation of schizophrenia,
    93, 101
Bonding of therapeutic
    relationship, 136
Borderline personality and
    process dimensions, 176, 177
Brief reactive psychosis, 94
Bulimia, 45
Bullard, Dexter M., 4
Burnham, Donald, 4

C

Cameron, John, 4
Case studies
  patient selection approach,
    10–12
  rationale and methodology, 3–6
  study of treatment process,
    methods and assumptions,
    123–127
  See also "Ben" case study;
    "Betty" case study; "Joanne"
    case study; "Mark" case study
Chestnut Lodge, 5
  practice of psychotherapy at,
    122
Chestnut Lodge Follow-up Study,
  8, 10, 123
Clinical psychiatry, case history
    perspective, 91
Cohen, Mabel, 4
Cohen, Robert, 4
Cold wet sheet packs
  patient attitudes towards,
    68–69, 154
  use of, case examples, 18–19
Columbia Psychoanalytic
    Institute, 176
Commitment level in therapy, 136
  case illustrations, 143–144
Communicating process level
  case illustrations, 164, 169
  description, 131

Compulsive eating, presenting
    symptom, 41
Containment concept, 139–140
    "being-with" patient, 141,
        158–159
    capacity for soothing, 140,
        156–157
    case evaluations, 153–159
    limits for mutual safety, 139,
        153–154
    therapeutic regression,
        139–140, 154–156
    therapeutic restraint, 140–141,
        157–158
    tolerance of dysphoria, 140,
        156
Couch, early use of, 16
Counter-projective statement, 169
Course of illness, 99–101, 109
    as indication of unique aspects
        in individuals, 100

D

Defenses
    mature, 106
    primitive, 106
    use of, case examples,
        105–107, 166–167
Defensiveness maturity
    as measure of illness severity,
        104
Deficit syndrome
    examples from case studies,
        101–102
    patients relationship with
        therapist, 129
Deinstitutionalization, 56
Delusions, 94, 96
    case examples, 13
    in childhood, case example, 75
    grandiose, 20, 30, 95
    persecutory, 14, 30, 44, 95
Denial
    defensive function, case of
        "Mark," 76
    prototypic of schizophrenia,
        104
Dependency needs, "Joanne"
    case, 60–61

Depression, case illustrations, 14,
    102–103
Descriptive empathy, 138
Deterioration of functioning, 94
Developmental vulnerabilities,
    113–114
    evaluation of cases, 114–117
    for predicting course and
        outcome, 111
Diagnoses, 94
    of case studies, 94–96
    paranoid schizophrenia, 27
    schizophrenia, catatonic, in
        partial remission, 16
    schizophrenic disorder with
        paranoid trends, 48
    schizophrenic psychosis with
        withdrawal and depression,
        36
    schizophrenic reaction,
        catatonic type, 72
    schizophrenic reaction,
        chronic, undifferentiated
        type, 14
    use of process dimension
        profiles, 176
Diagnostic and Statistical Manual
    of Mental Disorders, Third
    Edition (DSM-III), 11, 94, 123
Direct analysis, 8
Disillusionment and mourning
    phase in internalization
    process, 134–135
Disordered thought patterns, 94
Doctor-patient relationship. See
    Dyad relationship
Dreams
    about patients, 129
    "Ben" case, interpretations, 14,
        20
Drug treatment. See Medications
DSM-III. See Diagnostic and
    Statistical Manual of Mental
    Disorders, Third Edition
Dyadic match in therapy
    relationship
    case illustrations, 144–145
    description, 136
Dyad relationship
    bonding, 136
    confident in loss of, 135
    containment of conflicts and

Dyad relationship (*cont.*)
    dysphorias, 139–140
    as focus of therapy, 133
    levels of interaction, 127–135
    patient rejection of importance
        of, 167
    primacy in treatment, 6
    as prototypic of patient's
        relationships outside the
        dyad, 124
    recognition of respective roles,
        130
    setting limits for mutual safety,
        139
    tolerance of dysphoria, 140
    See also Patients; Therapist;
        Treatment process
Dynamic empathy, 138
    case example, 144–145
Dystonic aspects of self,
    acceptance of, 134

E

Eating disorders
    bulimia, 45
    nonedible substances, case
        example, 43
    use of food to prevent panic, 46
    See also Obesity
Electroconvulsive therapy (ECT),
    14, 30, 72
Empathic projective statements,
    169
Empathy in treatment process,
    138–139
    case illustrations, 150–153
Employment capacity,
    relationship to prognosis,
    117–118
Engagement process level
    case illustrations, 161–163,
        167
    description, 129
Existential empathy, 138–139
Eysenck, H.J., 9

F

Families
    communication difficulties,
        case example, 43

    effect of criticism on relapse
        rates, 8
    emotional overinvolvement of, 8
    history of mental illness as risk
        factor, 114
    home-based asylum care, 186,
        189
    level of psychopathology as risk
        factor, 114
Family therapy, benefits, 8
Feelings
    acceptance of responsibility for
        aggressive wishes, 134
    elucidation in therapy, 131
    identification and naming
        capacity, 131
    See also Affect states
Field dependence of illness,
    treatment impacts, 99
Fortification process level
    case illustrations, 164–165,
        169–170
    description, 132
Frank, Jerome, 191
Fromm-Reichmann, Frieda, 4,
    48–64
    therapy techniques, 191–192
    See also "Joanne" case study

G

Gastrointestinal symptoms, 45
Genetic risk factors, 114
    case illustrations, 28, 73
Gestalt therapy, 191
Gestational infections, 114
Gibson, Robert, 4
Gomes-Schwartz, Beverly, 7, 8
Grandiose delusions, 30, 95
    treatment technique, 20
Greenspan, S.I., 123
Group therapy, case example,
    33–36

H

Hallucinations, 45, 94
    auditory, 14, 30, 72, 95, 96
    case examples, 13, 41
    "field dependent," 95
    olfactory, case example, 43
    visual, 30, 95

Havens, L., 169, 191
Hedonic tone of dyadic
     relationship, 137–138
   case illustrations, 148–150
Hogarty, G.E., 8
Homosexuality
   case illustrations, 14, 15
Homosexual panic, 94, 112
Hospitals, as facilitator of good
     dyad relationship, 5
Host factors
   conflict, in "Joanne" case,
     111–112
   developmental regression, in
     "Betty" case, 113
   developmental vulnerabilities,
     111, 113–114
   premorbid dimensions, 111
   sexual inhibitions, 112–113
   story line dimension,
     111–113

I

Identification with therapist, 134
Illness history
   constructing a story line,
     111–113
   establishing continuity between
     "well" and "sick" stages, 171
Illness severity
   case evaluations, 105–107
   dimensions, 103–105, 109–110
Imitative behavior
   case example, 80
   as signal of attachment to
     therapist, 129
Individual psychotherapy, 122
   existential empathy for
     individualizing care, 138
   as perspective on the case
     histories, 91–92
Individuation process
   as factor in illness onset, 97
   and internalization process,
     135
Insight-oriented therapy, 8
Insulin coma treatments, case
     example, 72
Integration process level
   case illustration, 170
   description, 133–134

Internalization process level
   case illustration, 171–172
   description, 134–135
Interpersonal therapy, 191
   research support for, 8–9
Interpretations, use in reversal of
     regressions, 171–172
Introjection, operational result of,
     134
Invasiveness of personality as
     measure of illness severity,
     104
Investigative techniques in
     therapy, 125

J

Jaspers, Karl, 192
"Joanne" case study
   affective presentation, 102
   attained process level, 166–173
   "being-with" relatedness, 159
   commitment level to therapy,
     143
   containment of dysphoric
     affects, 156
   course of illness, 99–100
   degree of relatedness, 108–109
   desire for limits during therapy,
     154
   developmental vulnerabilities,
     116
   diagnosis, 95–96
   empathy during treatment
     process, 152–153
   flexibility during therapy, 148
   hedonic tone of dyadic
     relationship, 150
   illness severity, 106–107
   instances of therapeutic
     restraint, 158
   narrative description, 41–64
   onset, 97
   potential outcome with
     contemporary treatment, 183
   premorbid adjustment
     assessment, 118
   range and heterogeneity of
     relatedness, 146–147
   record of outcome, 64–70
   relationship with therapist,
     144–145

"Joanne" case study (*cont.*)
  ritualized interactions, 146
  therapeutic regression,
    155–156
  time structure, 145

K

Kafka, John, 4
Kohut, H., 149
Kraepelin, Emil, 93, 97
  use of illness course to define
    schizophrenia, 100–101

L

Language
  establishment of common
    symbols, meanings and
    syntax, 131, 169
  private, case example, 44–45,
    46
Long-term psychotherapy, 8
  developmental sequencing
    aspects, 126

M

"Mark" case study
  affective presentation, 101–102
  attained process level, 162–163
  avoidance of interaction, 108
  "being-with" relatedness, 159
  commitment level to therapy,
    143
  course of illness, 99, 100
  diagnosis, 96
  empathy during treatment
    process, 150–151
  hedonic tone of dyadic
    relationship, 148
  illness severity, 105
  instances of therapeutic
    restraint, 158
  lack of containment of
    regression, 154–155
  lack of limits during therapy,
    153–154
  narrative description, 71–84

  need for interactiveness, 108
  onset, 97
  outcome results, 84–87
  possible genetic vulnerability,
    114–115
  potential outcome with
    contemporary treatment,
    181–183
  premorbid adjustment
    assessment, 117
  prognosis, 186
  relationship with therapist, 145
  ritualized interactions, 146
  time structure, 145
Medical illnesses
  case example, 41
  as possible source of
    schizophrenia vulnerability,
    114
Medical model of therapy, 125,
  131
  limitations of, 127
Medications, 5
  neuroleptics, 183
  potential benefits, case
    illustrations, 182
  potential of process levels for
    drug compliance, 178
  research studies on use of, 7
Metaperspective, development of,
  133–134
Mosaic Test, 47
Mother-child relationship
  awareness and tolerance for
    maternal failures, 53
  maternal dependency, case of
    "Mark," 79
  See also Families

N

National Institutes of Health (NIH)
  recovery process studies,
    124–125
Natural history of schizophrenia
  influence on outcome, 184–187
Need/fear dilemma, 129
Negative schizophrenia, case of
  "Mark," 188
Negative syndrome patients and
  therapist relationship, 129

Negative transference
  case illustrations, 156,
    169–170
  See also Transference
    relationship
Neuroleptics, 183
Neurotic personality and process
  dimensions, 176, 177
Nightmares, 45
NIH. See National Institutes of
  Health

O

Obesity
  alternation of self-deprecation
    with grandiosity, 46
  and need for affection, 46
  presenting symptom, case
    example, 41
  therapy techniques, case
    example, 54–55
Object relations, capacity for, 25
Onset, 94
  descriptive features, 97, 109
Outcome
  contribution of treatment to,
    187–190
  controlled comparison studies
    using process dimensions,
    179–181
  correlation with analytic
    process level, 176
  natural history effect, 184–187
  for patients at fortification
    process level, 132
  premorbid factors for prediction
    of, 118
  problems of defining quality, 7
  relationship to treatment
    process levels, 6, 123,
    127–135
  validation of effects of social
    skills training, 8–9

P

Pao, Ping-Nie, 4
Parental disagreements,
  techniques for coping with, 74

Participant observation, patient
  capacity for, 133
Patients
  capability to detail history
    phenomenologically and
    interactionally, 133–134
  conscious efforts to change
    therapeutically, 135
  emphasis on assets and strong
    points of, 131–132
  role playing capabilities, 137
  See also Host factors
Perceptual motor tasks testing,
  16
Persecutory delusions, 14, 30, 44,
  95
Personality
  concomitant development of
    normal and schizophrenic,
    118
  illness invasiveness, 104
Play techniques, use in adolescent
  cases, 57
Positive schizophrenia
  case of "Ben," 103
  case of "Betty," 188
Premorbid dimensions, 111
  case evaluations, 117–118
  impacts on prognosis, 117
  for predicting course and
    outcome, 111
Primary gain from illness
  case examples, 105
  as measure of illness severity,
    104
Privacy, respect for patient's
  limits, 140
Problem solving process level
  case illustration, 164, 169
  description, 131–132
Process levels, 127–135
  attachment, 129–130
  case illustrations, 161–173
  communicating, 131
  concurrent validity testing, 178
  correlations with patients, 128
  description, 120
  engagement, 129
  fortification, 132
  as goals/techniques in
    therapeutic work, 191
  integration, 133–134

Process levels (*cont.*)
  internalization, 134–135
  linkage with outcomes, 123
  no engagement, 127–129
  problem solving, 131–132
  relationship, 130
  relationship with parameters,
    178–179
  research implications, 175–181
  termination, 135
  treatment implications,
    181–184
  working alliance–analytic,
    132–133
  working alliance–supportive,
    130–131
Process parameters, 135–141
  commitment level, 136,
    143–144
  concurrent validity testing, 178
  containment, 139–141
  dyadic match, 136
  empathy, 138–139, 150–153
  as goals/techniques in
    therapeutic work, 191
  hedonic tone, 137–138
  relationship with levels,
    178–179
  research implications, 175–181
  structure of relatedness,
    136–137
  treatment implications,
    181–184
Prodromal symptoms, 96
Prognosis
  effect of natural history of
    schizophrenia, 185–186
  impact of premorbid
    dimensions, 117
  use of process dimension
    profiles, 176
Projection, 104
Psychoanalysis, 8, 122, 191
  "direct analysis" study results,
    7–8
Psychodynamic formulations
  for establishing intactness of
    patient, 113
  use in establishing patient
    story line, 111
Psychoeducational family therapy,
  effectiveness of, 8

Psychological tests
  "Ben" case results, 16
  "Betty" case results, 30, 36
  "Joanne" case results, 44,
    47–48, 59–60
  "Mark" case results, 72, 76–77
Psychometric studies, 178–179
Psychosis
  case of "Ben," 13, 94
  presenting symptoms, 41
Psychosocial treatments, 8–9
Psychotherapy, 5
  criticisms of use for
    schizophrenia, 7–8
  developmental perspective, 126
  proposed integrated treatment
    plan, 190–192
  studies in support of, 8–10
  studies on use with
    schizophrenia, 6–10
  See also Individual
    psychotherapy; Long-term
    psychotherapy; Treatment
    process
Psychotic experiences, integration
  and outcome relationship,
  125
Psychotic personality and process
  dimensions, 176, 177
Puberty, as factor in illness onset,
  97

R

Rage
  necessity of expression in
    therapy, 83
  See also Affect states
Reaction formation, 104
  case of "Joanne," 106
Reality, techniques for fostering
  acceptance of, 132
Reality testing
  case illustrations, 105–106
  in internalization process,
    134–135
  as measure of illness severity,
    103–104
Recognition of illness, 96
Rehabilitation programs, 5, 182,
  183–184

Relapse rates, effects of family criticism, 8
Relatedness, 109–110
  as affecting treatment process, 107–108
  alienating schizophrenia, 107–108
  capacity to form attachment with therapist, 130
  case illustrations, 145–153
  interactive schizophrenia, 107
  structure in treatment process, 136–137, 145–153
Relationship process level, description, 130
Relationships
  shift towards extradyadic relationships, 135
  with therapist. See Dyad relationship
Research studies
  outcome as independent variable, 10
  psychoanalysis patient outcomes, 176
  psychotherapy of schizophrenia, 6–10
  standard prospective research design, 9
  use of medication in treatment, 7
  use of process dimensions for predicting outcome, 178
Residual symptoms, 96
Restraint, use of, 18
Rioch, David, 4
Rioch, Margaret, 4
Risk factors. See Host factors
Rogerian therapy, 8
Role playing in treatment process, 137
Rorschach test
  "Betty" case results, 31
  "Joanne" case results, 47
  "Mark" case results, 72
Rosen, John, 7–8

S

Schizoid withdrawal, 31
Schizophreniform psychosis, 94

Schizophrenogenic theory, 114
Schizotypal personality disorder
  case of "Joanne," 166
  criteria, 96
Schulz, Clarence, 4
"Sealing-over" process. See Fortification process level
Searles, Harold, 4
Secondary gains from illness
  case of "Mark," 79
  impact on treatment, 104–105
  letting go of, 171
  as measure of illness severity, 104–105
Self
  acceptance as adult rather than patient, 135
  acceptance of dystonic aspects as real, 134
Self-analysis, role in therapy process, 133
Self-generated distortions, patient recognition of, 170
Self-mutilation
  as expression of negative feelings against therapist, 60, 62
  "Joanne" case, 54
Self-object differentiation
  as basis for understanding emotional relativity, 133
  lack of, and long-term outcome, 129
Self-observation, patient capacity for, 19, 52
Self-therapeutic functioning, 134
Separation anxiety, 29
  from therapist, 167
Sexual obsessions, 15, 72
Sharfstein, S.S., 123
Short-term psychotherapy, 8
Smith, M.L., 9
Social activities, participation in, 132
Social behavior and relationships
  avoidance measures, 5
  maladaptation as factor in severity of illness, 98
  relationship of capacity level to prognosis, 117–118
  social isolation, case example, 41

Social skills training, effects on
    outcome, 8–9
Stimulus modulation in therapy,
    140
Stone, Michael, 8
Stress
    illness onset relationship with,
        97, 98
    as measure of field dependence
        versus independence of
        illness, 99
    as risk factor, 114
Sublimation, 104
Suicidal feelings, patient
    techniques for dealing with,
    55
Suicide attempts, case example,
    13–14
Sullivan, Harry Stack, 5, 191
Supportive-adaptive therapy, 8
Supportive alliance process level
    case illustration, 164
    description, 131
Supportive techniques in therapy,
    125
Suppression, 104
Symptoms, 94–97
    discernment of meanings from,
        111–113
    encouragement to ignore and
        suppress, 132
    "Joanne" case, 41
    patient distress, 103
    prodromal symptoms, 94
    for schizophrenia diagnosis, 94
Symptom structure
    case of "Joanne," 106
    as measure of illness severity,
        104

T

Termination process level, 135
    case illustration, 172
Thematic Aperception Test (TAT),
    16
Thematic story line of illness
    case illustrations, 111–113
    purpose of, 111
Therapeutic regression
    containment of, 139–140

    containment of, case
        evaluations, 154–156
Therapist
    acceptance of negative feelings
        against, 134
    attachment to, 38
    balance between closeness and
        distance, 140, 157–158
    capacity for soothing and
        stimulus modulation, 140,
        156–157
    demonstration of fallibility and
        humaneness, 48–49
    effect of absences on attached
        patients, 129
    empathy of, 138–139, 150–153
    establishment as a real person,
        133
    identification process, 80, 82,
        134
    imitation of, case example, 81
    presentation both as person
        and instrument, 140–141
    relatedness containment, 141
    role of "practical" relationship
        with patient, 55
    solving relationship problems
        with, 133
    See also Dyad relationship
Therapy techniques. *See*
    Treatment process
Thorazine, 14, 15, 17
Thought disorder, 96
    case of "Mark," 75
Thoughts, elucidation in therapy,
    131
Thymoleptics, 183
Time structure in therapy, 136
    case evaluations, 145–146
Transference psychosis, 129
Transference relationship
    case illustrations, 18, 170
    negative transference, case
        illustrations, 156, 169–170
    patient discrimination as a
        distortion, 133
    patient use for fortification
        against disease, 132
Treatment efficacy studies,
    179–181
    sample design for using process
        dimensions, 180

Treatment process
    active intervention, 50
    as collaboration between
        therapist and patient, 63, 68
    concept, 121–123
    implications of natural history
        effect, 186–187
    individuality of, 122
    integration of "therapy" and
        "asylum," 191–192
    investigative techniques, 125
    parameters, description, 120
    perspectives for describing
        relatedness, 136–137
    process levels, description, 120
    recurring themes, 4, 121–122
    research implications, 175–181
    supportive techniques, 125
    technical interventions,
        125–126

See also Dyad relationship;
        Process levels; Process
        parameters
Treatment records, 12
Treatments
    interpersonal, 119

W

Will, Otto, 4
Winnicott, D.W., 139
Working alliance-analytic process
        level
    case illustration, 165–166,
        168–169
Working alliance-supportive
        process level
    case illustration, 164
    description, 130–131